The Journey of BECOMING the Soul Alchemist

A Sacred Journey of Reclaiming Your Power,
Remembering Your Light, and Embodying Your Truth

KAY SANDERS

ISBN: 979-8-218-70886-3

Published by Sacred Path Publishing

With deep reverence, this book is offered in service to your awakening, your embodiment, and your soul's liberation. May each word meet you where you are — and call you home to who you truly are.

Dedication

To Ari—For your unwavering support, guidance, and mentorship, For holding space for every idea, every unraveling, every rising, For believing in me when I was still learning to believe in myself.

This book would not exist without your presence and support. Thank you for walking beside me as this vision became reality, for helping me bring it to life—not just in words, but in frequency.

With deepest gratitude and soul-full love, Kay

Table Of Content

Dedication...5

Table Of Content...7

Foreword...9

The Path of the Soul Alchemist................................11

Why I Wrote This Book 13

The Alchemical Path of the Soul Alchemist..............17

The Four Phases of the Journey..............................19

How to Walk This Path 21

Bonus Soul Alchemist Support Toolkit....................23

A Note from the Threshold 24

Invocation - The Path of the Soul Alchemist............26

✧ Part I: The Stirring ✧ 28

    Chapter 1: The Inner Knowing You Can't Ignore......30

    Chapter 2: When Life Stops Making Sense 38

    Chapter 3: Feeling Stuck Isn't Failure 48

    Chapter 4: Your Soul Is Trying to Get Your Attention 56

✧ Part II: The Transmutation ✧ 65

    Chapter 5: Letting Go of Who You Thought You Had to Be...67

    Chapter 6: The Layers You Didn't Choose.................80

    Chapter 7: You Are Not Broken—You're Becoming.................96

    Chapter 8: Meeting the Shadow Without Fear 108

    Chapter 9: Emotional Alchemy................................127

    Chapter 10 The Frequency You Choose to Embody.............153

    Chapter 11: Transmutation Practices That Work.............178

✧ Part III: The Embodiment — Living as the Soul Alchemist ✧
.... 200

Chapter 12: Embodied Alignment: Becoming the Frequency. 202

Chapter 13: Nervous System Alchemy............................... 221

Chapter 14: From Ritual to Reality 236

Chapter 15: Walking Through the World in Your Truth 248

Chapter 16: Let it Be Easy, Let it Be True.......................... 263

Chapter 17: Embodying Boundaries, Discernment, and Devotion
.... 275

Chapter 18: Living from Your Future Self Now 289

✧ Part IV: The Radiance — Becoming the Transmission ✧ 304

Chapter 19: Your Presence is the Message 306

Chapter 20: Purpose Without Pressure 323

Chapter 21: Wealth as an Energetic Expression 337

Chapter 22: Becoming the Portal for Others 359

Chapter 23: Co-Creating with the Quantum Field 374

This Is Just the Beginning.. 387

✧ The Alchemist Commitment ✧ 389

Continue Your Soul Alchemy Journey.................................... 392

About the Author.. 394

Foreword

by Ari

There are some books that teach, others that guide—and then there are those rare, living texts that transform. This is one of them.

The Journey of BECOMING the Soul Alchemist isn't just something you read. It's something you remember. It's a mirror that reflects back the deepest essence of who you are beneath the conditioning, the wounds, and the noise. It's a path back home to your soul.

I've walked beside Kay through every page of this book—from the raw beginnings to the final words you're about to read. I've witnessed the energy she poured into each chapter—not just the wisdom and teachings, but the frequency behind them. These are not intellectual insights copied from elsewhere. They are lived codes. They are transmissions forged through fire, heartbreak, healing, and the relentless devotion to truth.

What you hold in your hands is not just a collection of chapters. It's an initiation. A permission slip to feel. A doorway into remembrance. And an invitation to reclaim the parts of yourself you were told to abandon.

If you are here, it's not by accident. Your soul brought you to this moment for a reason. And as you journey through these pages, you will find yourself shedding, awakening, softening, and rising—again and again—until the truth of who you are is no longer a distant idea but an embodied knowing.

Kay has done more than write a book. She's offered a transmission of her essence. And in doing so, she's created a sacred space for yours to awaken.

So take a breath. Open your heart. And let the alchemy begin.

With reverence,
Ari

The Path of the Soul Alchemist

A Sacred Journey of Reclaiming Your Power, Remembering Your Light, and Embodying Your Truth

This is not simply a book. It is an activation—a living, breathing transmission encoded with light frequencies meant to stir something deep within you. Every word, every page, every invocation holds an energetic signature designed to awaken what you already carry in your soul. This is a return to truth. A sacred re-entry into the fullness of who you are.

You did not arrive here by accident. If these pages have found their way into your hands, it is because something within you is ready—ready to rise, to remember, and to reclaim the parts of yourself you've long buried beneath the noise of the world. This journey is not about becoming something new. It is about remembering who you've always been beneath the masks, the patterns, the pressure to fit into spaces you've long outgrown.

This book is for the ones who know there's more—more within them, more available to them, more meant for them. You may not be able to name it, but you can feel it. That quiet inner knowing, that stirring in your chest, that ache that whispers you didn't come here to play small. You came here to awaken to your own brilliance. You came here to embody the truth that your soul has always known.

If you allow this journey to move through you—not just as information, but as transformation—something within you will shift. Not in your mind, but in your field. In your body. In your being. You will begin to feel more aligned, more empowered, more deeply connected to the version of yourself who is no longer derailed by circumstances, but grounded in frequency. You will stop chasing wholeness and start living it. You will become the Soul Alchemist—the one who knows how to move energy, transmute patterns, and consciously create reality from the inside out.

This is your invitation to come home to yourself. To release the weight of limitation. To remember the light you came here to be. The world is shifting, and with it comes a call—a call to rise, to shine, and to become the beacon you were born to be. You do not need to know the way. You only need to say yes to the next step, and the step after that. The path will reveal itself to the one who walks it.

The frequency of this work is here to guide you gently but powerfully into your own remembrance. It is here to stir your soul awake and call you into a deeper way of living, being, and creating. It is not meant to be rushed or consumed quickly. It is meant to be felt, integrated, and lived. Allow the energy to move through you. Let the incantations open you. Let the practices root you into your body and your truth.

Because once you say yes to this path, you are no longer just reading—you are activating. And the version of you who is already whole, already radiant, already aligned, is waiting on the other side of this journey, ready to meet you in your fullest expression.

Welcome, Soul Alchemist.

Why I Wrote This Book

My journey began in 2016 when I experienced what I can only describe as a deep inner awakening. Something shifted inside me, and from that point on, nothing was ever the same. It wasn't dramatic or sudden, but it stirred something undeniable—something I couldn't ignore. That awakening sent me into years of intense inner work, reflection, and discovery. I found myself navigating through what felt like one long dark night of the soul. Life asked me to look inward, to heal, to release what no longer served me, and to find my way back to who I truly am.

During those years, I was doing everything I could to survive—trying to grow a business, raise my son, and simply keep moving forward. I faced deep financial struggles. In 2019, I nearly lost everything. That was a breaking point for me. I remember asking myself, "Is this really it? Is this what my life is going to be?" I couldn't accept that. I knew, deep down, there had to be more. I could feel it. I wasn't meant to live a life that felt this limited. I wasn't meant to constantly struggle. I knew I was here to be more, do more, and experience something far greater than what I had known up until that point.

So I went deeper. I worked with the Akashic Records. I had my light language unlocked—and that experience changed my life. Things began to shift, but there was still something missing. I couldn't quite place it, but I knew the path hadn't fully revealed itself yet.

Everything changed in 2024. That's when I received the clarity I had been searching for. Through intense shadow work, a deep dive into my Gene Keys, and continued energetic recalibration, my true purpose began to come forward. That was when I received the guidance that I am a Soul Alchemist. That this—this path, this frequency, this embodiment—is what I came here to teach, to transmit, and to live.

It wasn't just a title or a concept—it was a truth that had been waiting for me all along. It was through every struggle, every challenge, and every quiet moment of devotion that I learned how to rise. Not by forcing or fixing, but by becoming. I didn't just apply the teachings. I embodied them. I lived them. And over time, I realized—I was the work. I wasn't trying to become aligned. I was living in alignment. I had reached a place within myself where I didn't want anything because I already had everything I truly needed. There were even moments I didn't know what to manifest because I felt so deeply content.

My business was still moving slowly at that time, and for a while, I didn't understand why. But I came to realize something important: I hadn't yet fully embraced who I truly am. I knew I was meant to be a teacher, someone who activates and supports others—but I hadn't fully embodied that version of myself. I was still waiting. Still hiding. And as long as I stayed in that energy, the results I wanted couldn't come.

Everything began to shift the moment I chose to be the teacher. I stopped waiting for permission and began showing up in my fullness. I created my membership, Transcendence, as a sacred space for others to come home to themselves. I started running challenges and holding live spaces where I could connect with beautiful souls who were also on their journey. That in itself was a huge milestone for me—because I had to become the guide, the mentor, the activator I always knew I was meant to be.

It also required me to release the idea that I needed to teach the way others do. I'm not here to fix anyone. I'm not here to hold someone's hand or give them a list of steps. I'm here to be the embodiment of what's possible. To be the activation. That truth was both liberating and a little terrifying—but I knew it was right. I knew this was what I came here to live and share.

That's when the vision for this book arrived.

It came through during a time of powerful energetic openings—a time when I was already shifting, expanding, and receiving downloads more clearly than ever. The message was clear: this book wasn't meant to be written in a traditional way. It wasn't meant to be just another personal development book filled with strategies or mindset hacks. This was meant to be a transmission. A living body of work that would activate and support others in becoming the Soul Alchemist they already are.

This book is the culmination of everything I've lived, everything I've remembered, and everything I now embody. It's a journey back to self—not through logic, but through frequency. You won't find formulas or step-by-step plans in these pages. What you will find is resonance. Truth. Activation. And guidance to help you reclaim the version of you that has been waiting to rise.

I'm not here to give you answers. I'm here to hold space as you remember your own.

This book is for you if you've felt like there's more within you but you haven't quite been able to reach it. If you've done the work, but still feel like something is just out of reach. If you're tired of trying to fix yourself, tired of the noise, and ready to live from a place of truth, alignment, and ease.

This is not a book to rush through. It's a sacred journey—a living initiation. And if you let it, it will support you in awakening what's already within you.

I'm honored to walk beside you.

The Alchemical Path of the Soul Alchemist

A Living Journey Through Awakening, Transmutation, Embodiment, and Radiance

This is not just a journey of healing or personal growth—it's something far deeper, something sacred. The alchemical path is a return to the truest essence of who you are. It's not about improvement. It's about remembrance. This book is not meant to be read and mentally understood. It's meant to be felt, to be embodied. It is meant to activate something within you that you may not even be able to name yet—but you'll recognize it the moment it stirs.

Most personal development books offer steps, practices, or formulas. They make promises: do this, and your life will change. But what's often missing in those teachings is the most vital element of all—embodiment. Because without embodiment, the inner shifts don't hold. Without embodiment, you remain mentally aware but energetically unchanged. You continue looping through the same patterns, carrying the same energetic signatures, wondering why your external reality hasn't caught up with all the work you've done.

This path is different. This path will take you beyond what you know and into who you are.

Every page of this book is infused with light codes and frequencies designed to support your awakening. If you allow yourself to receive—not just read—the activations within these words, something will unlock within you. Not on a mental level, but in your field. In your body. In your soul.

Now let's talk about what it means to walk the Alchemical Path. To live as a Soul Alchemist.

A Soul Alchemist doesn't avoid the work. They welcome it. They use their outer experiences as mirrors for what still needs to be seen and shifted within. A Soul Alchemist knows that nothing outside of them will truly change until something inside of them shifts first. When resistance, fear, or lack arises, they don't bypass it. They tune in. They ask: What is this here to show me? They transmute fear into trust, lack into abundance, heaviness into clarity. They turn lead into gold—not metaphorically, but energetically.

To be a Soul Alchemist means to no longer operate from reaction or unconscious patterns. It means becoming deeply aware of what you're holding, what you're projecting, and what you're aligning with. You begin to catch the subtle fears, doubts, or imprints that are in direct conflict with what you desire to create. And instead of trying to do more on the outside, you go inward. You clear. You realign. You become the frequency of what you want to experience—and from that place, you receive.

The Soul Alchemist lives from embodiment. This is not about spiritual rituals or surface-level mindset work. It's about being the version of you who already holds the vision, already walks in alignment, already knows who they are and what they're here for. Over time, this becomes second nature. It becomes effortless. Because being a Soul Alchemist isn't something you do. It's something you are.

The Four Phases of the Journey

The journey ahead is structured in four phases, each one a living part of the transformation you're here to experience. Together, they form the roadmap to your liberation—not in the sense of reaching a destination, but in reclaiming your path forward as a Soul Alchemist.

The Stirring is where your awakening begins. It's the quiet inner pull that led you to this book—the whisper that says, there's more. It's the part of your journey where you feel the restlessness, the longing, the curiosity that leads you to seek something deeper. It's the moment your soul taps you on the shoulder and says, it's time.

Transmutation is where the alchemy begins. Here, we go deep. We face the shadows, the limitations, the emotional patterns that have held us back. This phase is not about bypassing discomfort—it's about using it. You'll learn to turn struggle into softness, fear into power, and doubt into clarity. You'll begin transmuting what no longer serves you, shifting the inner landscape so you can move forward unburdened and fully empowered.

Embodiment is where the inner work becomes a way of being. This is where you learn to live as your highest self—not someday, but now. You'll align with new timelines. You'll show up differently. Life begins to feel lighter, more spacious, even fun—because you're no longer chasing alignment, you are the alignment. Even when life wobbles, you'll know how to return to your truth and hold your center.

Radiance is the natural result of embodiment. In this phase, you're no longer becoming the Soul Alchemist—you are the Soul Alchemist. You live it. You transmit it. Whether you feel called to teach, lead, or simply embody your truth in your everyday life, you become a ripple of light in this world. You begin to leave an energetic imprint not by doing more, but by being more fully yourself.

This journey isn't linear. These phases may cycle, spiral, and repeat. But with each pass, you'll rise into greater alignment and clarity. You're not being led to a final destination. You're being called home—to yourself.

How to Walk This Path

Approach this journey with an open heart and a an open mind. This book is not a quick read—it is a sacred journey you walk, word by word, page by page, breath by breath. Let it meet you where you are. Let it hold you through what you're releasing. Let it awaken what you're ready to remember.

The words you'll read here are encoded. They carry light, truth, and transmission. This is not about concepts. This is about frequency. The power of this book is not just in the teachings—it's in what the teachings activate within you. The moment you open your heart and allow yourself to receive, the alchemy begins.

The practices are not assignments. They are invitations. Invitations to return to yourself. To reconnect with your energy. To shift your field and choose again. The incantations are not affirmations. They are spells of remembrance. They are energetic recalibrations designed to bring you back into alignment with your highest self.

You may feel emotional. You may feel stirred. You may feel lit up, seen, or even uncomfortable at times. That's part of the process. Don't resist it. Let it move through you. The discomfort is often where the light breaks through.

Give yourself permission to pause. To breathe. To let things integrate. Come back to certain passages again and again if you feel called. Each time, they'll meet you at a different level of your journey.

And above all else—be honest with yourself. You are not here to become more. You are here to come home to who you truly are. This is your space to return, to soften, to shed, to remember, and to rise.

Walk this path like you would walk through a temple: with reverence, presence, and devotion. You're not just reading a book. You're walking yourself home.

Bonus Soul Alchemist Support Toolkit

To support you as you continue your journey of becoming the Soul Alchemist you were always meant to be, I've created a bonus collection of tools and activations designed to help you deepen the work from this book. These resources will assist you in clearing energetic blocks, stabilizing your frequency, and anchoring into the embodiment of your soul's truth—one aligned step at a time.

You can access your free Soul Alchemist Toolkit at: www.kaysanders.com/bookbonus

This is your next step. Not to gather more information—but to expand into deeper embodiment.

This free gift is a taste of the deeper journey available inside Transcendence, my sacred membership space for soul-aligned expansion. You'll find more details at the back of this book if you feel called to explore further.

A Note from the Threshold

If you are here, it's because your soul knows that something within you is ready to rise. This moment is not just the beginning of a new journey—it is a return. A return to who you truly are, and a sacred turning point in your evolution.

You've likely walked a long path already. You've done the work. You've healed, released, explored, and questioned. And still, something inside of you whispered that there is more—not more to chase, but more to embody. A deeper truth that's been waiting to be remembered. A frequency that's always been there, underneath the layers you've had to carry.

Now you are standing at the doorway.

You may not fully understand why this book called you in. You may not know what's waiting on the other side of this journey. That's okay. You don't need to know. Your soul already does. It knows that this is the moment you've been preparing for, whether consciously or not. And it knows that what's awakening within you is far greater than anything you've ever tried to become through effort or force.

You are not broken. You never were. You are not lost. You are remembering. You are not behind. You are right on time.

This journey isn't about figuring anything out. It's about softening into who you already are. It's about clearing the noise so you can hear your soul again. It's about releasing the layers that were never really yours so you can finally feel the power, the clarity, and the peace that comes when you live as your truest self.

Let this book stir something ancient within you. Let the words activate the knowing that has lived within you all along. Let the incantations, the practices, and the frequency of these teachings awaken something sacred in your bones. This is not a read-through. It is a remembrance. It is an energetic initiation. It is a call home.

You are not being asked to become someone new. You are being invited to live as the version of yourself that's been waiting to rise. This version of you does not seek validation or wait for permission. She is already aligned. He is already powerful. You are already enough.

You are ready. You've always been ready. Now is the time to step across the threshold and begin walking as the Soul Alchemist you were always meant to be.

Invocation - The Path of the Soul Alchemist

Before you continue reading, I invite you to pause and return to yourself.

Let this be more than words on a page. Let this be a moment of remembrance — a sacred recalibration. You have not come this far to stay on the surface. You are being called into deeper truth, deeper embodiment, and deeper devotion to the path you chose long before this lifetime.

This invocation is not meant to inspire you. It is meant to *activate* you — to call forth what already lives within you, waiting to be claimed. Speak it aloud. Whisper it if you must. But let your body feel the vibration of every word. Let your soul recognize itself in this remembering.

I now choose to walk the path of my becoming.

Not to strive, fix, or force—but to remember what has always lived within me.
I release the versions of myself shaped by fear, doubt, and survival.
I release the noise, the pressure, the masks, and the smallness.

I call back every part of me I abandoned to belong.
I call back every fragment I gave away to feel safe.
I call back my light, my truth, my power, my presence.

I now choose to see my life through the eyes of my soul.
I now choose to turn every shadow into gold.
I now choose to lead from within.

With every breath, I return home to myself.
With every page, I open more fully to my truth.
With every word I read, I activate the frequency I came here to embody.

I am not here to follow someone else's path.
I am here to walk my own—with clarity, courage, and devotion.

I am the alchemist of my life.
I am the keeper of my light.
I am the creator of my reality.

And I am ready.

✧ Part I: The Stirring ✧

"Something deep within you has always known... you were never meant to stay asleep. The stirring is your soul remembering that there is more."

This is where it begins. Not with clarity, not with certainty—but with a quiet, undeniable knowing. A sense that something is shifting. A restlessness that can't be soothed. A feeling that the life you've been living is no longer in alignment with who you're becoming. And maybe, if you're being honest, it never really was.

The Stirring is the soul's first whisper. It's the part of the journey where everything you've known starts to unravel—not to punish or confuse you, but to create space for truth to rise. It is in this moment, when what used to work no longer does, that you are being called into deeper awareness. Into deeper presence. Into the first breath of remembrance.

You may not know exactly what you want. You may not be able to explain what's wrong. But you can feel it. You can feel that something is no longer resonating. Something inside of you is done pretending. Done performing. Done trying to make a version of yourself fit into a life that's too small for your soul.

And that knowing—that inner recognition—is sacred.

This phase isn't about action. It's not about figuring things out. It's about *noticing*. It's about slowing down long enough to feel what's been rising beneath the surface for years. It's about admitting to yourself that the version of you who created the life you've been living is not the version of you who's going to create what comes next.

This part of the journey invites you to honor the longing without judgment. To acknowledge the ache without rushing to fix it. To make space for the voice of your soul, even when your mind still doesn't understand what it's saying.

You are not here to get it all right. You are here to wake up. To remember. To feel. To let what no longer serves you begin to fall away. And to trust that what's stirring inside you is not the end of something—it's the beginning.

Welcome to the Stirring. Let your soul speak. Let yourself listen.

Chapter 1: The Inner Knowing You Can't Ignore

The soul's whisper and the restlessness of staying small

There comes a time when the life you've built no longer fits—not because it's wrong or broken, but because *you've outgrown it*. It's a subtle ache at first. A quiet discontent that lingers in the background of your days. It's like an itch you can't quite scratch, a restlessness that no amount of success, productivity, or external validation can soothe.

This inner knowing often shows up as a feeling that your life—as it currently stands—simply doesn't align anymore. And maybe, if you're honest with yourself, it never fully did. You feel it in your body, in your emotions, deep in your core. You might feel anxious for no reason. Tired of the same routines. Disconnected from the things you once poured your energy into. You sense that something needs to shift... even if you don't know what that something is.

This is not just dissatisfaction. It's not boredom. This is your soul speaking.

The inner knowing rarely screams. Instead, it whispers. It nudges. It pulls. At first it's easy to ignore, to explain away as stress or overthinking. But over time, if you don't listen, it gets louder. And eventually, it will show up in a way you can't dismiss. Sometimes it arrives through challenge—trauma, heartbreak, financial hardship, or loss. When we ignore the gentle nudges, life has a way of turning up the volume.

You may find yourself questioning everything—your work, your identity, your relationships, your purpose. And still, you can't quite explain what's happening. You just know, deep in your gut, that you're not meant to keep living like this. You're not meant to keep fitting yourself into spaces you've outgrown.

This is the moment of awakening. And it's sacred.

When the Life You Built No Longer Fits

You may wake up one morning and ask the question that changes everything: *Is this really all there is to life?* You may not have the answer yet, but the question alone is a signal. It's a doorway opening. It's the part of you that knows there is more—more to discover, more to become, more to live for.

For many of us, the life we created was built on survival. On expectations. On programming. We made choices based on what we thought we were supposed to do. We did what seemed "right" or "realistic." We built structures that served us for a time—but no longer reflect who we are now.

When that reality begins to feel misaligned, you may feel like an imposter in your own life. You go through the motions, but your heart isn't in it. You feel disconnected, maybe even numb. It's as if you're living someone else's story—not your own. That discomfort is not a problem. It's your soul calling you home.

And when your soul speaks, it does so with a kind of truth that bypasses logic. Your mind may resist it. Your ego may fear what it means. But deep within, something has already shifted. The old way no longer feels livable. The new way is still unclear—but you know you can't go back.

You are being called to rise. Not to achieve more or do more, but to become more aligned with who you *already are*. You are being asked to remember the purpose your soul came here to fulfill—not through effort, but through *embodiment*.

And that's why you're here.

Why We Resist What We Know

Even when the soul speaks clearly, most people don't listen right away. Not because they don't want to—but because listening means change. And change, especially the kind that calls you into full alignment, often asks you to let go of everything that kept you comfortable.

You may be afraid of what you'll lose. Relationships may shift. Friendships may fall away. The people you've built your life around may no longer understand you, and that fear of being alone—misunderstood, judged, or even rejected—can keep you stuck for years. You may find yourself questioning if the whispers you feel are real or just a fantasy. You may wonder, *What if I'm just making this up?*

It's not uncommon to feel like you're going crazy, especially when your outer world no longer reflects what's rising within you. You try to stay grounded, rational, responsible. You listen to the voices around you telling you to be practical, to stop dreaming, to get back to "real life." But what they don't realize is that your real life—the one your soul came here to live—is just beginning.

This is where the inner work begins. Because as you awaken, you must also face the parts of you that have spent a lifetime trying to stay safe. The ego. The survival self. The version of you that learned how to get by through pleasing others, staying small, and playing by rules that were never meant for you. And as much as that part of you has helped you get here, it cannot lead you forward.

The moment you begin to feel the inner knowing, you are being invited to trust—deeply. To trust yourself. To trust your soul. To trust the guidance you're receiving, even when your mind can't make sense of it. You are being asked to trust in divine timing, in a plan that is unfolding even if you can't yet see the full picture.

That level of trust doesn't come from logic. It comes from surrender.

It comes from giving yourself permission to stop seeking approval, to stop playing by someone else's rules, and to finally honor the path that's been quietly calling your name for a long time.

Signs You're Already Awakening

If you're reading this chapter and resonating with every word, you're already in it. You're already walking the path. You've already said yes—even if you didn't realize it until now.

You may be feeling a low-grade restlessness that never fully goes away. A sense of being dissatisfied with the life you've created, even if everything looks "fine" on the outside. You might feel confused, unmotivated, or disconnected from the things that used to excite you. You might have moments of deep clarity followed by waves of doubt. You want more, but you can't yet define what "more" means.

That's not failure. That's awakening.

These feelings are not problems to fix. They are *invitations*. They are the markers that your soul is trying to get your attention. That inner nudge, that sense that there is more to life, that pull toward something you can't quite explain—that is sacred. That is truth.

And the more you allow yourself to feel it, without needing to justify it or rush to fix it, the more clarity will come. Not all at once, but in pieces. In whispers. In nudges that feel both subtle and undeniable.

A Message to Your Soul

If you're feeling the stirring, the restlessness, the quiet voice inside you that says, *there's more,* then listen—because that voice is not wrong. It's not a fantasy. It's not wishful thinking. It's your soul trying to guide you home.

This isn't something to fear or push away. This isn't a sign that something is wrong. It's a sign that something is waking up.

You are not broken. You are not behind. You are awakening.

Your soul is trying to lead you—not toward someone else's version of success, but toward the life you were always meant to live. A life of alignment, truth, ease, and embodiment. A life where you don't just *survive*, you *create*. You *feel*. You *radiate*. You *become*.

If you've been waiting for someone to tell you it's okay to follow that nudge—to listen to your intuition, to explore what's rising within you, to trust what you've always felt but couldn't explain—then let this be it.

You don't need permission from anyone else. The only permission that matters is your own. Give yourself that permission now. To pause. To listen. To trust. To act.

Give yourself the freedom to follow the path that makes no sense to your mind but feels undeniably true in your heart. Give yourself space to become the most authentic, empowered version of yourself—the Soul Alchemist who lives and leads from within.

My Story of Resistance

For a long time, I didn't listen either. Even though I was deeply spiritual and already doing the work, I resisted. I was tuning in, receiving the messages, feeling the nudges—but I wasn't truly acting on them. I told myself I was doing all the right things, but I wasn't embodying what I knew. I wasn't fully trusting what I felt.

I was stuck in fear. I was stuck in doubt. And for years, I stayed there—doing the rituals, setting the intentions, but deep down still living from limitation. I was afraid to really let go. Afraid of what might happen if I actually followed through on what my soul was asking of me.

So I struggled. My spiritual business wasn't growing. I felt like I was doing everything right and still getting nowhere. Eventually, I launched a marketing consultancy just to create some financial stability. And oddly enough—that business took off with ease. It brought in the money I needed. It grew without much effort. And yet, it wasn't where my heart was.

Every time I thought about walking away from my spiritual work, that inner nudge came back stronger. *No*, it said. *This is what you're here to do.* Even when nothing made sense, even when I wanted to give up, I couldn't. Something deeper was holding me to the path.

And I had to finally admit something to myself—something that changed everything.

I created all of it.

Not consciously, not deliberately—but energetically, I was holding patterns that were keeping me stuck. I was embodying lack. Doubt. Fear. I didn't truly believe I could be abundant doing what I loved. I didn't fully believe that I was meant to lead, guide, and activate others. And so, nothing moved.

It wasn't until I got brutally honest with myself that everything started to shift.

I stopped blaming the outside world. I took full ownership. I realized that the version of me who kept showing up to do the work wasn't yet *being* the one who believed in the work. I was still operating from the version of me that didn't think it was possible. And that energy was running the show.

Once I claimed my power—once I acknowledged that *awareness gives you the power of choice*—things began to change. I still didn't have all the answers. I still had to trust. But I gave myself permission to keep going, to keep showing up, to follow the breadcrumbs even when the whole path wasn't clear.

And now, you're reading these words. And I'm here, not as someone who figured it all out—but as someone who finally stopped ignoring the knowing.

The Inner Knowing Is the Alchemical Spark

This moment—right here, right now—is not just a feeling. It's a sacred turning point. It is the beginning of your alchemical path.

The inner knowing you're feeling is more than a whisper from your soul. It's the first flicker of fire that starts to burn through what no longer serves you. It's the invitation to return to your essence, to your truth, and to your power—not someday, but now.

This is the moment when you begin to see your life through new eyes.
And in that moment, **awareness gives you the power of choice.**

Without awareness, you continue to live by default—repeating the same patterns, reacting to the same challenges, staying stuck in the same cycles. But once you become aware, *truly aware*, you have a choice. You can shift. You can release. You can transform. You can create.

Awareness is the moment you reclaim your power. It is the spark that turns your life into gold.

This stirring is not here to frustrate you—it's here to awaken you. It's not here to push you—it's here to *call you forward*. It's not a problem to fix—it's the sign that you're ready to become.

Because when you start paying attention to that inner knowing, you start looking for answers. You start seeking truth. You find yourself drawn to teachers, tools, and practices that help you dig deeper. And little by little, you begin shedding the layers that have kept you small. You begin transmuting old energy. You begin to rise.

And even though the path ahead may still feel unclear, you no longer feel lost—because you've remembered that you have *always been the alchemist of your life*.

This is just the beginning. And yet, it is everything. You are no longer waiting. You are no longer wondering. You are listening. You are awakening. You are becoming.

Welcome to the first breath of your return. The soul alchemy begins now.

Chapter 2: When Life Stops Making Sense

Recognizing when what used to work no longer does

There comes a time on this journey when everything that used to make sense suddenly... doesn't. You may not know exactly when it started, or how you got here, but you can feel it—deep in your body, in your thoughts, in your emotions. What once felt like a stable, structured life now feels like a box you've outgrown. The edges press in on you. The routine dulls your spark. You look around and realize: *this life I've built no longer fits.*

Emotionally, it can feel like frustration that simmers beneath the surface. A restlessness you can't explain. A sense of being stuck that no amount of trying seems to fix. You begin to question your path, your purpose, and even your identity. *Why am I here? What am I meant to do?* These questions echo inside of you, and yet no clear answer comes. There's only a deep knowing that something has to change.

You may find yourself lying awake at night, wondering what would bring you fulfillment. You try new things. You chase new experiences. But nothing fully quiets the ache. Because this isn't about needing something external—it's about remembering something internal.

Energetically, it's like trying to squeeze into a space you've outgrown. You don't fit anymore. Not in your job. Not in your relationships. Sometimes not even in your own skin. You may feel like a stranger in familiar places, or like the "weird one" among your family and friends. Your desires start to shift. Your viewpoints expand. You're drawn to new things—things others may not understand or relate to.

You begin to feel squeezed, constricted, unsettled. And yet, this discomfort isn't a sign that something is wrong. It's a sign that something deeper is awakening.

Confusion. Isolation. Guilt. Fear of being "too much" or "too different." All of these feelings may arise. And while it may seem like everything is falling apart, the truth is: something new is preparing to emerge.

This is not the end. This is the unraveling. And it is sacred.

When the Life You Built Begins to Crumble

In this phase, the unraveling often begins in the places where you've invested the most energy—your work, your relationships, your identity.

Your career may feel increasingly unfulfilling. You might dread going to work, feel constant friction with coworkers, or sense that no matter how hard you try, things just aren't working. You may even lose your job, face a demotion, or feel pushed out—all nudges from your soul, inviting you into something higher, something more aligned.

In your relationships, a shift begins to unfold. You start to grow, but others around you may not. And as you evolve, the people who once felt like home may no longer feel aligned. Some connections dissolve. Others stretch or break. You may grieve people who are still living because the energetic contract between you has completed. And while this can be painful, it's also purposeful. Every relationship—whether it lasts or fades—serves your evolution.

Your beliefs begin to crumble too. You start to see how much of what you once accepted as truth was actually rooted in fear, limitation, or programming. What once seemed black and white now feels fluid. You question everything—and in that questioning, space opens for something new to rise.

Your roles begin to shift. The version of you who lived to please, to perform, to prove—they begin to fade. You no longer want to be the one who always has it together, or the one who plays small just to keep the peace. These identities fall away because they no longer serve who you are becoming.

And the more you try to hold it all together, the heavier it feels. Your old life starts to feel hollow, unsustainable. And your soul becomes louder, trying to get your attention—not to punish, but to redirect.

First it whispers. Then it nudges. Then it shakes.

You may find yourself caught in a crescendo of discomfort. First it's subtle. Then it grows. Until one day, you wake up and feel like you've hit a wall. And if you still don't listen—if you keep pushing through, pretending, conforming—that's when the rock bottom moments tend to arrive.

But even that collapse is a blessing. Because nothing truly falls apart without making space for something new to unfold.

When You've Done Everything "Right" and Still Feel Lost

You may have followed all the rules. You did what was expected. You worked hard, stayed committed, built a life based on what you thought would bring you success, stability, and purpose. And yet, even after doing everything "right," you still find yourself waking up with this deep ache in your chest, a feeling that something isn't quite right. You wonder how you can feel so unfulfilled, so disconnected, when you've done everything you were supposed to do. And you're not alone in that experience.

The truth is, your soul didn't come here to live a life that simply checks the boxes. It didn't incarnate to fit into a mold or play it safe. You weren't meant to settle for a life that keeps you small. You came here with a mission, a deeper purpose, and a fire within that simply cannot be contained by the structures of a "normal" life. That inner fire may have been quiet for years, but it was always there—waiting for the moment you would finally begin to listen.

When your outer world starts to unravel—even if you've done everything "right"—it doesn't mean something has gone wrong. It means your soul is activating. It means the life you built before you awakened is no longer aligned with who you're becoming. And while it can feel painful, confusing, even unfair, it's actually the beginning of something profoundly sacred.

This unraveling is not a sign of failure. It is the signal that you are no longer willing—or able—to live in misalignment with your truth. It is the moment when your soul begins calling you into a higher timeline, one that you may not fully understand yet but can already feel pulling you forward.

And so, the old begins to dissolve—not because it was bad or wrong, but because it cannot hold the magnitude of who you are here to be. That's the deeper reason behind the collapse. You are not being punished. You are being redirected. The version of your life that was built before you awakened is making way for something more true, more alive, more aligned with your soul's purpose.

The Sacred Purpose of the Unraveling

What often feels like chaos is actually a divine recalibration. The breakdowns, the losses, the endings—they are not here to destroy you. They are here to bring you back into alignment. When everything is "fine," we rarely feel compelled to change. It's when life becomes uncomfortable, when the pressure builds, when we feel like we can't take another step in the wrong direction—that's when we begin to awaken. That's when we start looking deeper.

The unraveling is grace in disguise. It is the soul's way of clearing what no longer serves so that space can be made for what's meant to come through next. Often we resist this part. We try to hold everything together, cling to what once brought us comfort or safety. But the truth is, the things that are falling away are doing so because they were built from a version of you that no longer exists.

The discomfort is a signal, not a punishment. It's asking you to slow down, to listen, to stop pushing forward in the same old ways. It's asking you to surrender—not in defeat, but in devotion. Because in the surrender, the clarity comes. In the letting go, the new begins to rise.

This is the space between identities. The sacred in-between. The moment when you are no longer who you used to be, but not yet fully anchored in who you are becoming. And while this space can feel incredibly disorienting, it is also full of power. It is a space of possibility, a space where the soul begins to lead and the old self begins to soften its grip.

The old must fall apart not to break you—but to bring you back to the truth of who you've always been. What's crumbling is the illusion, the conditioning, the roles and beliefs that were never truly yours. What's rising in its place is you—your essence, your power, your truth.

A Message for the One in the Middle of It All

If you find yourself in this space right now—where life feels confusing, where everything that used to make sense is dissolving, where you're no longer sure who you are or what comes next— please know this: you are not doing anything wrong. You are not broken. You are not behind. You are in the middle of becoming.

This space you're in may feel incredibly uncomfortable. You may be gripped by fear, consumed by doubt, or overwhelmed by the intensity of everything you're experiencing, learning, and feeling. But even in the mess of it all, there is meaning. There is purpose. There is grace.

It may not feel like it now, but this is a sacred passage. The unraveling is making space for something truer to emerge. You are being invited to release the old patterns, to loosen the grip of control, to allow the pieces that no longer serve you to fall away—so that what is meant for you can finally arrive.

You are being prepared for something greater. Something more expansive. Something more *you*.

The discomfort you feel is not here to hurt you—it's here to awaken you. And when you allow the discomfort to be your teacher, your guide, even your mirror, that's when the alchemy begins.

You are not meant to go back to the way things were. You are being invited to move forward—not with force, but with presence. Not by figuring everything out, but by opening to the next step, the next breath, the next truth that rises within you.

You don't have to have all the answers right now. You only have to stay open. Surrender—not by giving up, but by letting go of the version of yourself that no longer resonates. Trust that this space you're in is preparing you for everything your soul has been waiting to embody.

This path will ask you to move slowly. Gently. With presence. It will ask for your honesty, your willingness, your devotion. It will challenge you to meet yourself in your fullness—your pain, your power, your shadow, your light. But I promise you: the version of you waiting on the other side of this season is more radiant, more grounded, and more aligned than you can yet imagine.

This is not the end. This is the beginning of your return.

My Journey Through the Unraveling

For me, life never really made sense—not in the way it seemed to for others. I've always felt like an outsider, the black sheep, someone who never quite fit. From a young age, I carried an intensity I didn't know how to explain. What I now understand as my dragon energy—powerful, passionate, untamed—was once the part of me I tried hardest to suppress. I didn't know how to hold it, let alone embody it.

I went through years of challenges, deep hardship, and emotional pain. In 2006, I moved to the United States with my son, brought here by my ex-husband—who left us just two months later. There I was, in a new country, far away from my family, completely alone, raising a child without support. My ex put me through hell, and there were moments I truly thought I wouldn't survive it. I was exhausted, broken down, and full of despair. The only thing that kept me going was my son. Without him, I don't know if I would still be here today.

In 2016, my spiritual journey began—but instead of bringing peace, it brought chaos. I left a toxic job because my health couldn't take it anymore, and that decision triggered a cascade of struggle. For years, it felt like one rock bottom moment after another. I tried to build my spiritual business, but nothing worked. I poured my heart into it, yet I barely stayed afloat. The frustration was overwhelming. I felt like I was doing everything "right," and yet still, I was stuck.

At one point, I even started a marketing consultancy to create some financial stability. And ironically, that business took off with ease. It provided for me, helped me feel safe, but it wasn't my soul work. Every time I thought about walking away from my spiritual path, I felt a deep, resounding *no*. I knew I couldn't give up. I knew something more was waiting.

And eventually, I realized something that changed everything: I had created this. Not because I wasn't worthy. Not because I was cursed. But because I had still been living from a version of me that didn't believe. I didn't fully believe I could be abundant doing what I love. I didn't believe I could lead and guide others from my own wisdom. And so, I kept showing up in energy that reflected lack and fear—and life mirrored that back to me.

The moment I got honest about that, everything shifted. I didn't blame the world. I didn't blame others. I took ownership. I realized that the outer misalignment was reflecting an inner misalignment—and that realization gave me the power to choose differently. I finally stopped resisting my essence. I stopped seeing my dragon energy as "too much," and began embracing it. Not toning it down, not hiding, but owning it. Fully.

I no longer regretted the path I had walked—even the pain. Because every moment, every heartbreak, every dark night of the soul carved me into the woman I am now. If I hadn't gone through all of that, I wouldn't have found my way here. I wouldn't have discovered my gifts. I wouldn't have written this book.

The unraveling was my rebirth.

And now, I offer this chapter to you as a reflection, a reminder, and an invitation to trust your own.

The Space Between Who You Were and Who You're Becoming

This part of your journey is not something to fix, rush through, or bypass. It's not a mistake. It's not a detour. It is a sacred transition—one that will become the foundation for everything that follows.

When the life you once lived no longer fits, and the new version of your reality hasn't yet fully arrived, you are standing in the threshold. This is the space between identities. The version of you that was built from fear, protection, survival, and programming is falling away—not because you failed, but because you are growing beyond it. You are no longer willing to live a life that costs you your truth.

This part of the path will challenge you to be still. It will ask you to sit in the discomfort of not knowing. It may stretch your patience, test your trust, and shake your foundations. But it will also prepare you to rise.

So much of this work—this sacred soul work—is not about rushing toward the light. It is about allowing the darkness to show you what still needs your presence. It is about allowing the unraveling to soften your grip on what no longer serves. It is about facing the version of yourself that you once needed to survive, and gently letting her go. It is about creating space for the version of you who no longer lives from fear, but from truth.

This transition is not just emotional. It's energetic. Somatic. Cellular. It moves through your body. It challenges your nervous system. It invites you to expand your capacity to hold discomfort without collapsing. It teaches you how to meet yourself with compassion, even when everything feels like too much.

And perhaps most importantly, it shows you that the greatest work you will ever do is not just to heal—but to fully embody your soul.

The truth is, you will be the first thing that gets in your way. Your old self will try to keep you small. It will resist change. It will question everything. And in that resistance, you'll be given the opportunity to choose—again and again—who you are becoming.

That's why this part of the journey matters. Because it is here, in this space between stories, that you reclaim your authorship. It is here that you begin to create not from fear, but from frequency. Not from what has been—but from what is rising within you now.

Give yourself the space to dissolve. To let go. To shed. Give yourself the grace to slow down. To listen. To trust. And give yourself permission to walk forward—not as someone who has it all figured out, but as someone who is ready to live from a deeper truth.

This is not the end of the world you once knew. This is the beginning of the world your soul is here to create.

Chapter 3: Feeling Stuck Isn't Failure

Why stagnation often precedes your next evolution

There's a very specific kind of ache that comes when you feel stuck. It's not just frustration—it's this quiet inner friction that seems to rub against everything you do. You might wake up and feel like you're carrying a heaviness that you can't explain. You want more, you desire change, you've even taken steps toward what you think will get you there… and still, nothing seems to shift.

You try the practices. You set the intentions. You journal. You visualize. But instead of momentum, you feel like you're walking through quicksand. Every step forward feels like it's followed by three steps back. And then come the questions: *Am I doing something wrong? Why isn't this working? Is this all there is?*

Mentally, it's exhausting. Emotionally, it can feel defeating. And physically, you may notice the effects too—fatigue, restlessness, a lack of energy or drive. The body often responds to spiritual stagnation in subtle but powerful ways. And what makes it even more challenging is the judgment we pile on top. You start believing that something must be wrong with you. That you're failing. That if things were working, you wouldn't feel this way.

But here's what I want you to know: feeling stuck is not failure. It's an initiation. And beneath the surface of that discomfort, something powerful is trying to get your attention.

Why We Think Stillness Means We're Failing

We live in a world that glorifies movement, output, and results. From an early age, we're taught to hustle. To strive. To earn our worth. Productivity becomes a currency for value, and if we're not actively doing something, we begin to feel like we're falling behind.

Stillness, in this society, is often mistaken for laziness. But the truth is, many of us stay busy as a form of distraction. We keep doing, hustling, working, and striving so we don't have to face what's actually happening within us. Because if we were to pause—if we became still—we might finally feel the dissonance. We might finally notice just how misaligned we are. And once we become aware, we have to choose. We either stay the same or we change.

And here's the thing, **awareness gives you the power of choice.**

Without awareness, there is no choice. You're simply reacting to life. But the moment you become aware—aware that something doesn't feel right, that something's not working—you have a choice. You can do something about it.

That's why we resist stillness. Because stillness reveals truth. It's where we meet ourselves without distraction. It's where the soul begins to whisper what the mind has tried to avoid.

But if you can trust the pause—if you can surrender to it rather than push through it—you'll find that it isn't the absence of progress. It's the space where real transformation begins.

What's Really Happening Beneath the Surface

Seasons of stuckness often coincide with dark nights of the soul—those periods of deep challenge, emotional heaviness, and internal disorientation. And while they may seem like detours or dead ends, they are, in truth, *portals*.

These moments show you what's misaligned. They bring to the surface the fears, doubts, and limitations that have been quietly shaping your life. When we ignore the early nudges—those small signs that something isn't working—the soul begins to turn up the volume. And if we still don't listen, that's when we experience the shake-ups, the rock bottoms, the breakdowns that force us to pay attention.

These are not punishments. They are initiations. And they are guiding you to shed what no longer serves.

During these times, you'll likely face shadow aspects of yourself—old wounds, limiting patterns, unconscious beliefs. But this isn't something to be afraid of. When you understand how to work with them—how to feel without attaching, how to lean into discomfort without resistance—everything changes.

This book will give you the tools, the practices, and the activations to help you move through these seasons with grace. Because it's not the darkness itself that creates the pain—it's the resistance to it. The more we push away what's rising, the more it lingers. But when we finally embrace what's coming up, when we meet it with compassion and curiosity, we move through it faster, with more ease.

Every moment of stillness, every wave of discomfort, holds within it a message, a lesson, and a gift. And when you choose to receive that gift, to integrate it and embody its wisdom, you become the version of you who no longer carries the weight of what once held you down.

The Energetic Wisdom of the Pause

What most people don't realize is that the pause is not an absence of progress—it's where alignment begins. The pause is sacred. It's where we come back to the present moment. It's where we reconnect with ourselves, our breath, and our frequency.

We're often so entangled in the past or anxiously reaching for the future that we forget to be *here*. And yet, it's only here—in the now— that we can step into a new timeline. That we can embody the version of ourselves who already lives the life we desire. That we can access the wisdom of our higher self. But to do that, we have to become still. We have to release the noise and return to the center.

The pause brings with it a sense of peace, of grounding, of presence. It gives us the space to respond rather than react. It gives us the opportunity to ask, *"Is this action aligned with who I'm becoming? Is this reaction coming from love or from fear?"* And in that space, we grow. We align. We reclaim our power.

When you learn to trust the pause, you no longer fear stillness. You no longer rush to fill every space with action or effort. You begin to understand that the space itself is medicine. The breath between the chapters is part of the story. And when you honor the pause, you open the door to everything you've been calling in.

For the One Who Feels Like Nothing Is Working

If you're in a place right now where you feel like you've done everything you're supposed to do—if you've visualized, meditated, taken action, practiced affirmations, tried to shift your mindset, followed the signs—and still nothing seems to be changing… I want you to know this:

There's nothing wrong with you. You haven't failed. And you're not being blocked by the Universe or denied what you want. What you're experiencing is a very real, very sacred part of the journey.

It doesn't mean you're not meant to have what you desire. It doesn't mean you're not aligned or not doing "enough." What it *does* mean is that you're likely missing one key piece of the puzzle—a piece that most people never realize they've overlooked.

You don't need to try harder. You don't need to do more. What's required is not more striving—it's *embodiment.*

You need to become the version of yourself who already has what you desire. Not just mentally, not just spiritually, but energetically. You have to calibrate your entire field to that frequency. And when you do, things begin to shift—not because you forced them to, but because you became available to receive what was always meant for you.

That's what this book will walk you through.

Embodiment is the piece most people skip—and it's also the one thing that changes everything.

Once you truly become the version of you who lives the life you've been trying to manifest, that life begins to meet you. It stops being something you chase and becomes something that *naturally unfolds.*

So if you're feeling tired, frustrated, or like you're spinning your wheels, please know: you are not stuck. You are preparing. You are becoming. And everything you've been asking for is already orbiting your field, waiting for you to meet it from the inside out.

My Story of "Stuckness" and What It Taught Me

There have been so many times in my life when I felt like I was doing all the right things, and yet everything felt like it was standing still—

or worse, falling apart. I've talked about the challenges I faced raising my son alone, starting over in a new country, and going through years of deep struggle. But what I haven't fully shared is how long I stayed in that place of stuckness, even after I started doing the spiritual work.

I took the courses. I read the books. I cleared the blocks. I followed the steps. But no matter how much I "did," it was like something kept pulling me back into the same cycle of lack, of frustration, of stagnation.

I now know why.

I hadn't yet become the version of me who believed it was possible. I was still operating from an identity that didn't feel worthy, that doubted herself, that feared failure. I was doing the work—but I wasn't embodying the frequency of what I truly wanted.

When that realization landed for me, everything changed. I got honest with myself. I stopped blaming the external. I stopped looking for the next tactic or technique. And instead, I asked myself, *"Who do I need to be in order to create the life I want?"*

That question broke something open. I started showing up differently. I began to trust in my power. I stopped hiding. I owned my voice, my presence, my dragon energy—and I let myself *be seen.*

And from there… things moved.

The path began to open. The clarity came. And I stopped waiting for permission. I became the woman I had been looking for.

So if you feel stuck, if things aren't flowing, don't give up. You might just be standing at the edge of your next expansion. And this book is here to guide you through that edge—with grace, with power, and with the exact tools to move through it.

The Space Before the Shift

Feeling stuck is not a sign that you're doing something wrong—it's a sign that something deeper is trying to rise. And the moment you can recognize that, everything begins to change.

Awareness gives you the power of choice. The simple act of naming that something doesn't feel right opens a doorway. It gives you the opportunity to pause, reflect, and begin asking the real questions: *What am I holding onto that's no longer aligned? What is trying to be released? What is asking to be transformed?*

When you acknowledge your stuckness with compassion instead of shame, you start to soften. You begin to make space for truth. And that space is exactly what we need before we begin the deeper healing work ahead.

Because the truth is—there's more beneath the surface than most people realize.

Like an iceberg, we often only see the small portion that rises above the water—the visible struggles, the conscious patterns, the surface-level fears. But below that is an entire structure of unconscious energy. Old wounds. Limiting beliefs. Childhood imprints. Unspoken fears. Energetic residue from past lifetimes. Things you may not even be aware of... but that are still shaping how you move through the world.

And whether you acknowledge them or not, they're there. They influence your choices, your manifestations, your relationships, your sense of worth. They affect what you allow yourself to receive and what you believe is possible for you.

That's why we're about to go deeper.

In Part II, we begin the sacred work of transmutation. We go into the fire—not to burn, but to be refined. We'll explore the shadows, the stories, the old identities that no longer serve who you are becoming. We'll look at what's been hidden beneath the surface and start the process of alchemizing it into gold.

Because without this inner work, embodiment isn't sustainable. You can try to manifest all day, but if your unconscious beliefs say *you're not ready,* your results will always match your deeper resonance—not your surface desires.

This is the part that many people skip. It's also why so many on the spiritual path—whether teachers, healers, or seekers—still find themselves stuck. They've awakened. They've done the rituals. But they haven't gone deep enough. Or they've only skimmed the surface of their shadows. And then they wonder why the abundance, the impact, the clarity still hasn't arrived.

So I want you to know: it's not because you're not meant for it. It's simply that this part matters more than you may have been taught.

And that's where we're going next.

In Part II, I'll walk with you through the most essential part of the alchemical path. Not to fix you—but to help you transmute the energy that has been blocking your light. You'll be supported, guided, and equipped with what you need to move through your next layer with grace and power.

This is where the real work begins.

And it's also where you begin to reclaim your truest self.

Chapter 4: Your Soul Is Trying to Get Your Attention

Hearing the whispers beneath the noise

There is a whisper that lives inside you. A quiet, steady presence that has always been with you. Sometimes it rises as a gut feeling or a soft inner pull in a direction that your mind doesn't understand but your body somehow knows. At other times, it moves through you in the form of restlessness—an ache that tells you something about your life no longer fits, even if you can't quite name what needs to change. It might even show up as tears that come without warning or a deep emotional wave that catches you off guard. These aren't just reactions to the moment. These are messages from your soul.

Soul doesn't always communicate in words. In fact, it rarely does. Its language is subtle, energetic, and deeply personal. It speaks through emotion, sensation, intuition, imagery, and frequency. It nudges you gently at first, offering signs through dreams, synchronicities, inner knowing, and quiet realizations. You might begin noticing the same number patterns repeating over and over, or overhear a phrase that hits you right in the chest like it was meant just for you. You might feel inexplicably drawn to a specific book or video or have a conversation that brings through the exact words you've been needing to hear. This is not random. This is how soul moves—through resonance, timing, and sacred alignment.

But soul's voice isn't only something that happens to you from the outside. You can actually learn to deepen that connection, to cultivate it intentionally, to strengthen it like you would a sacred relationship. And the more you engage in that relationship, the louder and clearer your soul's guidance becomes.

One of the simplest and most powerful ways to open that channel is to speak directly to your soul. You don't need to do anything complicated. Just bring your awareness into your heart. Let yourself settle. Place your hand on your chest, close your eyes, and begin by saying—either aloud or silently—"I now call forth my soul. Please connect with me now. I now call forth my higher self. Please connect with me now." Then allow yourself to feel what shifts. You may notice yourself sitting up straighter, feeling more complete, or sensing a calmness that washes through your body. You may not hear words, but you'll feel presence.

From that space, you can begin to commune with your soul. You can ask questions, tune in for answers, or simply sit in the quiet frequency of connection. Some prefer to do this through journaling, letting the words flow in automatic writing. Others choose to speak aloud or hold internal dialogue in stillness. There is no one right way—what matters most is that you approach it with openness, presence, and genuine desire to connect.

And over time, the more you listen, the more you'll start to notice: your soul has been speaking all along. You just needed the space to hear it.

Soul vs. Ego – Learning to Discern the Difference

One of the most important things you'll learn on this path is how to distinguish the voice of your soul from the voice of your ego. Because they sound very different—but only when you know how to listen.

The voice of ego often feels loud, fast, and heavy. It speaks from fear and doubt. It needs to protect you, control the outcome, and avoid risk at all costs. It creates stories, attaches to limitations, and gets easily overwhelmed by uncertainty. The ego wants guarantees. It wants safety and logic. And it tends to kick in the moment you begin stepping into something bigger.

Your soul speaks differently. Soul doesn't yell—it whispers. It doesn't panic—it invites. And while your soul's guidance may stretch you, it never comes from fear. You may feel discomfort at what it's asking you to step into—but underneath that discomfort, there's always a sense of expansion. A quiet *rightness*. An inner knowing that says, *This might be big… but it's mine.*

The energetic signature is clear when you tune in. Ego feels tight, constricted, and reactive. Soul feels open, grounded, and calm—even when the path ahead feels unknown.

One way to check in is to simply ask yourself: *How does this feel in my body?* If it feels like contraction, confusion, urgency, or fear—it's likely coming from your ego. If it feels like peace, clarity, or a calm inner "yes," even if it's scary—it's likely your soul.

Learning to discern between these two inner voices is essential—because on this alchemical path, the soul must lead. And the more you practice tuning in, the easier it becomes to recognize the difference.

Creating a Daily Dialogue with Your Soul

Your soul doesn't just show up in the big, life-changing moments. It wants to walk with you daily—through the little decisions, the ordinary moments, the subtle redirections.

But that relationship needs tending.

One of the most powerful ways to create a deeper relationship with your soul is to simply invite it in. Start your day by placing your hand on your heart, taking a few conscious breaths, and saying—aloud or silently—*"I now call forth my soul. Please connect with me now. I now call forth my higher self. Please connect with me now."* Then listen. Feel. Even if you don't hear a clear answer, trust that something inside you is shifting.

You may begin to feel a greater sense of presence or stillness. A deepening in your breath. A calming of your thoughts. That is your soul settling into the field of your awareness.

From that space, you can start an inner conversation. Ask a question, then let your pen move across the page. This is where automatic writing becomes a powerful practice—not because you're "channeling" something outside of yourself, but because you're giving voice to your deeper knowing. Your soul knows. You just have to give it space to speak.

You can also reflect in the evenings by asking: *Where did I follow my inner guidance today? Where did I ignore it?* You're not doing this to judge yourself—you're doing this to become aware. Because as I've shared many times before: awareness gives you the power of choice. And with choice, you can shift.

If you don't make space for these daily check-ins, you might start feeling lost or uncertain. But the moment you reconnect, even for just a few minutes, your sense of direction comes back. You feel more grounded, more centered, more open.

Over time, this becomes a way of living. You start making choices that feel right without needing to justify them. You begin trusting your own resonance over what others say. You speak to your soul the same way you'd speak to a trusted guide or friend. And it becomes a natural part of your everyday life.

Because this isn't about becoming "more intuitive." It's about returning to what you've always known. It's about remembering how to live in connection with the part of you that has never been separate from Source.

And as we begin the deeper work in the next phase of the journey, this connection to soul will become more important than ever.

Here are a few ways to attune to your soul's guidance on a daily basis:

- **Start your day by checking in.** Before you get out of bed, place your hand on your heart and ask: *What do I need to hear today?* Then listen.

- **Use automatic writing.** After calling in your soul (as described earlier), allow yourself to free-write without censoring. Let the words flow, even if they don't make sense at first. You'll be surprised what comes through.

- **Practice stillness.** Even five minutes of sitting with your hand on your heart, breathing deeply, and simply *being* can open the channel.

- **Reflect at night.** Before bed, ask: *Where did I ignore my inner knowing today? Where did I follow it?* This isn't about judgment—it's about cultivating awareness.

- **Speak aloud.** Yes—out loud. Soul responds to voiced intention. The more you include your soul in your process, the more active that guidance becomes.

Most importantly, keep the dialogue gentle. You're not trying to "get" answers. You're deepening a relationship. One that already lives within you.

When You Wonder: "Is This Even Real?"

If you've ever asked yourself, *"Am I just making this up?"* or *"What if I'm imagining all of this?"*—you're not alone. Every awakening soul, especially early on, has questioned whether the guidance they receive is real or valid. We've been conditioned to dismiss what we can't measure or logically explain. But inner guidance doesn't come from logic—it comes from resonance. It comes from a deeper place, a knowing that bypasses the mind and speaks directly to your truth.

Learning to trust your intuition, your soul nudges, your inner guidance is a process—and in the beginning, it's normal to wobble. This is why it's so important to stay present with how it feels in your body. Soul guidance feels grounded, clear, expansive. Even when it stretches you, it holds a certain "rightness," a sense of aligned possibility. Ego guidance, on the other hand, tends to feel urgent, scattered, or fear-based.

Over time, the more you listen, the more your system begins to calibrate. Your nervous system learns what soul feels like. Your inner compass becomes stronger. You no longer second-guess everything, because you've had enough moments of trusting yourself and seeing what unfolded when you did. That trust becomes embodied.

You don't need proof to trust what you feel. You don't need a sign for every decision. You don't need permission from anyone else. The resonance you feel inside—when you slow down, breathe, and really check in—that's enough.

And yes, you will still have moments of doubt. That's okay. The point isn't to be perfect or to get it right every time. The point is to keep choosing to listen. To reconnect. To return to your soul again and again, especially when things feel uncertain.

Why Soul Guidance Matters in What Comes Next

As we prepare to move into *Part II: The Transmutation*, this connection to your soul becomes more than just a nice concept—it becomes a necessary support system. Because what's coming next is the alchemical fire.

In Part II, we begin to peel back the layers. We confront the aspects of self that have kept you stuck, the unconscious programming that's been running the show, the parts of you that have been operating from fear, from wounds, from roles you didn't choose. This is where we meet the shadow—not to judge it, but to reclaim what's been lost beneath it. This is where true liberation begins.

And walking through that fire isn't something you do alone. Your soul will walk with you. It will guide you through the discomfort. It will show you what's ready to be released. It will bring you face to face with old patterns so that you can finally, truly, clear them—not by bypassing them, but by understanding the message they carry.

This is why learning to attune to your soul now, in this moment, matters. The work ahead will stretch you, but it will also free you. And the more attuned you are to the voice of your soul, the more gracefully you'll move through what's coming.

Because the truth is, the journey of the Soul Alchemist isn't about fixing yourself—it's about becoming who you really are.

The Path Ahead

If you've made it here, you're already listening. Your soul has led you to this moment, to this book, to this very sentence. And something within you is ready—not just to read more words, but to *embody* the frequency of what's unfolding.

This is not a passive journey. It is sacred. It is transformational. And what comes next will ask more of you—not in the form of pressure, but in the form of presence. It will ask you to feel what you once avoided. To hold yourself through discomfort. To release what no longer serves. And to rise—not through willpower, but through embodiment.

But you won't be doing it alone.

You'll be guided—by your soul, by your truth, by the energetic frameworks within this book. You'll have tools, practices, incantations, and reminders. And most of all, you'll have access to your inner wisdom every step of the way.

So take a breath. Place your hand on your heart. And say: *"I trust my soul to lead me. I am ready to transmute."*

The path of liberation is not a straight line. It's a spiral, a dance, a remembering.
And you, beloved Soul Alchemist, are ready to walk through the fire.

Let's begin.

Closing Incantation: The Stirring

Before you step into the alchemical fire, pause. Breathe. Let all that has stirred within you settle deeper into your being. You are not who you were when you began this journey—and you're only just beginning to remember what you came here to become.

Let this incantation seal what has awakened. Let it ready your field for what comes next.

Incantation - I Hear My Soul

I allow myself to feel what I once tried to silence.
I welcome the quiet knowing that keeps calling me home.
I trust that this stirring is sacred, even when my mind can't explain it.

I give myself permission to listen—deeply, fully, now.
I choose to honor the whisper of my soul above the noise of the world.

With every breath, I open to the truth that lives beneath my doubts. With every heartbeat, I remember: the path begins within.

I will not rush this moment. I will not judge what I find.
I will meet myself with honesty and reverence, knowing that awareness gives me the power of choice.

And so I listen. And so I begin.

✧ Part II: The Transmutation ✧

"The fire doesn't burn you to punish—it burns to purify,
to alchemize, to reveal the gold you forgot was yours."

This is where the real work begins.

You've heard the call. You've felt the stirring. You've begun to listen more closely to your soul. And now, you've reached the threshold of the fire. Not the kind that burns for destruction—but the kind that purifies, that alchemizes, that frees.

Transmutation is not about fixing. It's not about chasing healing or endlessly trying to solve what's "wrong" with you. It's about meeting the parts of you that have been buried, silenced, distorted, or hidden—and bringing them into the light so they can be reclaimed. This is the space where the old self begins to dissolve. Not because you force it to die, but because you are no longer willing to carry what was never yours to begin with.

In this part of the journey, we will uncover the layers you've worn for a lifetime—layers inherited from your family, your culture, your past experiences, and your own survival strategies. We'll look at the masks and identities that once kept you safe, but now keep you small. We'll meet the shadow, not to shame it, but to understand the gifts it guards. We'll feel the emotions you've been told are "too much," and learn how to work with them as energy—not as problems to solve.

This work is sacred. It is not always easy. But it is necessary if you want to become the alchemist of your own reality.

The transmutation phase will teach you how to work with what's heavy, dense, and distorted—and turn it into clarity, power, and truth. You'll be given tools, energetic practices, rituals, and activations to help you release what no longer serves and call your power back from the places you've left it behind.

What lies ahead is not just about letting go—it's about liberation. And liberation begins with truth.

You are not here to bypass your pain. You are here to honor it, to listen to it, and then to choose something new.

Let the fire begin. Let the alchemy unfold. Let the Soul Alchemist within you rise.

Chapter 5: Letting Go of Who You Thought You Had to Be

Dismantling survival identities and inherited roles that no longer fit

There comes a moment on your alchemical journey when you realize—you can't take your old identity with you. The version of you who learned how to stay safe by dimming her light, playing small, following the rules, and trying to be what everyone else expected... she can't walk the path you're now being called to walk.

Letting go of an identity means releasing a version of yourself that, in some way, became a prison. That version may have helped you survive. It may have protected you. It may have been the only way you knew how to belong, stay safe, or navigate the world. But at some point, what once kept you safe becomes what's holding you back.

We carry so many identities—some conscious, some deeply hidden. The woman who always plays it safe. The one who doesn't trust herself. The one who's convinced money is hard to come by. The version of you that doubts her gifts, hides her voice, avoids being seen, or fears failure. These identities become woven into your sense of self, but they're not who you really are. They're masks. They're roles. And many of them were never truly *yours* to begin with.

Even the "good" identities—like being the nurturing one, the strong one, the spiritual one, the independent one—can become limiting if they're tied to proving your worth or staying in control. The work isn't to discard every version of you. The work is to become conscious of what's true and what's inherited, what's empowering and what's outdated. The expansive aspects of you are meant to be nurtured and evolved. But the limiting identities? Those need to be seen, honored for the role they played—and then lovingly released so your true essence can emerge.

What once felt like truth can start to feel tight. That's the sign you've outgrown it.

Maybe you used to believe that following your soul's path meant sacrificing your income. Maybe you learned that love has to be earned, that safety means shrinking, or that being spiritual means not desiring wealth. And maybe those beliefs helped you make sense of life for a time. But now they feel off. They don't quite fit anymore. That's because your energy has shifted. Your soul is ready for more. And anything that no longer aligns with that evolution begins to feel heavier—like wearing someone else's clothes.

That's the nature of this path. You grow. And as you grow, you start to see through the illusions, the partial truths, the stories you once believed were just "the way life is." But they're not. They were just the lens you were looking through.

And letting go of those lenses is hard—not because they're true, but because they're *familiar.* The ego would rather stay in a known discomfort than risk stepping into an unknown potential. Even if you're not happy with who you are right now, at least you know how to survive as this version of you. And that perceived safety is exactly what makes it so hard to let go.

There's also the honesty this work requires. To become someone new, you must take full responsibility for who you've been. You must look at yourself—at the patterns, behaviors, choices, and stories you've been living—and say: *This is mine. I created this. And I'm ready to create something different.* That kind of ownership takes courage. It requires compassion. It might stir up grief, shame, or resistance. But it also opens the door to your liberation.

And that's what this chapter is here to help you with.

We're not here to fix you. You're not broken. You're becoming. And part of becoming is shedding. Releasing the old roles, survival strategies, and outdated truths you've outgrown. Some of them will fall away easily. Others may cling on for dear life. But don't worry— I'll walk you through it all.

Because once you let go of who you thought you had to be, you make space for who you *actually are* to rise.

How Survival Identities Are Formed

The identities we carry didn't just appear out of nowhere. They were shaped by experience—by moments that left an imprint, by situations that hurt, by the need to stay safe, be accepted, or avoid pain. At some point in your life, you learned that being all of who you are wasn't always welcome. And so, you adapted.

Let's say the first time you fell in love, you were wide open. Your heart was pure, unhurt, and trusting. But then the relationship ended—and it hurt. You questioned yourself, you felt the sting of rejection or betrayal, and somewhere deep within, a decision was made: *I won't let that happen again.* You didn't consciously decide to build a wall, but you did. You became the version of you who is a little more guarded, a little more hesitant, a little more skeptical.

Then another relationship comes along. And you carry that baggage with you. Maybe you don't open up as quickly. Maybe you hold back parts of yourself. Maybe you expect disappointment before it even arrives. And if that relationship ends, it only confirms the identity you've created: *See? It's not safe to trust. It always ends this way.* And so, that identity becomes more solidified.

This doesn't just happen in love. It happens with money, too. Maybe you grew up in a home where money was tight. Your parents struggled. You overheard arguments about bills. You saw stress in their eyes. You internalized the message that money is hard to come by. That you have to work yourself into the ground just to scrape by. That abundance is for *other* people. And so, you adapt to that belief. You live from it. And even if you begin to make more money, you might notice it disappears just as quickly. Something always comes up—an unexpected bill, a repair, a setback—something that reinforces the identity: *See? I can't hold onto money. It's just how life is.*

We take on these survival identities as a way to protect ourselves, but over time, they become prisons. They shape our lives without us even realizing it. And it's not just about love or money—this applies to every area of life.

You may have learned to be the caretaker because that's how you felt loved. Or the overachiever because success gave you a sense of worth. Or the strong one because being vulnerable never felt safe. Or the "good girl" because disappointing others felt unbearable. Each of these roles might have served you once. But eventually, they limit you. They keep you from being *you.*

And then there are the masks we wear to fit in.

You mold yourself into who you think others want you to be. You become agreeable, likable, easy to be around. You downplay your passions. You silence your voice. You hide your gifts. And you begin to shrink into a version of yourself that feels safe in the world—but not free.

I've been there. For a long time, I believed I was "too much." Too intense. Too deep. Too sensitive. So, I dimmed my light. I tried to tone it down. I made myself smaller so others would feel more comfortable around me. But all that did was disconnect me from my power. It left me feeling frustrated, misunderstood, and unseen. The moment I gave myself permission to fully *be* me—without apologizing for it—everything shifted. My energy changed. My life changed. People began to respond differently because I was finally aligned with who I *really* am.

When we hide who we are, when we live from a false identity, we create friction in our system. It feels like being out of sync with yourself. You start to feel stuck, disconnected, frustrated, or like something is missing. And that's because you're not living as your full self. You're living as a version of you that was created out of necessity, not truth.

The roles we play—caretaker, achiever, peacemaker, the one who holds it all together—aren't inherently bad. But they are often rooted in old survival strategies. And if we never question them, we risk spending our whole life being someone we're not.

That's why this work matters. That's why this chapter is here. To help you see what roles you've taken on. To help you remember who you are underneath them all.

The Signs That It's Time to Let Go

There comes a moment when your current reality starts to feel heavy—off—like you're walking around in clothes that don't quite fit anymore. This is often the first sign that a version of yourself is ready to be released.

You might start feeling friction in areas of your life that used to feel manageable—relationships feel strained, money stops flowing, you're suddenly more reactive or anxious, your body starts speaking louder through fatigue, tension, or physical symptoms. It may even feel like life just isn't "clicking" the way it used to. That's not failure—it's feedback. That friction is your soul whispering: *You've outgrown this version of you.*

This internal dissonance shows up everywhere. You might find yourself constantly bumping up against others, feeling like you're speaking two completely different languages. And in a way, you are. There's what you say and do on the surface—and then there's the energetic language of who you *actually* are beneath the masks. When those two don't match, people can feel it. Even if they can't name it, they sense something's off.

But when you begin to let go of the masks and show up as your authentic self, something powerful happens. Your energy, your essence, and your expression come into alignment. The friction dissolves. Your nervous system starts to regulate. And you begin to relate to the world from a place of truth, rather than defense.

That's when you know you're stepping into a new chapter—not just clearing old energy but *transcending it.*

The body always reveals misalignment before the mind catches up. You might feel chronic tension, nervous system dysregulation, emotional instability, or even cycles of illness that don't seem to make sense. That's because unprocessed energy creates stress in your system—and the longer you wear identities that don't match your truth, the more your body has to compensate for the energetic strain. You may find yourself constantly exhausted, sensitive to your environment, or overwhelmed by things that used to feel easy. These are not just signs of burnout—they're signals of misalignment.

Eventually, the work becomes less about continuing to heal and more about *transcending.* There's only so much clearing you can do before the next step becomes clear: *embody something new.*

Let's say you're working with the identity of someone who's been heartbroken. You do the inner work—you clear the pain, release the grief, and remove the energetic imprint from that original wound. That's powerful. But if you stop there, you stay in the loop. You might feel lighter, but you haven't yet chosen a new frequency to embody. And so you find yourself repeating the same experiences, attracting similar relationships, and needing to heal all over again.

True transformation happens when you draw a line in the sand and say, *No more. I'm done carrying this.* That's when the shift occurs—because you're no longer defined by the wound. You're ready to ask: *What was the deeper message in all of this? What was the lesson? What gift was hidden in that experience?*

And once you uncover that gift, you don't just acknowledge it—you *embody* it. You live from it. You let it reshape the way you think, feel, choose, and create. You take new actions that align with who you've become—not who you used to be.

That's how the old version of you falls away—not through force, but through remembrance and integration. Not because you hate who you were, but because you've outgrown that version. You've harvested the wisdom. And now, you're ready to evolve.

The Unraveling Before the Becoming

Once you start to recognize the limiting identities you've been living from—and trust me, every single person has them—it can feel a little overwhelming at first. You might notice resistance rising up, or even a sense of fear about what you'll uncover if you truly "go there." That's normal. You're not doing anything wrong by feeling that way.

But here's the truth: those identities are playing out in the background whether you look at them or not. They're running the show, influencing how you move through life, how you relate to others, how you create, love, trust, and lead. You might not see it on the surface, but those old patterns have been quietly shaping your experiences the whole time.

So when you finally bring the courage to face them—to work with them—that's when everything starts to shift. That's when you take the wheel back.

Up until now, it's been like your limiting identity has been driving the car while you sat in the passenger seat saying, "Why are we going this way? This doesn't feel right!" And that identity just kept driving, ignoring you like the annoying backseat voice. But now? Now you're getting back into the driver's seat. This book, this work—it's your roadmap back to sovereignty. You are no longer a passive passenger in your own life.

Of course, that dismantling doesn't happen in a vacuum. It ripples out into every area—your relationships, your business, your visibility, your creativity, and especially your trust in yourself.

Because when you start letting go of who you've *believed* yourself to be, and begin embodying who you truly are, your energy shifts. You become more vibrant. You begin showing up with less hesitation, more truth, more confidence. And not everyone will know how to handle that.

Especially if you used to play small, stay quiet, hide your voice, or shrink your light to avoid being "too much." If you were the peacemaker, the invisible one, the doormat—then suddenly stepping into your empowered, authentic self can feel like a shock to those around you. Not because you're doing anything wrong, but because they no longer recognize the old version of you they were used to.

And here's the thing—this dissonance often happens on an energetic level, not a surface one. They might not *say* anything's changed, but they feel it. Your energy no longer mirrors their expectations of you. And when that happens, it can cause friction or even distance. That's okay.

You're not here to stay stuck in the identity others are comfortable with. You're here to evolve. You're here to awaken. You're here to become the truest version of you.

So let me say this clearly: do not dim your light to make others comfortable. Do not shrink just to fit someone else's outdated perception of who you're supposed to be. That's not your job. Your only job is to be fully, unapologetically you.

And while the unraveling of those old versions can feel like a breakdown—it's not. It's a breakthrough.

It's the sacred moment where the false layers fall away and you finally start to remember who you've been all along. Beneath the roles, beneath the fear, beneath the survival masks—you're still in there. And you're ready to rise.

Reclaiming Your Power Through Letting Go

Holding onto false identities—those roles and versions of yourself you've outgrown—is one of the most common forms of energetic leakage. It creates internal friction that your system can barely keep up with. When you're pretending to be someone you're not, just to be accepted, liked, or to avoid judgment, you put an immense strain on your nervous system. And your energy has to work overtime to maintain that mask.

You might not even notice it in the moment, but you definitely feel it afterward.

Think about those family gatherings or social settings where you hide parts of yourself. Maybe you keep quiet about your spiritual path, the intuitive gifts you've discovered, or the energy work you've been exploring—because you don't want to be judged or dismissed. So you edit yourself. You filter your truth. You pretend to be someone you're not just to avoid the awkward stares or raised eyebrows.

And then you come home… completely drained.

You feel like you've just run an emotional marathon, even though all you did was sit around making small talk. That's the cost of holding misaligned energy. That's what happens when you deny who you truly are to maintain someone else's comfort. Your nervous system can't regulate properly because it's been overstimulated by trying to hold a frequency that isn't yours.

But here's the beautiful part—when you begin to let go of those false, limiting identities, everything starts to shift. The moment you release who you thought you had to be, you make room for soul embodiment.

You create space for your true self to rise. Your energy becomes coherent. Your nervous system begins to settle. You no longer waste energy trying to be something you're not—because being *you* becomes your default setting. Unfiltered. Unapologetic. Unlimited.

And no, it doesn't mean you'll never have to navigate others' reactions again. But it means you no longer abandon yourself to do so.

As these old identities fall away, they're replaced by new, more aligned expressions of who you've become. Not roles you wear to please others—but soul expressions that support you in moving forward. You're not pretending anymore. You're becoming.

Letting go isn't just about what you release. It's about what you reclaim. You reclaim your energy. You reclaim your truth. You reclaim your power.

A Message to Your Soul

You didn't come here to hide. You didn't choose this lifetime just to shrink yourself down or twist who you are to fit into boxes that were never meant for you. You didn't incarnate to be small, quiet, or manageable. You came here to be fully expressed. You came here to embody your truth and walk the path that only *you* can walk—unfiltered, unmasked, unapologetically you.

But somewhere along the way, you were told it wasn't safe. Maybe not in words, but through energy, through experiences, through what you absorbed from those around you. You learned to dim your light so others wouldn't feel uncomfortable. You learned to carry the weight of expectations that were never yours to begin with. You were handed roles to play, masks to wear, identities to hold—because at some point, they helped you feel safe, accepted, or simply able to keep going.

And maybe they did help you survive for a time. But they were never meant to define you.

Now those old roles feel heavy. They no longer fit. And deep down, you can feel it. You can feel the discomfort of pretending. You can feel the disconnect that comes from living out of alignment with who you truly are. And even though a part of you may still cling to the familiar, the truth is rising within you. The truth that you are *not* the masks. You are not the stories, the fears, or the false identities shaped through pain and protection. You are so much more.

It's okay to grieve the versions of yourself you've outgrown. It's okay to feel the fear that comes when the old stories start to unravel. You've held them for a long time. They became part of your rhythm, part of how you moved through the world. But they were never the fullness of you. They were fragments—coping mechanisms, survival strategies, roles you stepped into when you didn't yet know it was safe to be seen.

Now, the invitation is to lay them down. Not with shame. Not with judgment. But with reverence. They served you. But they are no longer needed for where you're going next.

This is not about fixing yourself. It's not about becoming someone entirely new. It's about returning to what's always been within you. It's about remembering the version of you that existed before the world told you who you needed to be. The version of you that never left—just waited patiently beneath the surface.

So take a deep breath, and give yourself permission. Permission to stop performing. Permission to stop apologizing for who you are. Permission to stop editing your truth so others feel more comfortable.
Permission to let go of the roles you never consciously chose, and to reclaim the parts of yourself you silenced just to belong.

You are not too much. You are not behind. You are not broken or lost. You are simply shedding the pieces that were never really yours—and remembering the power that was always there.

This is not a breakdown. It is a sacred turning point. You are standing in the doorway of something far more expansive than what you've known. And what lies on the other side of this letting go is freedom. Alignment. Radiance.

All that's required is your yes. A yes to your evolution. A yes to your soul. A yes to living your truth—not someday, but now.

Let this be the chapter where everything shifts. Let this be the moment you return to yourself—not in theory, but in embodiment. This is your time.

You are ready. You have always been ready. And now, the real journey begins.

Closing Incantation: Releasing Who I Thought I Had to Be

Before you move forward, take a breath. Feel into everything this chapter stirred in you—the identities you've outgrown, the ways you've shaped yourself to survive, the truths you're beginning to remember.

You don't need to have it all figured out. You don't need to know who you're becoming just yet. You only need to be willing to release who you are no longer.

This incantation is not a performance. It is a declaration. Let it land in your body. Let it ripple through your field. Speak it aloud—or whisper it to your soul—and let it begin the unraveling.

Incantation

I now release the roles I was never meant to play.
I lay down the masks I wore to feel safe, accepted, or loved.
I dissolve the identities shaped by fear, by lack, by survival.
I honor who I have been—and I choose now to become who I truly am.

I no longer pretend to be less than I am.
I no longer seek permission to be all of me.
I no longer anchor my worth in how others see me.

I return my energy to myself. I call back the fragments scattered through time, through story, through self-forgetting.
I bring them home—whole, clear, integrated.

I remember who I am beneath the noise, the programming, the performance. I am not a role. I am not a mask. I am the essence beneath them all.

From this moment forward, I choose truth. I choose alignment. I choose to walk as the Soul Alchemist I already am. So it is.

Chapter 6: The Layers You Didn't Choose

Clearing generational wounds, energetic imprints, and societal conditioning

As we grow up, we learn all sorts of things from our parents, caregivers, and the world around us—things that shape what we believe to be true, even when those beliefs aren't based in truth at all. These early messages, behaviors, and rules form a framework that becomes so familiar we rarely stop to question it. But just because something feels true doesn't mean it actually is.

These are what I call "the layers you didn't choose." They are the beliefs that were ingrained in you before you had the capacity to choose for yourself. Things like:

– "It's hard to make money."
– "Money doesn't grow on trees."
– "You have to work really hard to earn anything worthwhile."
– "Nothing good comes easy—you have to struggle, sacrifice, and prove yourself."
– "You only receive love when you're good, quiet, helpful, or successful."

These kinds of beliefs don't just shape your thoughts—they imprint deeply into your energy field. They plant seeds of lack, limitation, unworthiness, and fear. And the impact of those seeds can linger for decades.

If love was withheld when you made a mistake, you may have internalized the message that love is conditional or that you're not lovable when you're imperfect. If you were punished for expressing yourself, you may have learned that your voice isn't welcome, or that it's safer to stay quiet and small. These early experiences are powerful because they don't just leave psychological marks—they leave energetic signatures. They create deeply embedded patterns that influence how you move through life, how you show up in the world, and what you believe is possible for you.

Let's say you absorbed an energetic pattern of lack. That might show up as financial struggle, never quite having enough, or always living paycheck to paycheck. The outer experience reflects the inner imprint. If you carry beliefs around not being deserving or good enough, you might find yourself playing small, holding back from your dreams, or talking yourself out of opportunities before they even fully form.

These inherited layers shape your reality—and I call them "false truths." Not because they aren't real to you, but because they are not the *higher* truth. For example, you might believe deep down that making money is hard. That belief has become *your* truth. But the higher truth is that making money can actually be easy. There are countless people who have created abundance with ease, flow, and alignment. So your belief isn't *the* truth—it's simply a *truth* you've picked up along the way.

And the moment you recognize that, you gain power. You gain choice. Wherever something in your life feels limited, stuck, or out of alignment, that's a signal. It's an invitation to look within and ask:

What am I believing that might not actually be true? What truths have I been carrying that are ready to be released?

Because when you become aware of these layers, you can begin to peel them back. You can decide whether to keep holding onto beliefs that limit you—or whether you're ready to let them go and begin living from a place of higher truth, from a place of soul.

And the moment you choose that—something begins to shift. Even before you know what all the beliefs are, your willingness to release them starts the unraveling. The energy begins to move, the weight begins to lift. So let's begin with a simple but powerful practice to support that shift right now.

Practice:

Begin each day by setting the intention: "I now release any belief, imprint, or truth that is not mine or not aligned with my highest good." Place your hand on your heart and breathe deeply. Then repeat: **"I now clear and transmute all limiting truths across all times, space, reality, lifetimes and dimensions."**

Generational Wounds That Didn't Start With You

Now let's talk about the ancestral wounds that have been passed down through generations—layers of energetic and emotional inheritance that you didn't choose, but that still affect you deeply.

If you're experiencing lack, financial hardship, overworking, or constant sacrifice—like always putting career before relationships—those patterns may be playing out because of ancestral imprints running silently in the background. Think of it this way: your parents taught you what they believed to be true, and they learned those truths from their parents, who learned from their own, and so on. These beliefs, behaviors, and wounds don't start with you—they're handed down like invisible heirlooms, encoded into your subconscious and energetic field.

Now consider this: many generations ago, wealth and abundance were not widely accessible. People often lived in poverty or simply got by with very little. Their lives were shaped by struggle and survival. From that place, they developed deeply ingrained beliefs like "there's never enough," "you have to work hard to earn your worth," or "luxury is for other people." These were not just ideas—they were truths for them. And those truths became part of your energetic inheritance.

Even if you've done mindset work around money, worthiness, or success, if these generational patterns haven't been cleared energetically, they still linger. You might carry an internal sense of guilt around abundance or feel uncomfortable receiving too much, even though you consciously desire it. That's the hidden influence of ancestral imprinting.

It's also where the concept of sacrifice comes in—believing you have to choose between this or that instead of believing you can have both. That belief—of needing to give something up in order to receive something else—is another example of inherited limitation. It creates a perspective where life feels like a constant negotiation rather than a flow of aligned receiving.

These beliefs are so deeply embedded that they often feel like your own. But they're not. They're inherited truths—passed down, absorbed, and eventually embodied.

This is where you must choose to interrupt the pattern. You get to be the one who says, "No more." You get to clear what didn't start with you—but can end with you. This work isn't just for your own healing—it's for your lineage. When you clear an ancestral wound, you liberate yourself, your ancestors, and the generations to come.

And this is where your energetic practice becomes essential. Awareness opens the door—but it's the clearing that moves the energy. You're not just processing intellectually. You're releasing what your body, your nervous system, and your energetic field have carried for lifetimes.

So when you feel the weight of something that doesn't quite feel like yours—when grief, guilt, scarcity, or pressure rises—you can meet it with choice. You can meet it with intention. This is the statement I use in my own practice, and I invite you to try it for yourself:

Clearing Statement

"I now clear and transmute this (name the feeling) across all times, space, reality, lifetimes and dimensions."

Say it with presence. Whisper it with love. Feel the energy begin to shift as you speak. You don't have to know exactly where it came from. You just have to choose to release it. This is how you stop the cycle. This is how you reclaim your energy, your sovereignty, and your truth.

Ancestral Clearing Practice

1. **Create a sacred space**. Sit quietly with a journal, light a candle, or play soft music that helps you feel grounded and open.

2. **Tune into a recurring challenge in your life.** Ask yourself: "Does this really feel like mine? Or could it belong to someone before me?"

3. **Close your eyes, place your hand on your heart**, and say: *"If this is not mine, I now clear and transmute this (name the feeling) across all times, space, reality, lifetimes and dimensions."*

4. **Breathe deeply**, and imagine light flooding your field, dissolving the energy of that wound across your lineage.

5. **Afterward, write freely in your journal.** What came up? What shifted? What did you feel in your body?

What Energetic Imprinting Really Means

Energetic imprinting happens anytime you experience something—especially in childhood or early adulthood—that leaves a strong emotional charge. It's not just about what happens to you. It's about what that moment leaves behind in your energy field.

Let me explain it like this.

Imagine you're walking down the street, feeling relaxed, at peace, everything is good. And suddenly, out of nowhere, someone comes at you from the side and pushes you to the ground. You're shocked. Shaken. Every fiber of your being is activated by that jolt of fear and confusion. You pick yourself up, gather your things, and try to move on with your day. But later, even hours or days after the event, you still remember how it felt. You still feel the charge of it in your body.

That's an energetic imprint.

It doesn't go away just because time has passed. If the energetic charge is not cleared or dissolved, it stays with you. And it affects how you move through the world. You might avoid walking on that same sidewalk again. Or you feel a subtle but persistent unease every time you're in a similar situation. Your nervous system remembers, even if your mind tries to forget.

The same thing happens with heartbreak. With failure. With moments where you felt rejected, unseen, or not good enough. If something caused you to feel NOT OK—if it shook you in some way—it left an imprint. And that imprint becomes part of the filter through which you experience life.

So what do you do? You hold back. You play small. You tell yourself it's safer not to try again. That past experience—no matter how long

85

ago—still holds power over you because of the unprocessed energy it left behind.

And here's the key: it's not about the story. The story doesn't matter! It's not the details of what happened that matter—it's the emotional charge, the energetic punch that the experience left behind.

So if you want to truly release what's still holding you back, you must stop revisiting the story and instead focus on clearing the energetic imprint it caused.

That means tuning into the feeling, not the event.

What did that moment leave you with? Fear? Shame? Embarrassment? Heartbreak? Not good enough? Then work with *that*.

Use this clearing statement with full presence: *"I now clear and transmute this (name the feeling) across all times, space, reality, lifetimes and dimensions."*

Let the story fade. Let the emotion rise. And then release the charge. Letting it dissolve into the nothingness it came from. Once the intensity starts to ease, you can return to the experience and ask: *"What was I meant to learn from this? What was the message? What was the gift?"*

But do that only after you've cleared the energy. Because when you're still activated, you can't access the higher wisdom. You're too deep in the pain to see the lesson. When you clear the charge, something opens. You become available to new awareness. And that's when true transmutation happens—not by fixing the past, but by releasing the energetic hold it still has on you.

Energetic Imprint Clearing Practice

1. **Sit quietly and scan your body.** Where are you holding tension, heaviness, or discomfort?

2. **Bring to mind an experience that left you feeling NOT OK.** Let yourself feel the energy of it without going into the full story.

3. **Ask yourself:** What's the core emotion here? What energetic charge am I still carrying?

4. **Place your hand on your heart** and repeat the clearing statement with intention:
   "I now clear and transmute this (name the feeling) across all times, space, reality, lifetimes and dimensions."

5. **Breathe and release.** Let the energy dissolve. Imagine it being lifted from your field.

6. **Once the intensity softens, tune in again.** Ask: What was I meant to learn? What gift did this experience hold?

The Weight of Societal Conditioning

From a very early age, society teaches us that in order to belong, we must conform. We are conditioned to believe that it is safer to fit in, to stay in line, to follow the path already paved by others. We learn that if we show up as anything outside the accepted norms—if we speak too boldly, feel too deeply, or express ourselves too freely— we risk being judged, misunderstood, or outright rejected.

This kind of conditioning doesn't just influence how we behave; it begins to shape who we believe we are allowed to be. It teaches us to dim our light, to second-guess our truth, and to wear masks in order to be accepted. And for those of us who have embarked on a spiritual awakening journey, this creates a deep inner tension.

Because the more we awaken, the more we begin to return to who we truly are on a soul level. We start to see through the illusions. We begin to recognize the ways we've been programmed. And we feel the call to break free from the systems and identities that no longer resonate. Yet that very act of awakening can feel uncomfortable—not just for us, but for those around us who are still deeply asleep.

When you begin to shift, to open, to reclaim your truth, your energy naturally disrupts the old dynamics. People who have known you in your more conditioned form may not know how to relate to the new version of you. Your light can be triggering. Your awareness can stir discomfort in others, not because you've done anything wrong, but because your presence reflects back what they are not yet willing to face within themselves.

If you've ever felt rejected, excluded, or misunderstood as you've stepped more fully into your authentic self, it's important to understand that it's not about you. It's about what your energy evokes in others. You are awakening something in them that they may not yet be ready or willing to see. And while that can be painful at times, it is also part of your path.

We were not born to follow. We were born to lead. We are the rebels. The trailblazers. The wayshowers. We are here to challenge the status quo—not by force, but through embodiment. We are not meant to conform to outdated systems or rigid formulas that leave no room for the soul. We are here to forge a new way—one that honors authenticity, alignment, and truth.

But let's be honest: this isn't always an easy path to walk. It can feel lonely. It can feel vulnerable. There will be times when others don't understand you, when your choices don't make sense to those still operating within the matrix of societal programming. There may be moments when you question yourself, when the desire to belong whispers louder than the call of your soul.

And in those moments, it can be tempting to hide again. To filter what you say. To shrink just enough to make others comfortable. To stay quiet when your soul wants to roar.

But every time you do that—every time you dilute yourself in order to be accepted—you create an energetic mismatch. You show up one way, but your soul is speaking another language. You pretend to be someone you're not in order to fit in, but the cost of that is always disconnection—from self, from Source, and from the path you came here to walk.

This creates a deep inner sense of NOT OK.

You may not always be able to name it, but you feel it. A sense that something is off. A discomfort in your body. A tightness in your chest. A heaviness in your energy. That is the signal that you are out of alignment with your truth. And that discomfort is a gift—it is your compass.

As I always say: awareness gives you the power of choice. And with choice, you can shift. You can choose to no longer hide. You can choose to no longer play small. You can choose to no longer betray yourself in exchange for belonging.

Because true belonging never requires you to abandon who you are. True belonging begins when you finally accept yourself, when you reclaim your truth, and when you show up as the full expression of your soul—unapologetically and without permission.

Yes, it takes courage. Yes, it takes deep trust. Yes, there may be moments when the path feels steep and uncertain.

But what you gain is so much greater than what you lose. You gain freedom. You gain sovereignty. You gain the ability to walk through this world with your head held high, knowing that you are living in alignment with the truth of who you are.

When you stop trying to fit into the mold society created for you—and instead allow yourself to embody the vastness, the brilliance, and the uniqueness of your soul—that is when everything begins to shift. Your frequency becomes coherent. Your energy becomes magnetic. Life responds to your truth with deeper resonance and greater ease.

You were never meant to dim your light. You are here to shine, to awaken, to lead. And every time you choose authenticity over approval, you take another step into the embodiment of your divine self.

How to Discern What's Yours and What's Not

As sensitive souls—especially if you're an empath, intuitive, or energetically open being—one of the greatest challenges is knowing what's actually *yours*. So much of what you carry may not have originated within you at all. Thoughts, beliefs, fears, even physical tension can take root in your system when you unknowingly absorb them from those around you, your lineage, or the collective.

This is why developing discernment is so important. You must learn to pause and ask yourself: *Is this even mine?*

Let's say you find yourself spiraling in fear, overwhelmed with doubt, or gripped by a belief that you're not good enough, not ready, or not worthy. Instead of immediately trying to fight it or fix it, what if you paused for a moment and asked, *Where did this come from?* Was it something you were taught? Something you picked up from a parent, a teacher, a past partner, or even the collective energy swirling around you? Or is it something that still lingers in your field simply because you've never questioned it?

Anytime you feel constricted, heavy, uneasy, or disconnected from yourself, that's your cue. When you feel NOT OK, something is out of alignment. That's your opening to stop, breathe, and turn inward with awareness.

Start by tuning in to the feeling—not the story. **The story doesn't matter!** It's what keeps you spinning in old loops. But the story is not what needs clearing. What needs clearing is the *energy* the story activated in you—the imprint it left behind. When you focus on the feeling beneath the story, you move into the realm of true transformation.

And here's the thing: whether it's yours or not, you don't have to keep carrying it.

If it's not yours, release it. Return it to sender with love and consciousness attached. Or, if returning it would not serve the sender, simply transmute it into love and light. Either way, it's time to let it go.

If it *is* yours, that's OK too. You now have the awareness to do something about it. You can tune into the energetic charge it holds within you, meet it with compassion and neutrality, and clear it using your intention.

Use this clearing statement with presence and heart:

"I now clear and transmute this (name the feeling) across all times, space, reality, lifetimes and dimensions."

This is one of the simplest yet most powerful tools you can use. It honors the multidimensional nature of what you're releasing. It acknowledges that the energy may have roots beyond this lifetime, this body, or this moment—and that it's safe to let it go.

Remember, with awareness comes the power of choice. And every time you choose to stop, to tune in, and to ask, *Is this mine?* you reclaim your sovereignty. You become more conscious of what you allow into your field, what you carry, and what you are willing to release.

Over time, this becomes a way of life.

You become attuned to the subtle shifts in your energy. You start to notice when something feels "off," even if you can't name it. And instead of brushing it aside or pushing through, you pause. You create space to clear what doesn't belong, to integrate what does, and to choose how you want to move forward.

This is what it means to become energetically sovereign. It's not about perfection. It's about presence. It's about honoring your energy and committing to living in alignment with what is true, what is light, and what is *yours*.

What Happens When These Layers Begin to Clear

As you begin to release the energetic weight of the layers you didn't choose—ancestral imprints, conditioned beliefs, societal noise, and emotional residue—something profound starts to shift.

You feel lighter.

Not just emotionally or mentally, but energetically. There's more space within you. Your inner world feels less crowded, less tangled. The fog begins to lift. The tension softens. Your breath deepens. Life doesn't feel so heavy or hard. You start to sense a quiet spaciousness, a subtle expansion that wasn't there before. It's as if you've been carrying around a hundred-pound backpack for years without even realizing it—and suddenly, it's gone.

That's the moment you remember what alignment feels like.

Because when your field is clear, your light shines brighter. Your vibration lifts. You become magnetic—not because you're trying, but because there's less distortion in your field. Your essence can finally come through without being filtered or suppressed by outdated beliefs or energetic static.

This clearing also creates room for something new.

New energy. New thoughts. New inspiration. New possibilities.

When you let go of old energetic imprints, you make space for higher frequencies to move in—like ease, clarity, abundance, and joy. But this only happens when you intentionally release what no longer serves you.

Think of it like remodeling your home. You've decided it's time for a complete transformation. You want to create a space that feels beautiful, elevated, maybe even a little luxurious—a space that reflects who you are now, not who you used to be.

But in order to bring in new furniture, fresh paint, new artwork, and an entirely new aesthetic... you can't leave the old stuff where it is. There's no room. So you begin removing the outdated furniture, the clutter that's been sitting in corners for years, the colors and designs that no longer resonate. You create a clean slate. You clear the space.

Then, you begin filling your home with beauty. With intention. With the things that light you up. And once the remodel is complete, you can feel it in your entire being. You walk through your space and it lifts you. You feel energized, inspired, expansive. Your environment is no longer dragging your energy down—it's reflecting the vibration you now choose to embody. It's amplifying your essence.

The same is true for your inner world.

If you want to expand, to elevate, to align with the life you deeply desire—you must first make room. That means clearing out what's been weighing you down. That means releasing the energetic shackles of the past. That means choosing to no longer carry what was never yours to hold in the first place.

And once you do?

You feel more free. More at peace. More connected to yourself and the divine truth of who you are. Life becomes more fluid, more aligned. You start to attract people, opportunities, and experiences that reflect your higher frequency. You begin to live from your soul instead of your conditioning. You embody a higher level of alignment. And from that place, life flows.

This isn't a one-time thing. It's a practice. A commitment. A sacred devotion to your own energetic sovereignty. But every layer you clear brings you closer to yourself. Every false truth you release brings you closer to the truth. Every outdated imprint you dissolve brings you closer to the life you're here to live.

This is the gift of doing the deep inner work. It's not just about healing the past—it's about preparing your field for what's next. It's about remembering who you've always been underneath all the noise, and finally giving that version of you the space to rise.

Closing Incantation - Reclaiming What Was Always Yours

You've just moved through one of the heaviest parts of the work— uncovering the layers you didn't choose. The ancestral imprints, societal conditioning, and energetic residue you've been carrying were never meant to define you. But they've shaped you—until now.

As you begin clearing these outdated patterns and reclaiming your inner authority, you're not just letting go... you're coming home. Every time you choose to pause, to tune in, and to release what isn't yours, you're rewriting your energetic signature. You're shifting your field. And in doing so, you create space for a new frequency to take root—one that reflects your truth, your essence, your soul.

Let this incantation anchor that shift. Speak it aloud. Let it land in your body, your field, your bones. And as always, trust that even when it feels subtle, the energy is already moving.

Incantation:

I now choose to release the layers that were never mine to carry.
The ancestral burdens, the collective heaviness, the false truths I once believed—I set them down now.
I return to my center. I return to my sovereignty.
I call my energy back from all timelines, all lifetimes, all stories where I gave it away.
I now clear and transmute this heaviness across all times, space, reality, lifetimes, and dimensions.
I breathe into my body and feel the lightness returning.
I make space for clarity. For truth. For soul-deep alignment.
May all that is not mine dissolve into the light, with love.
May all that remains be a reflection of who I truly am.
Whole. Free. Unburdened.
And so it is.

Chapter 7: You Are Not Broken—You're Becoming

Reframing healing from fixing to reclaiming

There is a subtle, yet deeply ingrained belief in the personal development and spiritual growth space that you are broken. That there is something inherently wrong with you. That in order to manifest the life you desire—the money, the success, the freedom—you first need to be fixed. Healed. Corrected.

But let me say this clearly: You are not broken. You never have been. What you are is layered—with imprints, conditioning, programming, old wounds, and unresolved energy. And yes, these layers may cloud your vision, limit your potential, and make you feel disconnected from who you truly are. But having layers to work through does not mean you are broken. It means you're in the process of becoming.

I used to believe something was wrong with me. I genuinely thought that I was too wounded, too blocked, too energetically tangled to ever live the life I dreamed of. For years, I chased healing. I dove into clearing work, shadow work, trauma release—anything and everything that promised to "fix" me. But no matter how much I healed, the same patterns kept showing up. I would take one step forward, only to fall five steps back. And so the cycle repeated: dig deeper, clear more, try harder.

Eventually, something clicked. Not through another session or a profound teaching—but in a moment of quiet clarity. I realized: nothing was wrong with me. I didn't need to be fixed—I needed to transcend the outdated version of myself and embody the woman I was always meant to be. That was the shift. It wasn't about doing more healing. It was about stepping into embodiment.

Because here's the truth: you can do all the healing work in the world, but if you don't embody the next-level version of you—if you don't *choose* to become her—you'll stay stuck in the loop of endless clearing. You'll keep believing you're not ready, not healed enough, not whole enough. But healing is not the destination. It's part of the journey toward embodiment.

That realization was liberating. I could finally stop trying to fix myself and start becoming. I began showing up as the version of me who was already aligned with what I desired. I tapped into her energy, her essence, her confidence. And things began to shift—not because I was healed, but because I *became*.

That is the essence of Soul Alchemy. That's what you're learning to embody through this book. You're not here to be fixed. You're here to remember your power, to clear what no longer resonates, and to *become* who you already are at the soul level.

So let me say it again: you are not broken. You are becoming. And you're doing it beautifully.

How Healing Is Often Misunderstood

The desire to heal can sometimes carry a subtle but heavy message: that something is wrong with you. That you're not enough as you are. That you're missing something or that you're broken in a way that needs to be fixed.

And when you hold that belief—even unconsciously—it reinforces a state of lack. It feeds thoughts like *I'm not good enough, I can't do this,* or *This is too hard.* That kind of pressure creates frustration, fatigue, and resistance, especially if you've been doing the inner work for a long time and still find yourself circling the same patterns.

If you've ever caught yourself thinking, *Why is this coming up again?* or *Haven't I already healed this?,* you're not alone. I've been there too. I know how exhausting it can feel when it seems like the work never ends. But the truth is, healing isn't meant to be a lifelong destination you're trying to reach. It's a process of shedding, of becoming lighter, and of *remembering* who you already are underneath it all.

The path of the Soul Alchemist is not about spending all your time digging into the past, trying to uncover every wound or every hidden block. That approach can easily become a trap—one that keeps you locked in the belief that you're not yet whole, not yet worthy, not yet ready.

Instead, the Soul Alchemist walks forward—with vision, with clarity, and with presence. You hold the energy of where you're going, not as a distant goal to strive toward, but as a frequency to embody right now. You move toward it. You live from it. And when something comes up—a trigger, a fear, a limiting belief—you meet it. You pause, tune in, and ask, *What is this showing me? What's the lesson or invitation here?*

And then you work through it—not by spiraling into the story or making yourself wrong, but by clearing the charge, reclaiming your power, and returning to alignment. That's the dance of transformation. That's the rhythm of true healing—not as a stagnant ritual, but as a dynamic, embodied way of being.

The Soul Alchemist doesn't wait until everything is perfect before taking the next step. She moves. She evolves as she goes. She knows that clarity often comes through motion, and that what needs to be healed will reveal itself naturally *in the process* of expansion.

And that's what so many teachings overlook. When you believe you have to be fully healed in order to have the life you desire, you keep yourself stuck in the old paradigm—one where you're always chasing, always correcting, never arriving.

But healing can't be forced. You can't push yourself through a weekend of shadow work and expect lifelong transformation. Deep healing happens in layers, through presence and awareness, not urgency. It happens when you're in motion—when you stretch beyond your comfort zone and let the energy surface as you grow.

If you feel like nothing is coming up for you—no triggers, no fears, no resistance—it's worth asking yourself if you've actually been stretching at all. Because when we stagnate, when we stay in familiar territory, our edges aren't challenged. But growth happens at the edge. And that edge is where the alchemy begins.

So yes, things will come up. And when they do, that's your moment. That's your invitation to tune in, clear what's no longer aligned, and keep moving forward—without getting derailed, without needing to retreat, without making yourself wrong for having something to work through.

There's also a powerful shift that happens when you stop healing to become whole and start healing to *remember* that you already are. The purpose of releasing doubt, fear, and old pain isn't to fix you—it's to reconnect you to your authentic self. It's to uncover the parts of you that have always been whole, but were buried beneath layers of survival, programming, and protection.

Every layer you shed is not a step toward perfection—it's a step toward truth. A step back into alignment with your essence. And the more you remember who you are, the more naturally you begin to embody that truth in every area of your life.

That is what healing is meant to be. Not a burden. Not a cycle of inadequacy. But a path of reclamation. A return to your soul's original frequency.

Reclamation Is Remembering Who You Already Are

When you begin to reclaim the parts of you that got lost, buried, rejected, or hidden along the way, something profound happens—you come home to yourself. It's not about becoming someone new. It's about remembering who you've always been underneath the noise, the conditioning, the wounds, and the masks.

We often fragment ourselves to survive. We leave pieces behind in moments when we felt unsafe, unseen, or unworthy. We shrink in the presence of those who don't understand us. We silence our truth to avoid conflict. We disconnect from our light so we don't outshine others. Over time, those fragmented pieces of self get buried beneath the weight of shoulds, shame, and societal expectations.

But when you reclaim those pieces—when you gather yourself back up—you start to feel whole again. Not because you *fixed* anything. But because you *remembered*. You reconnected. You opened the door back to the truth that never left you.

I remember preparing for a call with my coach one day. I did what I always do—I tuned in to see what needed healing or clearing. But instead of a wound rising to the surface, something else came through: *nothing needs healing right now*. What needed to happen was a full, unapologetic embodiment of the version of me I had always been but kept doubting. The version of me that didn't need fixing. That already was whole, abundant, successful, and powerful.

And that awareness—simple as it may sound—hit me like a wave. It changed everything.

That moment was a homecoming. It was the moment I called my power back. I claimed all the parts I had abandoned along the way and stepped back into the wholeness of who I am. My energy shifted. My field expanded. I didn't *want* for anything anymore. I wasn't looking for the next thing to manifest or the next thing to heal. I was *present*. I was *whole*. I was at peace.

That's what true reclamation feels like.

It's not something external. It's not about acquiring a new skill or reaching a new milestone. It's an *inner awakening*. A remembrance that you've never actually been broken—you just forgot who you are. And when that remembering clicks into place, your entire life begins to reorient around that inner truth. Not because you forced something to happen, but because your frequency changed. Your field shifted. And the universe responds to that.

And here's the key: no amount of external success or spiritual growth will give you that sense of inner wholeness if you haven't claimed it within yourself. Chasing after more—more healing, more breakthroughs, more tools—will only take you so far. Eventually, you have to stop and come back to yourself. To your own breath. Your own body. Your own truth.

The real power, the real magic, is in remembering that it's all within you already.

So as you move through this chapter and the ones to come, I want to remind you: you are not broken. You are not behind. You are not missing anything. You are in the sacred process of becoming—by reclaiming the truth of who you've always been.

How Can We Begin to Shift from "Fixing" to "Becoming"?

The path of becoming begins with awareness—awareness that you're not here to fix what's broken but to transcend what's outdated. And that shift in awareness changes everything.

Fixing implies that something is wrong with you. That you're not enough. That you need to get somewhere else before you can feel whole or worthy. But *becoming*... that's different. Becoming is about unfolding into the truth of who you already are. It's about allowing the layers that never belonged to you to fall away so the brilliance underneath can shine through.

And to make that shift, you have to begin relating to yourself in a new way—with more compassion, more curiosity, and far less urgency or judgment.

When something triggers you, instead of spiraling into "What's wrong with me?" or "Why is this happening again?", pause. Breathe. Ask, "What is this showing me? What energy is surfacing here? Where is this trying to guide me?" You're not investigating yourself like a problem to be solved—you're meeting yourself as someone worthy of deeper understanding.

Self-inquiry becomes an act of love rather than an act of scrutiny. And your inner dialogue changes too. Instead of saying, "I should be past this by now," you start saying, "I'm in process. I'm becoming. I trust my path."

Comparison and self-judgment are two of the biggest saboteurs on this journey. Looking at others and thinking, *They're further along,* or *They're doing it better,* only pulls you out of your own center. The truth is, no one's path is meant to look like yours. Your process, your flow, your unfolding is sacred—and trying to force it into someone else's timeline will only create more resistance.

One of the most powerful things you can do is *hold space for your own evolution without making yourself wrong*. That means honoring the pace of your healing. That means giving yourself grace when old patterns resurface. That means celebrating the small shifts that no one else sees but you feel deep in your bones.

And when you approach yourself with that level of compassion, your transformation accelerates—not because you're trying harder, but because your energy softens. Your field opens. You become more available for your soul's guidance and embodiment to lead the way.

This is what it means to become a Soul Alchemist. You stop trying to fix yourself and start co-creating with the wisdom within you. You respond to what arises with presence, not panic. You hold yourself in awareness, not avoidance. And you step into your becoming—not as something to chase, but as something to *embody right now.*

Because the version of you that you are becoming? She already exists. She already lives within you. And she's just waiting for you to say yes.

How Can You Hold Space for Your Evolution Without Making Yourself Wrong?

The journey of becoming isn't a straight line. It's not always graceful or fast. Sometimes it's messy. Sometimes it feels like you're going in circles. And sometimes it feels like everything you've worked so hard to release comes crashing back in. But that doesn't mean you've failed. That doesn't mean you're broken. That doesn't mean you're doing it wrong.

It simply means—you're evolving.

There's a sacred middle space in transformation that most people try to rush through. That space where you're no longer who you used to be... but not quite who you're becoming. It's uncomfortable. It's tender. It's uncertain. But it's also incredibly fertile. This is where the real integration happens. This is where you practice trust. This is where you become.

The challenge for many is that we've been conditioned to associate growth with constant forward motion. To believe that if we're not leaping ahead, we're falling behind. But growth doesn't always look like a breakthrough. Sometimes it looks like sitting with yourself through discomfort. Sometimes it looks like honoring your need for rest. Sometimes it looks like saying, "I don't have the answers yet—and that's okay."

Holding space for your evolution means allowing yourself to be exactly where you are without self-judgment. It means resisting the urge to shame yourself for not being "further along." It means witnessing your process without making it mean something is wrong.

This is where compassion becomes your compass. Not just in how you speak to yourself, but in how you relate to the unfolding path you're on. You don't demand clarity before you take a step—you learn to walk with uncertainty. You don't rush the process just to arrive—you allow the process to shape you into who you're meant to become.

The truth is, your evolution is not a performance. It's not meant to be polished or perfect. It's meant to be *real*. Raw. Unfiltered. And it's in those raw spaces—where you're honest, where you're present, where you're still choosing to keep going even when it's hard—that you become unshakable.

So let yourself be in the becoming. Not with urgency. Not with pressure. But with reverence. Because the version of you that's emerging from this journey isn't fragile. She's forged in presence. In devotion. In truth.

And when you allow yourself to *honor the messy middle*, you begin to trust that even the parts that feel chaotic are part of something sacred. Something purposeful. Something that's leading you home.

What Becomes Possible When You Stop Believing You're Broken?

When you let go of the belief that something is wrong with you, a profound shift begins to take place—not just in your mind, but in your energy, your choices, and how you move through the world. The moment you stop identifying as someone who needs fixing, you start reclaiming your role as the creator of your life.

You're no longer trapped in the story that life is happening *to* you. Instead, you begin to understand that life is happening *for* you. Every challenge, every setback, every trigger becomes a messenger—not of your inadequacy, but of your readiness to transcend the old and step into something higher.

This shift pulls you out of victim energy and into empowerment. It allows you to take responsibility not from a place of blame or guilt, but from a place of sovereignty. You begin to ask new questions. Instead of, "Why is this happening to me?" you ask, "What within me created this experience?" or "What is this showing me about where I still hold limitations?" That kind of inner inquiry opens the door to liberation—because you're no longer reacting from emotional attachment, but responding with awareness and intention.

And this is where self-worth begins to expand.

You start to recognize that you are already whole—not because you've done all the healing, but because your wholeness was never lost to begin with. It was simply buried beneath layers of conditioning, pain, and programming. As you peel those layers back, you don't become someone new—you remember who you've always been.

When that remembrance settles in, your energy shifts. You stop chasing and start allowing. You stop proving and start embodying. Your desires begin to align with your soul—not with fear, lack, or urgency—but with clarity, trust, and resonance. You start to take action not because you're trying to fix what's broken, but because you're showing up *as* the version of you who already lives the life you desire.

And you begin to flow.

There is a freedom that arises when you stop fighting yourself. When you no longer believe you need to become someone else in order to be worthy. When you stop second-guessing and start trusting. You feel lighter. More present. More powerful. And most importantly, more *you*.

That is the power of releasing the belief that you are broken.

Because once you do, you're no longer ruled by limitation—you are led by your soul.

Closing Transmission: Becoming the One Who Already Is

You are not here to fix yourself. You are here to remember.

To reclaim the parts of you that were buried beneath the weight of conditioning, judgment, fear, and shame. To awaken the truth that you have always been whole, always been worthy, always been enough.

This chapter wasn't about convincing you of your wholeness—it was about helping you feel it. To offer you the space to return to yourself. To let go of the need to be "done," and instead to live from the energy of becoming.

The path of the Soul Alchemist is not about healing endlessly. It's about honoring what arises, working with it, and choosing to align with a higher version of yourself—again and again.

So take a breath. Feel into your body. Soften the part of you that still whispers "I'm not ready" or "I'm not enough." And let this incantation be a declaration of your power:

Incantation

"I now clear and transmute this feeling of not being enough across all times, space, reality, lifetimes, and dimensions. I now choose to embody the version of me who already is whole, worthy, and aligned. I remember who I am."

Let it be felt. Let it be claimed. Let it become the energy you carry forward as you continue your becoming.

Chapter 8: Meeting the Shadow Without Fear

Shadow work as sacred reclamation, not shame

Many people think of the shadow as this dark side of ourselves—something to be rejected, feared, resisted, and pushed away. But in all honesty, the shadow is part of us. It creates balance within us, and it can also be our greatest teacher. There can't be light without the dark. There can't be good without the bad. And there can't be our Soul Self or Higher Self without the limited shadow self.

But when we look at the shadow more closely, we realize that every shadow aspect playing out in the background... we created it. All of it. These aspects were created in moments of distress, fear, worry, agony. And they were created for one reason only—to protect us. To keep us safe. To guard our hearts from pain and suffering.

The thing is, these shadow aspects don't grow and evolve like we do. They stay the same. In fact, they often intensify whenever we go through similar experiences to the one that created them in the first place.

I mentioned this example before: the first time you got your heart broken, a shadow aspect was created—one that was meant to keep you safe moving forward. And it did an amazing job. You became more cautious, more guarded. You didn't open your heart as quickly or as fully. Then, let's say it happened again. You got hurt once more. So the shadow intensified its efforts. It dialed up the protection even more. Because damn it—you got hurt again. And this part of you that loves you so deeply just wants to protect you.

But what that shadow doesn't realize is that it's also interfering with what you truly desire. That guard it's holding up keeps love out. It makes you hold back, doubt, question your partner. It creates friction. It sabotages connection. And that can lead to the same painful ending all over again, which then confirms to the shadow, "See? I knew it. It's always the same. I better protect even harder next time." And on and on it goes.

But what if we chose to work *with* the shadow instead of letting it run wild—sabotaging us, holding us back, and keeping us stuck in old patterns? This is where shadow work comes in. And the name says it all—*shadow work*—working *with* the shadow.

Your shadow aspects can become your greatest guides. They show you what needs your attention, what's outdated and ready to evolve. When you lean into the discomfort instead of running from it, you can *transcend* those limitations and give that shadow aspect a new, higher role.

So, is the shadow bad?

I guess that depends on how you choose to see it. You might see it as bad because it reveals uncomfortable truths—things playing out in the background that you didn't want to face. It forces you to be honest with yourself and take responsibility for what you've unconsciously created. That's not easy. In fact, it can be messy and ugly. That's why some people say the shadow is bad.

But I see it differently. I see the shadow as my greatest teacher. It always shows me exactly what I need to look at in order to break through my limitations. Whenever something surfaces, I say, "Thank you for making yourself known to me. Now that I have the awareness, I can do something about it." And that's exactly what I do.

If the shadow hadn't peeked its head out, I wouldn't have even known something was lurking beneath the surface. It would have stayed there—affecting me, holding me back, getting in my way. But since it showed up, I was able to transcend it.

And here's the thing: whenever something comes into your awareness, it's because it's *ready* to be acknowledged. Ready to be worked through. Ready to be released.

Think of it like a knock on the door. If you don't open it, the knocking continues—and it gets louder and louder until you finally answer.

That's why so many people resist shadow work. That's why they fear the shadow or label it as bad. But the truth is, the shadow itself isn't the problem. **The resistance is.** The more you resist what the shadow is trying to show you, the louder the knock becomes. That's when things get really uncomfortable.

So when you ignore the knock—when you ignore what the shadow is trying to tell or teach you—it builds. It tightens. It gets louder. And you're left feeling trapped in a loop. But when you finally open the door and say, *"Alright. I'm listening,"* that's when the alchemy begins.

When the Shadow First Speaks

The shadow usually makes itself known when you're in the midst of changing your life, awakening to something deeper, or even just moving through the day. It's that part of you that gets **triggered**—when someone says or does something that doesn't sit right with you… when an old memory gets stirred… when a long-buried wound quietly rises to the surface.

Sometimes, you won't even know what exactly it triggered. You just feel... off. On edge. Not quite yourself.

Just think back over today—or even yesterday. **How many times did you feel NOT OK?** That subtle (or strong) sense that something's off... that something poked at your peace. Maybe you felt dismissed. Rejected. Not good enough. Or maybe it wasn't so intense—just a passing wave of discomfort or doubt. That, too, is your shadow speaking.

The feeling of NOT OK is often the very first sign. It's the gentle (or not-so-gentle) nudge that something has been activated within you. Some belief. Some memory. Some protective piece that got stirred awake.

And the truth is, this happens far more often than we realize. Our shadow aspects get poked throughout the day, but we rarely stop to notice.

If you were to pause more often—just to ask, *"How am I feeling right now? What's actually going on inside me?"*—you'd begin to notice the patterns. You'd start to feel when a shadow aspect is trying to get your attention. And this is where your power lies.

Let me say this again: **awareness gives you the power of choice.**

When you realize that a shadow just got poked, you can work with it. You can sit with it. You can ask, *What is this trying to show me? What do I need to feel right now?*

Because here's the truth: your shadow aspect loves you.

It's not trying to mess up your life. It's not trying to sabotage you. It's trying to protect you in the only way it knows how—by roaring, by stirring, by making you feel NOT OK just long enough for you to pay attention.

That discomfort is not punishment. It's a portal. A signpost. A messenger saying: "Look here. Something old is ready to be seen. Something within you is asking for love."

Why Shadow Work Is Feared

I've already spoken about resistance—because the truth is, shadow work *can* feel painful and messy. It asks something from you. In order to truly heal a shadow, you have to lean into it. You have to sit with the discomfort. You have to be radically honest with yourself and acknowledge that you created it—maybe unknowingly, but still, it came from you.

You have to open yourself up to uncover the message, the lesson, and the gift. Because every shadow carries a gift. There is a deeper meaning behind every shadow aspect. And when you do shadow work, that's what you're meant to uncover. But in order to get to the gift, you have to go through the shadow. And *that's* what so many people fear. That's what they resist.

But here's what you need to understand: the only thing that makes shadow work *feel* hard and painful is the **resistance to it**.

Your shadow is just trying to get your attention. It's saying, "Something isn't right. Something is NOT OK." The shadow perceives danger—even if there's no real danger at all. And when you begin shadow work, the invitation is to lean into that feeling. To face what's uncomfortable with presence, not panic.

Now, if you don't know how to do this from an empowered place, it can feel overwhelming. It can even be derailing. But that's exactly why I wrote this book. I want to guide you through this process in a way that doesn't have to be devastating or too intense to face.

Let me also say this: even when you *do* approach shadow work from an empowered place, it can still be emotional. Some feelings need to be felt fully in order to be released. Sometimes the energy has to move, the pressure has to release, the emotion has to be expressed before clarity can return. But when you feel with *intention*, rather than letting the emotion run wild and consume you, something shifts. You become the one holding the space. You don't get lost in it.

Another reason many people avoid shadow work altogether is because they're afraid of what they might uncover. They don't want to deal with it. They don't want to face what they might not like about themselves. So instead, they stay on the surface. They do just enough healing to feel better in the moment, but not enough to actually transform what's causing the pattern in the first place.

That's what spiritual bypassing is—trying to get to the light without walking through the dark.

It's the illusion of healing. A mirage. You *think* you're better. You *think* you've cleared it. But the real wounds—the deep ones—are still sitting in that locked-up box within your consciousness. You may have pushed them down so far you've forgotten they're even there. But just because you can't see them doesn't mean they're not still running in the background, affecting everything.

That's why surface-level healing isn't enough. That's why you have to be willing to go deeper. Because those buried wounds still carry energetic weight. They're still shaping your thoughts, your decisions, your emotional reactions, your energy.

For a long time, I resisted going that deep. I did so much healing work, but I still felt stuck in my life. Nothing really changed. It wasn't until I started working with my Gene Keys that I truly saw the shadow. I began to understand the specific shadow frequencies that had been active in my life for years—decades, really. I realized that these shadow aspects were in the driver's seat. They were dictating my actions, my choices, how I showed up in the world. And that realization hit hard.

At first, I felt shocked. I judged myself. I blamed myself.

But then... I felt **immense gratitude** for the awareness. Because awareness gave me the power of choice. I could finally do something about it.

So I went deep. I worked with every shadow outlined within my Gene Keys Profile. I leaned in. I felt the discomfort. I cleared the energetic charge. I released the emotional attachments. I looked at my shadows from different angles—in different areas of my life— and I kept clearing, layer by layer.

And then there came a point where it wasn't about healing anymore. It was about **transcending**. About integrating the gift that each shadow held. About living from a more empowered version of me— the one who had walked through the shadow and come out the other side.

It was messy. It was painful. But it taught me how to move with awareness. With compassion. With grace.

Now, when my shadow peeks its head, I welcome it. I lean in. I feel what needs to be felt. I clear what needs to be cleared. I integrate the gift. And I embody the version of me that lives from that gift—not the wound.

And *this*—this is what I want to teach you through this book.

These days, when something gets stirred in my field, I don't get derailed like I used to. It's not a spiral—it's more of an inconvenience. I make time and space to work through it. That's it. Before, I'd be stuck in the ick for days, weeks, months and even years. Especially during those dark nights of the soul. But now, I have the awareness. I have the tools. And I trust myself to move through what arises with grace.

That doesn't mean it never gets uncomfortable. It still does. But I know that as long as I feel the feeling *with intention*—rather than letting it take over—I'll move through it. And quickly.

This is what happens when you meet your shadow with compassion. When you give yourself space and time. When you work with the shadow instead of pushing it away.

Because once you do, it no longer has a hold on you. It no longer runs the show. It's not in the driver's seat anymore. It's grown. It's evolved. It's been alchemized.

Shadow Work as Reclamation

I hope by now you're beginning to see that shadow work isn't something to fear or resist. It's an act of reclaiming your power—of coming back home to yourself.

Because the more you work with your shadow, the more you release the layers of "stuff" that have been holding you back… the limitations, the energetic imprints, the old survival patterns. These are the things that have been overshadowing your authentic self. And every time you lean in, you peel back another layer—getting closer and closer to your core. You begin to reconnect with your truth, your essence, your sovereignty.

Shadow work places you back in the driver's seat of your life. That in itself is an act of empowerment. You're no longer reacting from wounded parts. You're choosing. You're leading. You're owning the process.

Because every time one of your shadows gets poked, and you choose to meet it, work with it, and transcend it—that is pure power. That is self-leadership. That is embodiment. You're deciding what you're available for, and anything that doesn't align? You get to shift it. You have the tools. You have the awareness. You're no longer at the mercy of old programming.

And here, I want to remind you of something we touched on earlier in this book:

You don't need to be fixed. Even if you're realizing that a *lot* of shadow aspects are still running the show—that doesn't mean there's anything wrong with you. You are not broken. You are simply carrying aspects that are outdated. Limiting. Ready to be upgraded.

That's what shadow work allows you to do.

The more you embrace your shadow and allow it to be your teacher—not your enemy—the more empowered you become. The more baggage you release. The more liberation you feel in your body, in your energy, in your life.

Just imagine…

If nothing was holding you back anymore—

If the old patterns were no longer running—

If the emotional charge was gone…

What would your life look like? What would you create? Who would you become?

That version of you—that life—is fully possible. But to get there, you must first transcend the parts of you that have kept you anchored in your current reality… the loops, the self-sabotage, the hiding, the hoping without action, the waiting for things to change while continuing to repeat the same patterns.

And I say this because I lived that.

I wanted more. I dreamed of success, abundance, freedom, joy… but nothing shifted in a lasting way. Sure, things got better here and there. But the *big breakthroughs*? The quantum shifts? They didn't happen until I stopped running and started working with my shadows.

I stopped trying to bypass. I embraced the discomfort. I welcomed the whole journey—the good, the bad, and the ugly.

And now, looking back, I'm so glad I did. Because if I hadn't... I wouldn't be writing this book. I wouldn't be making the impact I'm making. I wouldn't be living the joy, the abundance, the freedom that once felt out of reach.

So, was it worth it? Absolutely. Every moment of it.

The Power of Feeling NOT OK

The feeling of NOT OK is your first indicator that something isn't right. That something got poked. That something was triggered. Most of the time, we don't even realize it. We either react, shut down, or go on autopilot—and we completely miss what's happening beneath the surface. Or maybe we notice that we're off, but we can't pinpoint why.

That's where awareness comes in. When you feel NOT OK, it's a sacred invitation to pause. And in that pause, you create space— space to breathe, space to detach, space to tune in. That space allows you to ask: *What am I actually feeling right now?*

From there, you can start to explore what happened that triggered you. Was it something someone said or did? Something you said or did? When you become aware of the external trigger, you can then go deeper: *Why did that affect me so much? Where is this reaction really coming from? What's at the root of this feeling?*

This is shadow work in action. But it's important to meet these moments without judgment. You're connecting with a part of yourself that may be tender or raw. You need compassion here— immense compassion. You're meeting your shadow with presence, and that's a powerful act of love. When you uncover what's at the root of your discomfort, you can then begin to release the emotional charge it's carrying. This is where you can use my clearing statement:

"I now clear and transmute this (name the feeling) across all times, space, reality, lifetimes, and dimensions."

Say it with intention. Say it with clarity. Let the energy move.

Once the intensity has softened, ask: *What is the message in this? What is the lesson? What is the gift?* Because there is always a gift waiting beneath the feeling of NOT OK. But if you brush it off, you miss it. And that's what most of us do.

We ignore the discomfort. We push it aside because we don't have time, or we simply don't want to deal with it. We pretend we're fine, but deep down, we're not. And whether you acknowledge it or not, you're still making a choice—either to bypass or to face what's asking for your attention.

Awareness gives you the power of choice. And when you *do* become aware, you can no longer act like you don't know. You are choosing. Bypassing might feel easier in the moment, but that discomfort? It's going to come back. Maybe not right away, but it will return—louder, heavier, and more disruptive than before.

So instead of avoiding it, why not honor it? Why not treat the feeling of NOT OK as a sacred portal? Because that's exactly what it is. It's not a problem to fix—it's an opening. When you slow down, when you listen, when you go within, you reclaim your power. You stop reacting from the shadow and start responding with presence. And that's when the alchemy begins.

How to Meet Your Shadow with Power and Grace

Let me outline how to do this beautiful shadow work in a way that feels empowering and deeply transformational.

It all begins with awareness. Without awareness, you don't have the power to make a different choice. So your first step is to start noticing. Start tuning in. Pay attention to when you feel off, when you feel triggered, when you notice the sense of *I'm not OK*. That moment of awareness is everything—because now you have a choice. You can choose to meet what's coming up, and that in itself is a powerful act.

Once you've recognized that a shadow aspect has been activated, the next step is to emotionally step back. That means detaching from the story of what happened. The story doesn't matter. Let me say that again: the story never matters. Let go of the details. Let go of who said what or how it played out. What matters now is the feeling— what's happening within you.

Tune into that. Ask yourself, *What am I feeling right now?* Maybe it's unworthiness, rejection, sadness, or the sense of not being heard. Whatever it is, acknowledge it without judgment. This is you allowing yourself to be present with your shadow, and that's a sacred thing. Be gentle. This part of you might be tender or raw. Meet it with compassion.

From there, ask yourself: *Where is this coming from? When was the first time I remember feeling this way?* There's always a deeper root—an earlier experience, often from childhood or your younger years, that seeded this wound. And what triggered you today? That was just the activation, not the origin. When you uncover the root memory or energetic imprint, don't dive into the story—just stay connected to the feeling.

Now, with intention, allow yourself to feel that feeling. Let it move through you. You're not indulging it—you're allowing it to release. You might even turn up the intensity slightly so it can be fully felt and expressed. After a few minutes, you'll likely notice the energy beginning to shift. The emotion loses its grip. The charge lessens. You've taken out the steam.

At this point, you can use the clearing statement to help clear any remaining energy, imprints, or attachments still connected to that shadow:

"I now clear and transmute this (name the feeling) across all times, space, reality, lifetimes, and dimensions."

Say it with intention. Stay connected to the energy you're releasing. Let it move.

Once the emotional and energetic charge has cleared, tune back in and ask: *What was I meant to learn from this? What is the message, the lesson, the gift?* There's always something there—an insight, a shift, a deeper truth. And when you receive that message, it's time to integrate it.

Integration means choosing something new. It means changing the behavior or pattern that led you to this experience in the first place. If the gift is about believing in yourself more, then you commit to doing that. If it's about setting clearer boundaries, then you act on that. Integration is about living from the gift—not just understanding it intellectually, but embodying it. This is how you transcend the old shadow pattern and reclaim your power.

You can't do the healing, clear the charge, uncover the gift—and then go back to doing things the same way. That only reactivates the shadow all over again. You must act from the new awareness, from the higher place, as the version of you who has integrated the lesson and now chooses differently.

But the most important part of this entire process is this: be gentle with yourself. No judgment. No guilt. No shame. This work requires openness, compassion, and grace. And when you do it this way, shadow work becomes one of the most empowering and transformative things you can do. You stop being tossed around by your shadow and instead walk beside it, with your eyes wide open and your power fully intact.

This is what it means to work **with** your shadow—rather than being dragged by it, confused by it, or unconsciously sabotaged by it. And this is what I want to guide you into.

If You're Afraid to "Go There"

If you're afraid to "go there"—to face the parts of yourself you've kept hidden—then I want to offer you a gentle invitation. You don't need to dive headfirst into your deepest trauma or emotional pain. Start small. Begin with something that doesn't carry as much weight or energetic intensity.

Practicing this process with smaller triggers helps you build trust in yourself. It gives you the confidence to face the heavier stuff when you're ready—because you'll have already experienced what's possible.

And if something does feel too big or overwhelming, don't force yourself through it alone. Some wounds are layered and deep. It's okay to ask for support. Find someone who can help you hold space for the process, someone who can guide you gently through the healing so you're not carrying it all by yourself.

Even with that said—shadow work is still one of the most empowering and life-transforming practices you will ever do. It gives you the ability to free yourself from the energetic grip of past experiences. It helps you reclaim your power. And once you learn how to work with your shadow in the way I just shared with you, you'll begin to realize that nothing can truly derail you anymore.

Yes, you'll still have challenges. Yes, pain and frustration may still arise. But now, you'll know how to meet it. You'll know how to process it and move through it with more ease, with more grace, and with far less suffering.

That's why I believe shadow work is the key to transformation. It's the foundation of becoming a Soul Alchemist.

Because a Soul Alchemist doesn't run from the dark. They meet it. They work with it. They transmute it.

And in order to consciously create the life you desire, you must be willing to meet what's still living in conflict with those desires. Those limiting patterns, those unconscious fears, those unresolved wounds—they often live in your shadow. And the moment you stop fearing them and start listening instead? That's the moment your real power returns.

When the Shift Becomes Who You Are

Integration is one of the most important—yet often overlooked—parts of shadow work and inner transformation. You can do all the healing, all the clearing, all the energetic releasing in the world... but without integration, you're missing a vital part of the journey.

Because it's during integration that everything clicks into place. It's where your nervous system catches up to the change. Your mindset recalibrates. Your emotions settle. Your whole system—mind, body, energy, and soul—adjusts to the shift that just occurred.

When you release the emotional or energetic charge, when you transcend a shadow aspect and uncover the gift it holds, the process isn't complete until that gift is embodied. And embodiment takes time. Your system needs space to recalibrate.

You're aligning to a new frequency—one that reflects the version of you who sees differently, feels differently, acts differently. That requires an energetic settling period. Integration is where you attune to your new energetic baseline.

And sometimes, that adjustment period can feel intense. You might feel tired. Emotionally raw. Even physically detoxing. That's all part of the shift. The energy is still working through you, still digesting. It's not a sign that something went wrong—it's a sign that something is moving.

I've seen this over and over again—not just in clients, but in myself. There were times when I went from one healing to the next, bingeing light language activations, doing multiple sessions back-to-back. And while it felt powerful in the moment, I later realized that I had skipped the most important step: integration. Without taking time to let the energy settle, I missed out on the depth of the transformation. The healing happened, but the embodiment didn't.

That's why I now say: don't rush it. Don't skip the stillness. Let the shift settle.

So how do you know when something has truly been integrated?

It often starts subtly. You begin to feel different. A little lighter. More clear. Less reactive. You notice that your thoughts are shifting—your beliefs are shifting. You respond to situations differently than before. You might find yourself making different choices, holding firmer boundaries, or feeling less triggered by things that used to knock you off center.

Then, your outer reality begins to reflect the shift. Sometimes people drift out of your life. Sometimes new people come in. Relationships might change. Tensions might soften. Opportunities that once felt blocked begin to flow. The changes aren't always loud or dramatic—they're often quiet. Gentle. Organic. Like something realigning itself behind the scenes.

And eventually, you notice… *something's different*. You're not showing up the same way. You're not stuck in the same loops. You're no longer carrying the same weight. You've shifted—and now life is shifting with you.

That's what it means to integrate. And that's how you know: The shadow has been met. The charge has been cleared. The gift has been claimed. And now… You're living from it.

The Shadow's Message to the Soul Alchemist

Before we close this chapter, I invite you to receive this message— not from your mind, but from your body, your field, your soul. This is the voice of the shadow itself, speaking to you, the Soul Alchemist. These are not words to analyze. They are here to be felt. Let them move through you. Let them awaken something dormant within you. Let them guide you home.

***

Do not fear me, do not resist or reject me. I am here to guide you, to teach you, to help you find your way home. When you embrace me fully and completely, and you open yourself up to my nudgings—my way of trying to get your attention—I can help you shift old and outdated energies, imprints you have ingrained long ago that no longer serve you. I am the light in the darkness. I am the guide that takes you into the abyss of your subconscious. I show you what you are unable to see for yourself. I bring to the forefront that which is ready to be released.

Fear me not, as I am here to help you grow, to help you heal, and to help you transform and transcend into the Soul Self you came here to re-embody.

When you open yourself up to my wisdom, yes, you will face many uncomfortable feelings. You will uncover things you may not like or want to become aware of. But know this: just because these things are uncomfortable for the human part of you does not mean they are not still affecting you. I do not wish to cause you harm. I wish to assist you in your growth, in your ascension. But it is the human self— the resistance you hold toward what I am here to show you—that causes you to fear me, to resist me, to feel challenged by me.

Because indeed, I am here to challenge you—not to hold your hand and tell you that all is well—but I'm here to push your buttons, to wake you up, to help you face what has been hidden deep beneath the surface. I'm here to push you to grow, to let go of what was but no longer is. I'm here to help you shed the layers of density that have been overshadowing your light, keeping you in the dark, disconnected from your truth.

Open yourself up to join me on this journey, and your life will transform in ways you have not yet allowed yourself to imagine. Yes, there will first be a path of discomfort and even darkness, but the path can be crossed more quickly when you bring an openness, a readiness, and a willingness to co-create this inner transformation together—with me as your guide, your mentor, your teacher.

I love you for who you are. But it is now time to forget who you think you are and rediscover the truth of your being. It is time to come home to yourself.

I am here, waiting for your readiness.

Always and forever,

Your Shadow

Closing Incantation: I Welcome My Shadow Home

You've now walked into the very heart of the shadow—and you're still here. That alone speaks volumes. Shadow work is not for the faint of heart. It's not linear. It's not always graceful. But it is sacred. It's a reclamation of your power, your truth, and your wholeness.

You've begun to see that the parts of you, you once rejected or feared were never here to harm you. They were simply waiting—patiently, fiercely—to be met with love. They were asking to be acknowledged, heard, felt, and ultimately integrated.

This is not a process you rush. It's not something to "check off the list." This is a relationship. A partnership. A soul agreement between your human self and the light that lives within your dark.

So take a moment. Breathe into all that you've moved through. And when you feel ready, speak this incantation aloud—not as a command, but as a declaration of remembrance.

Incantation

I now choose to meet my shadow not with fear,
but with presence, with compassion, with truth.
I release the need to run, to reject, to resist.
I soften into what rises within me.

I welcome the parts of me I once denied.
I allow them to speak, to be felt, to be seen.
I listen. I honor. I receive the wisdom they hold.

I now clear and transmute the fear, the shame,
the heaviness and judgment I've carried—
across all times, space, realities, lifetimes, and dimensions.

I reclaim the power hidden in the pain.
I integrate the gift buried beneath the discomfort.
I embody the version of me who no longer fears my own depth.

I am no longer fragmented.
I am whole.
I am the alchemist of my shadow.
And I walk forward now—free.

Chapter 9: Emotional Alchemy

How to feel, process, and release energy that's been stuck for lifetimes

---

Emotional alchemy is not about managing your emotions, suppressing them, or pretending they don't exist. It's about learning to work with your emotions as they arise—meeting them with presence, not resistance. It's the process of becoming aware of what's moving through you and leaning in, not to dwell in it, but to transmute it. That's what alchemy is. It's about turning lead into gold. In this context, it means transforming lower-vibrational emotions into higher ones—liberating the emotional energy trapped beneath the surface so you can rise into a greater version of yourself.

So many of us go through our day feeling emotional and triggered without even realizing why. Sometimes we pick up on energies from others, sometimes we're carrying our own triggers, and often, we're tuning into the collective unrest without even knowing it. All of that creates emotional interference that we either try to push through or just live with—feeling off, moody, irritated, heavy—but not really knowing what's going on beneath the surface.

Emotional alchemy invites you to pause when you feel "NOT OK" and turn inward with curiosity. What am I feeling right now? What got stirred up in me? Instead of rushing to feel better or bypassing what's present, you take a moment to name the emotion. Is it frustration? Shame? Hurt? Anger? The simple act of naming what you're feeling brings awareness, and with awareness comes the power of choice. Once you recognize what you're experiencing, you can decide what to do with it. Do you want to stay in that emotional state—or shift it?

That's where the alchemy begins.

You don't shift by pushing the emotion away. You acknowledge it. You sit with it. You feel it—not from a place of victimhood, like "Why is this happening to me?"—but from an empowered place of presence. You give it attention, let it express itself, and allow the charge to move through you. This might take a few minutes, sometimes longer, depending on the intensity. But as you stay with the emotion with the intention to release the steam, you'll begin to feel a softening. The energetic charge loosens, and suddenly, you're no longer bound by it.

At this point, you can use the clearing statement: **"I now clear and transmute this (name the emotion) across all times, space, reality, lifetimes, and dimensions."** Say it with intention, stay connected to the feeling, and allow it to move.

Once the charge is released, emotional alchemy invites you to consciously tune into the vibration you'd rather feel. Because here's the truth: you've felt joy, love, abundance, freedom—at some point in your life, you've experienced those feelings. And if you've felt them before, that means the frequency of those emotions is already within you. You don't need something outside of you to activate them—you can call them forward yourself.

This is where the **Law of Reversibility** comes in. If a circumstance can create a feeling, then a feeling can create a circumstance. For example, if receiving an unexpected check makes you feel abundant, then intentionally tuning into the frequency of abundance now can begin attracting experiences that match that frequency. That's alchemy.

So instead of staying stuck in anger or fear, you choose to feel joy, peace, or trust. You think of a time when you felt that higher emotion—let it wash over you, turn up the dial, and really FEEL it. This is how you transmute lower energy into something elevated and magnetic. This is how you shift your field.

Emotional alchemy puts you back in control. You no longer have to ride the emotional roller coaster of life. You gain the tools to shift how you feel—not by force, but by conscious presence. And once you begin using this process consistently, you'll notice how much more stable, grounded, and aligned you feel. You'll bounce back from triggers faster, and you'll stop being consumed by emotional spirals.

But the most important piece in all of this is awareness. Emotions are energy in motion. They want to move, not be suppressed. When you ignore them, they don't disappear—they get trapped in your energetic body. And over time, they build up and create stagnation, even dis-ease. Physical symptoms. Chronic conditions. Illness. This is why it's so vital to do this work—not just for your emotional well-being, but for your overall health and vibrancy.

Sometimes, emotions don't even want to be "healed"—they just want to be heard. Like a child tugging at your sleeve trying to get your attention, they get louder the longer they're ignored. And the moment you turn inward and say, "Okay, I hear you. What are you trying to tell me?"—that alone can bring relief. That acknowledgment is often all they needed.

Now, that doesn't mean you need to indulge in every emotional wave or let it define your experience. But when you meet your emotions with presence and awareness, you gain the ability to move through them with intention instead of getting stuck inside of them. Sometimes you'll need to feel the feeling fully, and other times you'll just need to notice it, release the steam, and shift.

Later in the book, we'll explore frequency in more depth. But for now, know this: your emotions influence your frequency, and your frequency creates your reality. The Universe doesn't respond to your words—it responds to your energetic signature. If you're constantly dwelling in frustration, anger, or lack, you'll keep attracting experiences that reflect those energies back to you.

But if you learn how to shift—how to feel, process, and transmute—you'll begin creating from a place of alignment, clarity, and sovereignty. And that's what it means to be a Soul Alchemist. You work with your emotions consciously. You transmute the dense into light. You shape your reality through the frequencies you choose to embody.

And that begins here—by choosing to feel what's present... and then consciously shift into what you desire to experience.

Why We Carry Emotions for Lifetimes Without Realizing It

We are often energetic sponges, absorbing emotions from others, from our environment, from the collective, and even from unseen spiritual dimensions. This is especially true for those who are highly sensitive or empathic. You're not just feeling your own emotions—you're picking up on emotional residue from people around you, from the energies of a space, from the unspoken pain of society. And unless you're consciously working with your energy, all of it gets stored within your energetic system.

But it's not just emotions from this lifetime. We carry emotional imprints across time. Past lives, ancestral patterns, soul contracts—these all leave energetic traces. If you lived a past life where you were betrayed, cast out, or harmed in ways that were shocking or traumatic, the emotions connected to those experiences can stay embedded in your soul's energetic field. These imprints don't just disappear when your physical body dies. If they go unprocessed, they carry forward into your next incarnation—unfinished, unacknowledged, unresolved.

That's how emotions become trapped.

Let's bring it into something more relatable. Think back to your very first heartbreak. Even if it happened decades ago, if you never fully processed and released those emotions, they didn't vanish. They became part of your inner emotional landscape—perhaps quiet and dormant most of the time, but still present, still shaping how you show up in relationships. They might resurface as fear of intimacy, as walls you put up, or as patterns you keep repeating. This is what it means to carry emotional energy through time.

One of my clients, who was extremely intuitive and empathic, had unknowingly been carrying emotional weight for years. She had taken on other people's pain for so long—family, friends, even strangers—and had no idea how much of it wasn't even hers. When we worked together to release what had become trapped, it felt to her like a hundred-pound sack was lifted off her shoulders. That weight, that heaviness, had been silently influencing every area of her life. And until she released it, she had no idea how much lighter she could feel.

This is why emotional alchemy and energy hygiene aren't just "nice to have" practices. They are essential. Just like you brush your teeth every day to stay clean and healthy, your energy field needs regular care and cleansing. If you're constantly absorbing and suppressing without releasing, you create a backlog. That backlog doesn't just weigh on your emotional state—it distorts your perception, clouds your intuition, blocks your ability to manifest, and alters how you respond to life. You become reactive instead of intentional. You feel heavy when you want to feel free.

And these trapped layers of emotion don't just affect how you feel—they shape what you create.

Unprocessed emotions create friction in your energy field. That friction becomes static, distortion, interference. It blocks the clarity and flow needed for effortless creation. It clouds your inner guidance and makes you question your intuition. It shows up as resistance, procrastination, doubt, or fear. You might think you're stuck because you're doing something wrong—but in truth, you may just be carrying too much that was never yours to begin with.

This is why soul-level transformation requires emotional clearing. You cannot manifest a new reality from an energy field that's still saturated in the frequencies of past pain. You can't become the Soul Alchemist you're meant to be while dragging bags of emotional weight behind you—bags you didn't even realize you were carrying.

You came here to be free. To create, express, and expand as your highest self. But that requires energetic spaciousness. And that spaciousness comes from letting go.

It's not always about healing some massive trauma—it can be as simple as getting honest about how you feel, noticing when you're carrying something heavy, and choosing to let it go. Daily. Intentionally. Not with force, but with love and awareness.

Because the more space you create within your energy field, the more power you reclaim. The more light you hold. And the more effortlessly you begin to manifest a life that reflects the truth of who you are—not the pain of who you used to be.

The Signs That Old Emotional Energy Is Surfacing

When old emotional energy begins to surface, it doesn't always announce itself clearly. It often creeps in subtly, through your mood, your body, your thoughts, or the way life begins to feel slightly "off." But when you know what to look for, you can catch it early—before it spirals into overwhelm or becomes a pattern that throws you off course.

One of the first and most common indicators is a sudden wave of discomfort. You might feel irritable, anxious, unsettled, or even flat-out "not OK" for no apparent reason. There's nothing significant that triggered it, but emotionally, something feels heavy, out of sync, or agitating. This is your internal guidance system alerting you that something deeper is surfacing.

Physically, you might experience fatigue, headaches, tightness in the chest, tension in the shoulders or jaw, nausea, or restlessness in the body—especially in the legs and solar plexus area. These are some of the places where emotional energy often gets trapped, and when it begins to rise to the surface, the body speaks up. You may even feel like your body is trying to "shake something off," and in a way— it is.

Emotionally, this can look like overreacting to small things, crying unexpectedly, or feeling emotionally tender and raw. Old emotional layers don't always return with the same storyline—they often reappear as energetic residue that simply feels intense, sticky, or confusing. You may not know why you're feeling the way you are, but the emotion is real and valid. It's the energy of the past asking to be felt, acknowledged, and released.

Mentally, it might show up as looping thoughts, self-doubt, self-criticism, or an inability to stay focused. You might start telling yourself stories that spiral—stories of being unworthy, behind, not enough, unsafe. These stories aren't new; they're echoes of old wounds that are being activated so they can be witnessed and alchemized.

In your energetic field, this can feel like static—an inner dissonance or disconnect. You may feel out of alignment with yourself, disoriented in your intuition, or like you're energetically "off." You might find your manifestations feel blocked, your usual practices feel ineffective, or synchronicities seem to stop flowing. That doesn't mean something is wrong—it means something is ready to be cleared.

In your outer life, this might look like sudden miscommunications, tension with others, obstacles appearing, or familiar patterns reemerging that you thought you had already worked through. When this happens, it's not a sign that you're failing or backtracking—it's a signal that a deeper layer is ready to be released.

Here's what to look for:

- You're feeling emotionally reactive without understanding why

- You're exhausted, restless, or experiencing physical tension or heaviness

- You're having old memories, patterns, or people resurface

- Your thoughts become repetitive or disempowering

- You feel off energetically—ungrounded, disconnected, or chaotic

- You notice a strong desire to retreat, isolate, or escape

- Life feels like it's slowing down or forcing you inward

These are all signs that emotional energy is surfacing. Not to punish you, not to drag you back—but to give you an opportunity. An opportunity to alchemize.

The more you become attuned to these signs, the more empowered you become. You'll start to recognize that these moments aren't setbacks—they're sacred openings. Each wave of discomfort is an invitation to pause, turn inward, and transmute what's rising. With awareness comes the power of choice—and with choice comes liberation.

Feeling to Heal Without Being Derailed

One of the most empowering things you can do on your healing journey is to learn how to fully *feel* your emotions—without getting consumed or thrown off by them. When you learn how to do this, you're no longer at the mercy of emotional waves that knock you over and keep you down. Instead, you become the observer, the alchemist, the one who can lean into the discomfort and transmute it with presence, awareness, and choice.

This is what "feeling to heal" really means.

To feel to heal is to turn toward your emotions instead of away from them. It's to consciously allow yourself to feel what's moving through your body without trying to explain it away, avoid it, or bypass it. And yet, this is not about collapsing into emotion and letting it take you under. It's about meeting the feeling head-on—not from the story, not from the victim, but from the empowered place within you that *knows* this emotion is surfacing for a reason.

Sometimes, all an emotion needs is to be seen, heard, and honored. You don't need to psychoanalyze it. You don't need to know exactly where it came from. You just need to feel it. Give yourself a few minutes to sit with it intentionally. Tune into the sensation in your body. Let the emotion rise. If you can, even *turn up the intensity* of the feeling for just a moment—just enough to release the steam.

What you'll often find is that something breaks open. Like a pressure bubble bursting. The intensity dissolves. The edge softens. And then… something shifts. A sense of ease comes over you. A lightness. That's the moment when the energetic charge has been released. That's the moment you've moved the emotion through your body rather than letting it stay trapped inside.

And that's where you reclaim your power.

You become the driver of your emotional experience—not a passenger getting thrown around. Because no emotion, no matter how uncomfortable, can derail you when you know how to meet it, feel it, and alchemize it with intention. Emotional alchemy gives you the tools to do just that.

But here's the part most people miss—and this is what pulls them out of empowerment and back into spiraling:

The story.

The story is what keeps you stuck. It's what makes the emotion worse. The story feeds the fire, makes it bigger than it needs to be, and hooks your mind into a loop that's hard to escape. That's when you move from conscious processing into emotional spiraling—when you attach to the story and lose your grounded presence.

Let's break that down a bit more.

Conscious emotional processing is when you:

- Stay present with the *feeling* rather than the event that triggered it

- Witness your emotion without needing to justify or explain it

- Work with your body, breath, and energy to move the feeling through

- Honor what arises, and then choose what you want to feel instead

Emotional spiraling is when you:

- Rehash the same story over and over in your mind

- Try to make sense of why it happened, who did what, what you *should* have done differently

- Attach meaning to the emotion, reinforcing old beliefs like "I'm not good enough" or "This always happens to me"

- Sink into the victim state, feeling powerless and stuck

And this is why I always say: *stay out of the story.* Because the story is not the healing. The emotion is the portal. The story is the wrapping paper, the outer packaging that makes it look a certain way—but it's not what you're here to work with.

Think of it like this: Your emotions are the gift. The real, sacred treasure that's been wrapped up. But your mind wants to stay focused on the wrapping paper—the drama, the meaning, the why. But that's not what matters. When you do emotional alchemy, you're not here to fixate on what the box looks like. You're here to *open it* and work with what's inside.

So next time something triggers you, and your mind starts going into overdrive—pause. Notice it. That's your moment of choice. That's when you take a step back, drop out of your head, and drop into your heart. Tune in. What are you actually feeling right now? That's the only thing that matters in that moment. That's what wants your attention. That's the path to healing.

And when you do this consistently, something beautiful happens: you stop fearing your emotions. You stop running from discomfort. You meet yourself fully. And in that meeting, you transform.

The Nervous System: Your Inner Alarm and Anchor

Let's talk about your nervous system—because this is one of the most important pieces when it comes to emotional alchemy. Any time you're feeling NOT OK, your nervous system is activated. That's what causes the *feeling* of "I'm not OK." And that's also where a lot of those energetic imprints are stored. When something happens in your life, it's these imprints—conscious or unconscious—that get triggered, poking your system and setting off the internal alarm.

Think of your nervous system like the alarm system in your home. If someone tries to break in, the alarm goes off: *INTRUDER! DANGER!* Your nervous system works the same way. It is your first line of energetic defense. If something feels threatening—physically, emotionally, or energetically—it sends out a signal, warning you, *something's not right.*

That signal is what we call dysregulation. It's the unease in your body. The tightness in your chest. The shallow breath. The racing thoughts. The sense that something is wrong, even if you can't quite name what. From there, the emotions start spiraling. The mind kicks in. The discomfort grows. And suddenly, you're in the middle of a full-blown activation.

That's why it's so important to become familiar with your nervous system. To learn how to *read* it. Because once you become aware that your nervous system is activated, you can begin to do something about it. You can pause. You can breathe. You can regulate. You can take care of the part of you that's crying out, *Danger! Danger!*

But it's not just about responding in the moment—you also want to *cleanse*, *soothe*, and *calm* your nervous system after any emotional intensity or healing work. This is especially vital when doing deep emotional alchemy. Because even after you process an emotion or complete a session, your nervous system might still be buzzing. Still holding that memory of danger or emotional overwhelm in its field.

138

Remember the sidewalk example I shared before—where someone pushes you and you fall? Even if you stand back up, calm yourself down, and keep walking, hours later you might still feel that uneasy tension when you think back on it. That's your nervous system still running the alarm, even when the "danger" has passed.

If your nervous system stays in this hyper-activated state for too long, it creates a chronic sense of stress and ungroundedness. This is what happens with those who have experienced repeated trauma, like in PTSD. The nervous system gets stuck in a loop—always bracing, always scanning for threats, always on edge.

But even if you haven't lived through overt trauma, the emotional triggers of daily life can activate your system in subtler ways. A difficult conversation. A childhood wound resurfacing. A fear about the future. These things may not seem dramatic, but if you don't process them, they build up. Your nervous system becomes overwhelmed. You feel reactive. Impatient. Fragile. Or like you're constantly running on fumes with a short fuse.

Now layer in spiritual growth and ascension work—eclipses, solstices, cosmic downloads, full moons, activations, and energy work—and you've got even more input affecting your system. All of this can stretch your nervous system beyond what it's used to. That's not a bad thing—it's part of your expansion. But it means you need to be extra intentional about regulating your system as you grow.

Even listening to Light Language activations, participating in healing sessions, or doing deep internal processing work—*all of it* moves energy through your field and stirs your nervous system. That's why tending to this part of yourself is essential.

So, how do you work with your nervous system and calm it down when it's activated?

Start by tuning in to the energetic field around you. This is your nervous system's outer edge. Just take a moment to feel into that space. Where is the boundary of your field? How does it feel?

Does it feel calm—like a still lake? Or a little choppy—like some light waves splashing around? Or is it a full-blown storm—wild, frantic, chaotic?

This tells you exactly how activated your nervous system is.

If it's calm, great. That means your system is regulated. But if it feels wavy or stormy, it's time to calm it down. And here's the beautiful part: *you can do this with intention alone.*

Simply intend for the storm to settle. Imagine the waves slowing. See the waters becoming smooth. Let everything soften. Your nervous system is part of *you*, and that means you can shift it from the inside out. You don't need a fancy tool. Just presence and intention. Of course, if you know Light Language or other energy healing modalities, you can use those to support you—but it's not required. Your *choice* is the medicine.

If you find that your nervous system gets activated frequently—especially when you step outside your comfort zone—you may need to expand your nervous system as you grow. Think of it like a flexible, stretchable field that surrounds you. As you expand into more power, purpose, and truth, your nervous system needs to grow with you. Otherwise, it becomes tight, constricted, and reactive.

It's like wearing clothes that no longer fit. You wouldn't keep squeezing into a shirt that's three sizes too small—you'd buy a new one. And while you can't buy a new nervous system, you *can* expand the one you have. Just set the intention: *I now allow my nervous system to stretch and grow with me. I invite it to support my expansion in grace and harmony.*

Check in with your field often:

- If it feels too tight, expand it.

- If it feels too loose and disorienting, gently pull it in.

- If it feels stormy or chaotic, calm it down.

You are the steward of your field. You have the power to tend to your nervous system the same way you would tend to your garden—with care, consistency, and love.

And this brings us back to grounding.

Because when we talk about emotional alchemy, *grounding* is key. You can't do deep emotional work and expect to stay centered if your nervous system is flailing in all directions. The more activated your nervous system, the more ungrounded you feel. The more grounded you are, the calmer your nervous system becomes.

They work hand in hand.

And as you continue to grow, heal, and expand, let this be one of your sacred practices: to come back to your field, your body, your breath—and regulate from within. That is how you stay steady in the waves. That is how you alchemize in power, not panic.

Practices for Moving Energy

When it comes to emotional alchemy, it's not just about becoming aware of what you're feeling—it's also about *moving* the energy that's been trapped. Awareness gives you the power of choice, but embodiment comes through action. Through intention. Through practice.

Let's start with one of the most accessible and powerful tools of all: **breathwork**.

Your breath is a bridge between your inner and outer worlds. It's always with you, and yet we often forget how powerful it can be. When emotions feel stuck or overwhelming, take a moment to pause and *breathe with intention*. A simple technique you can try right away is this:

- Inhale slowly through your nose for a count of four

- Hold your breath at the top for four

- Exhale through your mouth for a count of six

- Repeat this for at least three minutes

As you breathe, imagine the emotion rising up with each inhale. With every exhale, release what no longer serves. Imagine the energetic debris melting away with each breath, softening and dissolving.

Now let's talk about a tool I personally use and teach in all of my work: **the clearing statement**.

This is a powerful way to release stuck energy on the spot. The practice is simple but deeply effective when done with full presence and intention. Here's how it works:

- First, *connect with the emotion*—not the story behind it, but the raw feeling itself.

- Drop into your body and ask, *What am I feeling right now?* Allow the sensation to rise.

- Then, repeat the clearing statement with intention:

"I now clear and transmute this [name the feeling] across all times, space, reality, lifetimes, and dimensions."

You can repeat the statement as many times as you need—until you feel a shift. The most important ingredient here is your *intention*. If you're simply saying the words without directing your energy toward release, you won't experience the same impact. But when you infuse the words with *deliberate* intent, something shifts. You'll feel it. A lightness. A release. The pressure lifting.

Now let's go a little deeper with **Light Language**.

Light Language is an energetic transmission that bypasses the logical mind and speaks directly to the soul. It's a multidimensional tool that carries frequencies of healing, activation, and remembrance. Each sound, tone, or symbol encodes a specific vibration—designed to shift energy, clear density, and support transformation at the soul level. It's not something you "understand" with the mind—it's something you *feel*.

If you already channel Light Language, you can use it much like the clearing statement. Tune into the emotion that's rising, allow yourself to feel it fully, and then let the codes flow. Speak or move the energy with intention, directing the transmission into any dense pockets that feel heavy, stuck, or charged. Let the Light Language move through you and blast open the layers that are ready to be released.

You can even amplify this process by combining Light Language with breathwork and the clearing statement. Breathe with presence, channel with power, speak the words of release—and allow your energy field to recalibrate in real time.

And if you're curious about Light Language or feel a nudge that you might carry this gift, I created a free mini course called *Discovering Light Language: A Beginner's Journey*. It's a great starting point to explore what Light Language is, how it works, and how to activate your own unique expression. You can access it here: https://www.kaysanders.com/discovering-light-language/

Another beautiful practice for emotional alchemy is **movement**.

This doesn't have to be anything complicated. Go for a walk. Stretch your body. Dance. Hit the gym and lift weights or do some cardio. What matters is that you *move your body with intention*.

When you move with the desire to move energy, something profound happens. As your muscles contract and stretch, you literally shake loose what's been stuck. That's why people often say they feel better after a walk, a workout, or even just a few minutes of stretching—it's not just the physical exertion. It's that the energy *moved*. You didn't let it sit and fester. You gave it somewhere to go.

So next time you feel upset, frustrated, or overwhelmed, don't just sit and stew in it. Go move. Breathe. Walk. Let the emotions move *through* you and *out* of you.

Other powerful practices include **journaling, singing, writing, or even talking out loud**. Each of these gives your emotions a voice—a way to express what's been locked inside. Here's how to use them intentionally:

- **Journaling:** Don't censor yourself. Let the emotions pour onto the page. Write from your body, not your head. You don't need to make sense—just move the energy. Let it flow until you feel something shift.

- **Singing or sounding:** Let your voice carry the emotion. You can sing actual songs or simply vocalize—humming, toning, or sighing. Sound moves stuck energy in powerful, ancient ways.

- **Writing:** Similar to journaling, but sometimes more focused. You can write letters you never send, or even write directly to the emotion: *Dear Anger, what are you trying to tell me?* Let the answers come.

- **Talking out loud:** Sometimes, speaking your truth out loud—just to yourself—is enough to release it. Let your voice vibrate the truth into the space around you.

That said, one thing I *don't* recommend is venting to others—especially if you're in a heightened emotional state. That's not processing. That's discharging—and it can actually amplify your emotion if the person you're talking to isn't grounded or starts adding their own energy to the mix. You may walk away feeling worse, more confused, or even more reactive.

Emotional alchemy is sacred work—and it's best done in a space of presence, not chaos. If you do want support, choose someone who can hold a clear and safe energetic space for you. A coach, healer, or mentor who won't feed the fire but can help you *process* and transmute the charge.

This isn't about avoiding connection or being isolated—it's about honoring the energetic responsibility of working with your emotions in a conscious, intentional way.

And remember, this isn't about perfection. It's a practice.

Some days, the energy will move quickly. Other days, it will take time. You may need more than one tool. You may need to revisit the same emotion more than once. That's okay. You're building emotional muscle. You're learning to stay with yourself. And every time you do, you reclaim more of your power.

Don't Rush the Process

There will be moments when you just want to *get it over with*. When the feelings feel too heavy, too overwhelming, too uncomfortable—and your mind screams, *Can't we just be done already?* But emotional alchemy doesn't work like that. You can't force it. You can't rush it. And if you try, you'll likely make things worse.

Some emotions need time to be fully seen, felt, and understood—especially when they're tied to deeper layers of your being or meant to reveal something important. As I shared earlier when talking about shadow work, each emotion holds a message, a lesson, or even a hidden gift. And if you're too caught up in the discomfort or attached to the story behind it, you might miss the deeper truth it's trying to show you.

There were times when I felt really *not OK*. Something would rise within me—dense, uncomfortable—and I couldn't immediately name it. I'd sit with it and ask, *What am I feeling?...* and sometimes I didn't get an answer right away. That's when I stopped trying to figure it out and simply chose to *be* with the feeling.

I remember one day I was just full of frustration. I felt pissy and bitchy for no clear reason—and instead of stuffing it down or pretending to be fine, I let myself *have a moment*. I owned it. I walked through my house repeating, *I'm so bitchy and pissy today!*—with full passion and energy behind it. I didn't take it out on anyone. I wasn't being careless or blaming. I was just letting the emotion move through me in a conscious, embodied way. I gave myself full permission to feel it.

My son looked at me like I was being weird (which, let's be real, I kind of was), but I told him I was having a moment, and he gave me the space I needed. I kept walking, kept declaring how pissy I felt— and after about 15 to 30 minutes, something shifted. The charge dissolved. The intensity softened. And once that space opened up inside of me, I was able to tune in and realize what had actually triggered the emotion in the first place.

Only then could I see the deeper truth—and respond in a higher, more empowered way. That clarity didn't come by trying to *get over it* or slap some light and love on top. It came because I *stayed with it*. I let the energy complete its cycle.

This is what I mean when I say: *you cannot rush emotional alchemy*.

Even when you use tools like breathwork, the clearing statement, or Light Language—these practices assist the process, but they don't bypass it. The energy still needs to be felt. The emotional wave still needs to crest and settle. You're not here to override or suppress your inner experience—you're here to *transmute* it. And that can only happen from a state of awareness and presence.

The moment you dive back into the story, reliving the situation and labeling yourself as a victim, you disconnect from the alchemy. You reinforce the very pattern you're trying to shift. That's why I say: don't attach to the story. Be with the *feeling*. Honor the *sensation*. Work with the *emotion* that's rising—not the narrative your mind wants to build around it.

Think of it like this: when a child is throwing a tantrum, and you ignore them, they only get louder. But if you sit with them, hold space for them, and let them *be seen*, they soften. They calm down. Emotions work the same way. If you ignore them, suppress them, or delay them, they build pressure. But if you meet them with presence, they'll pass through—and you'll feel the shift.

When you allow your emotions to complete their cycle, not only do you move through them more quickly, you do it in a way that strengthens your sovereignty. You reclaim your power. You choose to face what's rising instead of running from it.

And that is the essence of emotional alchemy.

You are not at the mercy of your emotions. You are the conscious creator working with them, transforming them, and allowing them to reveal what's ready to be seen, felt, and released.

What Happens When the Energy Releases

When old emotions finally release, you'll often feel it not just emotionally—but physically, energetically, even spiritually. It's not just something that happens in your mind. You'll feel it in your body. In your field. In your being.

You might notice an immediate drop in tension—maybe in your chest, your stomach, your shoulders, or somewhere else where you've been unknowingly holding it all in. If you're sensitive to energy, you may feel something move or shift in your field... a ripple, a softening, or even a wave that passes through you.

Sometimes, it triggers a flood of emotion. Tears might come—not from sadness, but from relief. It's like your system finally has permission to *let go*. Crying is one of the most natural ways the body clears emotional charge. But you may also experience other physical signs of release—burping, yawning, sneezing, or even an unexpected wave of exhaustion. That's the dense energy leaving your system. That's your body exhaling what it's been carrying for far too long.

And then... comes the calm.

Once things settle, you may feel lighter—literally, as if something has been lifted from your shoulders. You might feel a sense of spaciousness in your chest, as if you can breathe more deeply again. You may notice a subtle joy return, or a wave of peace wash over you for no apparent reason. Sometimes you even feel taller or more upright, as if your entire being has re-aligned itself.

These are all signs of alignment returning. Of energy recalibrating. Of you stepping closer to your center. Because here's the deeper truth: every time you release heavy emotional energy, you reclaim something sacred.

You reclaim a part of your power. You reclaim a piece of your sovereignty. You reclaim your clarity, your groundedness, your *self*. You come home to yourself—layer by layer, breath by breath, moment by moment.

This is why emotional alchemy is not just about healing... it's about *remembering* who you truly are underneath all that weight you were never meant to carry.

Emotional Alchemy as a Way of Living

When you release the emotional weight you've carried—sometimes for years, lifetimes even—something shifts. You begin to experience life differently. There's more space inside of you. More ease. More freedom.

You stop reacting so quickly. You respond instead—with presence, with clarity, with power. Things that once threw you off don't shake you as easily anymore. And when something *does* rattle you, you move through it more gracefully. You feel the emotions, you work with them, and you come out the other side lighter, clearer, more centered.

This is what changes your relationship to life.

Emotional alchemy puts you back in the driver's seat. It allows you to meet challenges not as a victim, but as a conscious creator. You no longer get swept away by emotional storms—you learn how to move with them, to dance with the discomfort, and to extract the gift that's always hidden inside.

And as you do this, your inner world begins to shift.

You become more grounded in who you are. More anchored in truth. You trust yourself more. You move through life with greater awareness, more emotional resilience, and a deep sense of self-honoring. You start attracting new experiences, new opportunities, even new people who are more aligned with your healed and expanded self. Or the relationships you already have begin to deepen and soften, because you're showing up with a clearer heart.

This is emotional freedom—not because you never feel anything challenging again, but because you no longer *fear* your emotions. You know how to work with them. You know how to meet them. You know how to move them. And that's power.

You stop resisting life. You start flowing with it. You stop spiraling. You start ascending.

The more you engage in emotional alchemy, the more you realize that everything is here to support your growth. Every trigger, every discomfort, every storm is just another invitation to reclaim your energy, your clarity, and your sovereignty.

That's the gift of this work. You're not just healing... you're evolving. You're transcending. You're becoming more of *you*.

Becoming the Alchemist of Your Emotional Body

To become the alchemist of your emotional body means you no longer let your emotions control you, consume you, or keep you stuck in repeating loops of pain and reaction. Instead, you meet them consciously. You work with them. You allow them to rise, move, speak, and release—without clinging to the stories or identifying with the storm.

You begin to understand that your emotions are messengers, not threats. Discomfort doesn't mean something is wrong with you—it means something is trying to get your attention. And rather than running from it, numbing it, or pretending it isn't there, you face it with open arms, open eyes, and an open heart.

That is emotional alchemy.

It's not about "fixing" yourself. It's about transmuting what no longer serves. It's about reclaiming your energy from all the places it's been scattered and calling yourself back—whole, sovereign, present.

You become the one who notices the wave rising and chooses to ride it with grace instead of drowning in it.

You become the one who no longer fears being "too much" or "too sensitive," because you've learned how to honor your sensitivity as a gift, not a burden. You become the one who walks into the fire of emotion and walks out lighter, clearer, and more aligned than ever before. And maybe most importantly, you stop judging yourself for feeling. You understand that your emotions are not the enemy. They are portals. Teachers. Catalysts.

And as you become more practiced in this alchemical work, you stop getting stuck in the same old patterns. You stop reacting from old wounds. You start responding from a deeper place of truth and embodiment. That is true empowerment.

This is your invitation to reclaim your role as the Soul Alchemist of your emotional body. To meet every wave with awareness. To honor every feeling with compassion. To choose presence over avoidance. To let the energy move, shift, and transform—because you are capable of holding it all.

Your emotions no longer rule you. They serve you. And that changes everything.

Closing Incantation: The Sacred Release

As we close this chapter, take a moment to honor yourself for simply being willing to face what's within. That alone is a powerful act of courage and sovereignty. Emotional alchemy is not about having it all figured out. It's about showing up—again and again—with presence, with grace, and with the unwavering commitment to meet yourself exactly where you are.

This is not a one-time fix. This is a way of being. A way of relating to your inner world with curiosity rather than fear. With compassion rather than judgment. With empowerment rather than avoidance.

Each time you lean into your emotions instead of running from them, you reclaim a piece of yourself. Each time you choose to breathe through the discomfort, to let the energy move, to feel without drowning, you are transmuting density into light. Pain into power. Resistance into peace.

And so, we anchor this chapter with an incantation—a vibrational declaration to remind your body, your being, and your soul: You are not the storm. You are the alchemist walking through it with sacred fire in your heart.

Incantation:

I now call back all fragments of my power from the emotions I have feared, suppressed, or avoided.
I open my heart and body to feel what is ready to be seen, to move what is ready to be released.
I release the need to rush, resist, or label what I feel. I allow. I witness. I transmute.
I honor my nervous system with compassion, grounding myself in presence as I move through each wave.
I release all stuck, heavy, or lingering energy into the nothingness from which it came.
I stand sovereign in my body, free in my emotions, clear in my energy.
With each breath, I become more anchored in truth, more embodied in power.
I am the alchemist of my inner world.
And so it is.

Chapter 10 The Frequency You Choose to Embody

Mastering your vibration as a conscious creator

In this chapter, we dive deeper into one of the most essential aspects of conscious creation—energetic alignment. Because here's the truth: being a Soul Alchemist isn't just about doing the inner work. It's not just about healing, clearing, and working through your emotions. Those pieces are vital, yes—but they're only part of the journey. The true transformation happens in **embodiment**.

Embodiment is the key that unlocks new timelines. It's about *being* the version of yourself who is already whole, already empowered, already aligned, sovereign, abundant, and free. Without this, you'll find yourself stuck in a cycle of clearing and healing—thinking you're making progress, only to feel like you've taken three steps forward and two steps back. Because you can't think or process your way into a new timeline—you have to *become* the version of you who already lives there.

This is why energetic embodiment matters. Every time you heal or transmute something, you're meant to rise into a higher essence. You've created an opening, and you now have the choice to move into a higher timeline by fully stepping into the frequency of the one who has already overcome the very challenge you just alchemized.

Let's say, for example, that one of your patterns was a lack of boundaries—people didn't take you seriously, walked all over you, or drained your energy. Through your inner work, you uncover the message and the gift: you're being invited to honor your own boundaries more deeply. You're being called to reclaim your worth and communicate your limits clearly. Now, this is where embodiment comes in. You ask: *Who is the version of me who already lives this truth?*

She's the woman who holds her head high. She's grounded in her truth. People respect her, honor her energy, and listen when she speaks. She feels empowered from the inside out. You begin to merge with her. You embody her essence—not just in your mind but in your posture, your decisions, your energy field. You don't wait to become her—you *become* her now.

This is what embodiment means. You're not admiring that version of yourself from afar—you *are* her. You *become* the vibrational match to the reality she lives in. That's how you shift timelines. That's how you grow into a new version of yourself and leave behind the limitations of your past. That's how you align.

So let's talk about what energetic alignment really means.

Energetic alignment is when your inner state and outer life begin to reflect harmony. You feel in sync—emotionally, spiritually, mentally, physically, and most importantly, **energetically**. It's when your actions feel guided, your choices feel true, and your energy is clean, clear, and powerful. You're not operating from effort—you're flowing from essence.

Now let's look at the opposite—energetic misalignment. Because that's likely where most of us spend more time than we'd like to admit.

When you're out of alignment, everything feels harder. You feel like you're dragging yourself uphill with a heavy backpack strapped to your shoulders. You're more easily overwhelmed, frustrated, or fatigued. You might wake up exhausted even after a full night's sleep. Your daily routine feels suffocating, repetitive, lifeless. Your inner being might be screaming, *There has to be more than this!*

You may feel extra sensitive to other people's energy—or to the collective. You take on their emotions or chaos without realizing it. The weight builds, and you start to feel like you're drowning in things that aren't even yours.

This is your cue to pause. To come back to yourself. To realign.

Becoming energetically aware means tuning into the subtle shifts—those barely-there nudges or internal alarms—and choosing to respond. You feel a little off? Don't push it aside. Drop into your heart. Tune into your body. Ask what needs to be seen, felt, cleared, or honored.

This is where the real magic happens. The more aware you become of your own energetic state, the quicker you can shift it. You won't stay misaligned for days or weeks—you'll catch it early and move back into harmony.

And if you're an empath, intuitive, or sensitive soul—this awareness is even more important. You can't afford to let energy fester in your field. You need to stay attuned, intentional, and clear. This is part of what it means to be a Soul Alchemist. You work with your energy field consistently. You don't ignore what's off—you lean in, transmute it, and recalibrate.

The more you prioritize your energy, the more your life begins to shift. You'll notice stronger boundaries—physically, emotionally, and energetically. You'll listen to your needs more. You'll honor yourself in deeper ways. And you'll feel more grounded, more empowered, and more *you*.

Now let's address one of the biggest cultural distortions we've been taught: **hustle is the key to success.**

We're taught to keep moving, keep striving, keep doing. But alignment is far more powerful than hustle. Rest isn't laziness—it's wisdom. Stillness isn't stagnation—it's sacred recalibration. When you align your energy first, things flow. You don't need to push. You don't need to fight. You become magnetic—not because of what you *do* but because of who you *are*.

From this place of alignment, life meets you where you are. Insight flows in. Guidance becomes clear. You become available for miracles. And the journey? It becomes lighter, freer, and more soul-led than ever before.

So the next time you feel out of sync, remember: you don't need to hustle harder. You just need to realign your frequency.

Your Frequency Shapes the Reality You Live In

Your frequency shapes your reality because *like attracts like*. What you emanate, you attract. What you send out vibrationally, you call back into your experience—whether you're aware of it or not.

Let's first clarify what "frequency" really means in energetic terms.

Everything is energy, and energy vibrates at different frequencies. Your frequency is the vibrational signature you emit based on your thoughts, emotions, beliefs, and most importantly—your embodiment. It's not just about what you *think* you want or what you *say* you believe. It's the energetic essence you live in, breathe in, and move from day in and day out.

So, if you constantly live in the energy of lack, frustration, or limitation, that becomes your dominant frequency. You start broadcasting that signal outward, and that same energy loops back to you in the form of more experiences that mirror that vibration.

For example, if you're always worrying about money—feeling anxious about bills, fearful of emergencies, or stressed that it's never enough—you're rooted in a lack frequency. Even if an unexpected windfall comes your way, it won't stay for long. The energy of lack repels abundance. You might suddenly need car repairs or lose a client or watch the money slip through your fingers just as quickly as it arrived. Why? Because your dominant frequency didn't shift, and your reality responded accordingly.

The same applies to relationships. If past pain led you to close your heart, mistrust others, or expect disappointment, then your energetic signature speaks louder than your words. You may be longing for love, connection, and deep intimacy—but the frequency you're holding is still infused with fear, hurt, and protection. You might unconsciously push people away, attract unavailable or emotionally immature partners, or recreate the same painful dynamics over and over again—because your internal frequency is still attuned to the old story.

Now let's talk about when your frequency *contradicts* your desires.

This is one of the biggest reasons people stay stuck. You might desire abundance, love, fulfillment, or freedom—but if your frequency is still soaked in doubt, fear, unworthiness, or lack, you are not a vibrational match to what you desire. Your energy is saying one thing while your mouth is saying another. And the universe always responds to your energy, not just your words or vision boards or journaling exercises.

You can't fake frequency. You *are* the frequency you live in.

That's why doing the deeper inner work, the emotional and energetic alchemy, is so vital. It clears out the distortions. It helps you recalibrate your field so you can align your energetic signature with what you truly want. And when you begin to embody the version of you who already lives in alignment with your desires—who feels safe, empowered, abundant, radiant—that's when you start tuning into a whole new frequency band. A reality that once seemed out of reach becomes your new normal, because you've shifted your baseline frequency and you're no longer a match to the limitations of your past.

The Subtle Forces That Knock You Out of Alignment

Energetic misalignment doesn't always come with flashing lights and warning signs. In fact, most of the time, it sneaks in quietly—through the noise of daily life, through unconscious habits, through subtle energetic shifts that go unnoticed until you suddenly feel off. That's why it's so important to understand *how* and *why* you fall out of alignment, so you can catch it sooner and return to your center before it throws off your entire day—or your trajectory.

It's not always easy to stay in alignment because life happens.

You may start your morning with a beautiful energy alignment practice where you feel deeply connected to yourself—your field calm, your nervous system settled, and your being anchored in presence. You feel empowered, grounded, and aligned. But then the day begins. Obligations start hitting you left and right, your to-dos start piling up, maybe you run into a coworker's mood or get hit with an unexpected expense, or you're simply pulled in a million directions—and just like that, without even realizing it, you've slipped out of that aligned state and into the chaotic energy of the 3D world.

And this happens to all of us. We're not just managing our own energy—we're interacting with people, environments, collective energies, and invisible frequencies that we unconsciously pick up on. Especially if you're a sensitive soul, an intuitive, or someone in a support role—whether that's as a healer, coach, caregiver, or even just a deeply empathetic friend—it's incredibly easy to absorb what isn't yours. You may not even realize you're carrying someone else's stress, sadness, fear, or frustration until your own vibration drops and your body starts feeling heavy or off. The truth is, your energy field is like a sponge. And if you're not intentional about cleansing and recalibrating, that sponge stays soaked with everyone else's stuff.

Now, when you're in alignment—truly anchored in your own energy, your own frequency—these external things don't shake you as easily. You can move through challenges with more grace, you recover more quickly from emotional dips, and you're far less likely to spiral or feel like everything is happening *to* you. But getting to that point requires consistent awareness and daily energetic hygiene—morning and evening practices to clear what you've picked up, to call your energy back, and to settle your nervous system.

If you don't, all that unprocessed energy builds up and begins to weigh you down. That's what causes misalignment—not just big emotional upheavals or major life events, but the accumulation of tiny unprocessed moments that stack up silently in your field.

And here's where unconscious patterning plays a massive role.

Most of what runs your life isn't what you consciously think or feel—it's the deep-seated, inherited, conditioned, and subconscious programming that lives beneath the surface. These are patterns formed from childhood experiences, ancestral imprints, societal expectations, and past life energies. They operate like invisible scripts running in the background, telling you who you should be, how you should behave, and what you should expect from life. And because they're so ingrained, you often don't even realize when one of those patterns gets triggered.

Let's say you grew up believing that you have to overgive to be loved. That belief forms an unconscious pattern that drives you to overextend your energy, ignore your boundaries, and put others first—even at the cost of your own well-being. That overgiving throws you out of alignment every single time, but because the pattern is so deeply embedded, you don't recognize it as misalignment—you think it's just who you are.

This is why awareness is your greatest power.

The moment you begin to feel *not OK*—even if it's subtle—you pause. You drop into your heart, you breathe, and you tune into your body and field. You ask yourself, *What just shifted? What triggered this misalignment?* That awareness gives you the power to choose differently—to clear, to realign, to protect your field, and to return to the version of you who lives in alignment with your truth.

Recognizing the Signs of Misalignment

Staying aligned is not just a nice-to-have on this journey—it's essential for your well-being and your ability to move through life in the most grounded, soul-led way. Alignment connects you to your soul's blueprint. Think of that blueprint as the roadmap your soul created for this lifetime—an energetic instruction manual showing you how to move through life in a way that brings fulfillment, clarity, and flow.

When you're aligned, you are walking that path. You're embodying your soul's intentions. You're in harmony with what your soul came here to do and experience. But when you fall out of alignment, things start to feel harder, heavier, more chaotic—and that's often your first clue that something isn't quite right.

So how do you recognize when you're out of alignment?

There are clear signs—on every level of your being:

Physically – You might feel squeezed. Everything feels harder than it should. It's like trying to move through mud, or carrying a heavy weight that won't let up. You may feel stressed, overwhelmed, constantly fatigued, or just not OK in your body. It's a felt sense of "off," even when you can't quite pinpoint why.

Mentally – You may experience intense self-doubt, fear, or worry. You start questioning your path, your decisions, your worth—even your purpose. Your mind is in overdrive, trying to make sense of everything but only spinning you deeper into confusion. The monkey mind takes the reins and turns your thoughts into a noisy, chaotic storm.

Energetically – You feel disoriented or disconnected from yourself. You might feel like your energy is split in half, scattered, or pulled in different directions. There's a constriction in your field, a lack of flow or spaciousness, and it can feel like you're not fully in your body—or not fully *you*.

Emotionally – Your emotions may swing wildly. One moment you're hopeful, the next you're irritated, discouraged, or just done. It feels like an emotional roller coaster that won't stop. You're more reactive, more triggered, and more easily thrown off center.

Intuitively – You feel it in your gut. Something's off. It doesn't matter if you can't explain it—there's a knowing inside that says, *This isn't it.* You might get signs, synchronicities, even dreams, but either you don't recognize them or you brush them off. That intuitive nudge grows louder the more misaligned you become.

These signs may vary in intensity, but they always point to the same thing: *your energy is not in alignment with your soul.* And when you're misaligned, life gets harder. What used to flow begins to stall. You might feel like everything is falling through the cracks, that you're constantly running into obstacles, or that no matter what you do, you're stuck in a loop of taking one step forward and five steps back.

As intuitive beings, it's critical that we listen to these nudges. Even the smallest whisper of "something is off" is worth exploring, because it's your inner guidance trying to course-correct you before you veer too far off track.

And just as it's important to notice misalignment, it's equally important to recognize what it feels like to be in alignment.

When you're aligned, things *flow*. Ideas come in easily and effortlessly. The actions you take lead to results with grace. You feel energized, empowered, and deeply rooted in your body and your truth. You're in a space of trust and ease—life works *with* you, not against you. That's alignment. That's your soul blueprint in motion.

Now, how do you discern what is aligned for you?

It's actually very simple: *you feel it.* Let's say you have an idea that seems okay on paper. Maybe someone told you it's the "right" strategy or the next best move. But instead of running with it right away, take a moment to *feel* into it. Does it feel expansive or tight? Exciting or burdensome? Do you feel like "I get to do this" or more like "I have to do this"?

True alignment feels like a deep inner yes—even if it stretches you beyond your comfort zone. There's still a knowing that says, *this is the path.*

Let me give you a personal example.

When I first received the intuitive download to write this book, I said to myself, *Okay, I've written books before—this'll be easy.* But once I began writing, I realized this book was going to require *so much more* of me. I wasn't just writing content—I was writing *my truth.* I was pouring my soul, my journey, and my energy into every single chapter. And

I'll be honest—I pulled back for a moment. It felt huge. It stretched me.

But even in that stretch, I *knew* it was aligned. I knew this book was meant to come through me, that it would be powerful for those who read it. So I leaned in, and allowed myself to expand into the truth of what this book really is.

Now, let me contrast that with a different story.

When I started my coaching business in 2015, I did what most new coaches do—I followed the experts. I took the courses, watched the webinars, hired the coaches. I learned all the "right" strategies—host a webinar, create a summit, launch a lead magnet. I did *all* the things I was told to do to grow my business.

But none of it felt good. I didn't feel comfortable showing up on a webinar. I felt like an imposter, like I was faking it. I didn't enjoy the process. And deep down, I felt squeezed. Guess what happened? Nothing. No clients. No income. No traction.

It wasn't until years later, when I started my spiritual awakening, that I finally understood why it never worked. I wasn't in alignment. I was building my business on someone else's path instead of my own.

That's why I now invite you to be the *rebel*. Yes, learn what you need to learn. Get support where you need it. But always take it with a grain of salt. Because no one—not a coach, not a course, not a guru—can tell you what is right for *you*. Only your *energy* can.

And here's the thing: Sometimes your mind will try to convince you something isn't aligned when really, it's just your fear talking. That's your monkey mind trying to keep you safe. When you're about to step outside of your comfort zone, it freaks out and pulls the alarm. But that doesn't necessarily mean it's misaligned—it just means you're growing.

So when something feels off, dig deeper. Ask yourself: *Is this resistance because it's not aligned? Or is it discomfort because I'm expanding?* Is this a "not now," a "not ever," or a "this is scary but true"?

Your body knows. Your energy knows. *You* know.

And that's why being present and honest with yourself is so important. Self-honesty isn't weakness—it's a superpower. It's how you take back your power and become the conscious creator of your reality. Because when you ignore the signs of misalignment—when you numb out or stay stuck in patterns of lack and limitation—you keep calling in experiences that match that energy.

But when you choose to become honest with yourself, when you say, *I don't feel OK and I want to shift this,* you reclaim your power. You start steering your life in a new direction—one that's aligned with your truth, your soul, and your highest timeline.

So let's make that your new normal: noticing the signs early, checking in with your energy often, and aligning with what truly resonates. Because that's how life becomes easier, more fulfilling—and a whole lot more magical.

Calibrating to a Higher Frequency

You hold the power to consciously calibrate yourself to a higher frequency, no matter how you're currently feeling or what's unfolding around you. Your frequency is never fixed. You are not a passive receiver of energy—you are its master. And with intention, you can raise your vibration and shift your energetic state in powerful, life-altering ways.

Just as you can spiral yourself into feeling tired, frustrated, or overwhelmed through your thoughts and focus, you can also guide yourself into feeling vibrant, aligned, empowered, and alive. You are *that* powerful. The key is intention and trust in your ability to choose something different.

Let's return to the law of reversibility I mentioned earlier. This universal law teaches us that if something in the outer world can make you feel a certain way, then by embodying that feeling first, you can draw the matching experience into your outer world. In other words—your inner state creates your external reality. Always.

So let's say you're feeling stuck, overwhelmed, or deeply misaligned. First, acknowledge it. Without judgment, simply bring awareness to how you're feeling. Then ask yourself: *Do I really want to keep feeling this way?* When you recognize that your current vibration is attracting more of what you *don't* want, you reclaim the power to shift.

Now choose how you *do* want to feel. Maybe you long to feel joy, peace, love, freedom, or abundance. Pick one. Then drop into your body and recall a moment—any memory, whether from childhood or adulthood—when you truly felt that feeling. Let it serve as an anchor. If you don't have a clear memory, just begin to *imagine* what it would feel like to experience that emotion. Either path works. What matters is that your body begins to recognize and hold the frequency.

Once you feel it, amplify it. Turn up the dial. Brighten it. Let it expand until it fills your entire being. Immerse yourself in the frequency. Breathe it in. Let it take up space in your body, in your field, in your awareness. Then set the intention: *This is my frequency. This is the energy I choose to embody.* Stay there as long as you'd like. When you return to your day, carry that essence with you. Let it radiate through your actions, your choices, your presence.

And then, take it further.

Check in with your energy field. Is it calm? Activated? Scattered? You can regulate it by simply setting the intention to ground, calm, and balance your nervous system. You are the master of your energetic system. Infuse this high-frequency emotional state into your energy field. *This is who I am now. This is what I emanate.* That's how you consciously calibrate to a new frequency—one that reflects the life you truly desire to live.

This is emotional alchemy in action. When you feel NOT OK, you now have the awareness to shift, to choose something different, to realign. That moment of conscious decision is where the power lies. As you walk the path of the Soul Alchemist, you're no longer the victim of your emotions, thoughts, or circumstances. You're the one who chooses what you embody—and by doing so, you change your life from the inside out.

Let me share with you a powerful daily energy hygiene practice to help you stay grounded, aligned, and connected to your highest frequency. Think of it as your energetic self-care ritual—one that helps you manage your energy field, embody your soul, and maintain vibrational sovereignty no matter what unfolds around you.

Morning Alignment Practice

Before you even get out of bed:

- Tune into your body and connect with your heart. Call forth your soul with intention: *"I now call forth my soul, please step forward and connect with me now."* Feel that warmth rise within you as your essence awakens.

- Imagine a waterfall of pure white light washing through your body and field, clearing away anything that's not yours and no longer serving you. Let it dissolve into the nothingness.

- Check in with your energy field and nervous system. If there's any activation, calm it down with your intention.

- Connect with the version of you who already embodies the life you desire. Not as someone far away, but as your current self. Feel her in your body. Embody her. Let that frequency anchor into your system.

- Intend to carry this energy into your day, infusing every action, interaction, and experience with this aligned version of you.

Midday Check-In

At midday or whenever you feel a shift:

- Pause and drop in. Ask: *How am I feeling? Is this aligned? Did I pick up something that isn't mine?*

- Invoke the waterfall of light or your inner flame to cleanse your field.

- Tune into your heart and see the fire within you growing stronger. Let it burn away what doesn't belong.

- Realign with the version of you that's empowered, grounded, and living the life you desire. Reclaim that embodiment.

- Shift into high-frequency emotions—love, peace, joy—and use them to reset your vibration.

- This can take just a few minutes, but it brings you back into alignment with who you truly are.

Evening Integration Practice

Before bed:

- Cleanse your energy field once again using the waterfall or flame. Let the day be washed away.

- Call back all parts of yourself that may have been scattered—through interactions, worries, or thoughts. Become whole again. Feel the return of your essence.

- Tune into your energy field and nervous system. Regulate and calm them as needed.

- Reconnect with the version of you that you're stepping into. Are you still carrying her essence? If not, simply realign—no judgment needed.

- Tune back into high-frequency emotions and let them carry you into restful, aligned sleep.

This kind of daily energetic recalibration isn't just spiritual hygiene—it's soul leadership. It helps you remain centered and sovereign in a world that constantly tries to pull you out of alignment. It helps you stay tuned into your essence, your soul blueprint, your creative power.

Because when you begin living like this—consciously, intentionally, energetically—you step fully into your role as the Soul Alchemist. And from that place, you don't just experience life... you create it.

Maintaining Alignment in a Chaotic World

Let's be real—life can feel messy, loud, and downright chaotic at times. And staying aligned in the midst of it all? That can feel like a full-time job. But here's what I want you to remember: being an embodied Soul Alchemist doesn't mean you're floating in high vibes all the time. That's not the goal. You're not here to bypass the human experience—you're here to embody your divinity *through* your humanity. That means feeling the full spectrum and choosing how you respond.

You will still have bad days. You'll still get triggered, overwhelmed, or knocked off-center. That's not failure—that's life. The difference now is in how you respond. When you embrace this path, when you begin living the practices in this book, you stop letting the chaos of the outer world dictate your inner reality. You stop spinning in reaction and instead ground yourself in intention.

You'll slip up. We all do. We're not just *human beings*—we're human *doings* most of the time. We get busy, distracted, pulled in too many directions. But what matters is this: when you notice you've slipped out of alignment, you don't judge yourself. You don't shame yourself. You simply *notice*, take a breath, and *choose again*. You come back to center. You clear your energy. You realign. And you move forward with more clarity, more strength, and more compassion than before.

That's the power of this work. It's not about perfection—it's about *presence*.

Now let's talk about something just as essential: **boundaries**. Not just physical ones, but energetic and spiritual boundaries too. These are your first line of defense when it comes to maintaining your alignment in a world that constantly wants to pull you into drama, fear, or obligation.

You have to decide—*what am I available for?* And just as importantly, *what am I no longer available for?*

If you're reading this book, chances are you're highly sensitive. You're probably an empath, a lightworker, a healer, or someone who feels *a lot*. You may work with energy, hold space for others, or be the go-to person in your circle who always listens, always gives, always cares. And while that's beautiful—it can also leave you drained, depleted, and disconnected from yourself if you don't hold clear boundaries.

Boundaries are not walls—they're *acts of self-respect*. They help you preserve your energy, your sanity, and your sovereignty. You don't have to be available all the time. You don't have to explain or justify your needs. You don't have to give from an empty cup just because you *can*.

It's time to honor your needs, your energy, and your time—*first*. That doesn't make you selfish. It makes you sovereign. And if there are moments when you *do* choose to go beyond your usual boundaries, let it be exactly that—a conscious *choice*, not an unconscious obligation.

Here's what I mean:

Let's say someone asks you for something and it goes against a boundary you've set. But maybe, for whatever reason, you decide to say yes. The shift happens when you say to yourself, *"I really don't want to do this. This isn't aligned with my boundary. But I choose to do it anyway because…"*

That's a powerful distinction.

When you choose from awareness, even if it's not ideal, you stay in your power. You're making a *sovereign choice*. But when you override yourself out of guilt, people-pleasing, or the belief that you "have no other option," you give your power away. And that will show up in your vibration. You'll feel the contraction. You'll feel resentment. You'll feel the disconnect.

Protecting your alignment means honoring your energy even in the small moments. It means staying aware of when your field gets pulled out of shape—by obligations, environments, people, or even your own thoughts. It means regularly coming back to your center and reclaiming your space.

And in a world flooded with fear, doubt, and noise, it also means choosing to *stay grounded in your truth.*

That might look like:

- Saying no when everyone expects a yes.

- Pulling back from the news cycle when it overwhelms your nervous system.

- Standing in your knowing even when no one else around you gets it.

- Choosing peace when others are choosing panic.

- Choosing expansion when others are choosing limitation.

It means asking yourself, *"Is this mine?"* every time you feel yourself pulled into heaviness or chaos. Is this your fear? Your doubt? Your urgency? Or are you picking it up from the collective, from your environment, from someone else?

That's energetic discernment. And it's how you protect your field and maintain your frequency.

You don't need to shield yourself or live in spiritual isolation. You just need to stay anchored in your truth, aligned with your energy, and committed to your path. This is a practice. It's not about getting it perfect. It's about noticing, adjusting, and coming back to alignment—again and again.

Becoming the Embodied Creator of Your Life

When you begin to live in energetic alignment—truly embodying the empowered, aligned version of yourself—your entire life begins to shift. The reality around you starts to rearrange itself to reflect who you've become on the inside. What once felt out of reach starts to feel natural. And what once felt heavy or impossible begins to flow with ease.

Now, I'll go deeper into this when we talk about embodiment and manifestation later in the book, but for now, I want you to understand this core truth: your outer world is a mirror. Every experience, relationship, pattern, or challenge in your external reality is reflecting something within you. It's all feedback. It's all pointing you back to yourself.

So if you want to create change in your life, it doesn't start by forcing something externally—it starts by going within. You have to look at what within you is in conflict with your desires. What belief, pattern, or frequency is getting in the way? That's where you do the inner work—the energetic alchemy I've been guiding you through in each chapter of this book.

As you keep coming back into alignment—as you embody the version of you who already lives the life you desire—your life will begin to shift.

You enter into flow state. Synchronicities appear. What once felt like a constant uphill battle begins to soften. Opportunities show up seemingly out of nowhere. Money begins to flow in new ways. Aligned people come into your world. Doors you didn't even know existed start swinging open.

And it doesn't feel like you're chasing anymore. It feels like you're allowing.

That's what energetic alignment creates. When you radiate the frequency of your future self—the version of you who already knows her worth, already lives in abundance, already feels safe, loved, and free—life responds accordingly. Your energy leads, and reality follows.

You'll notice that you begin to glow. People around you might comment on how different you seem. They might ask if you've fallen in love or changed your skincare routine. They'll see the shift even if they can't explain it—because it's your light they're noticing. Your energy becomes magnetic. Your essence becomes undeniable.

And more importantly, you'll feel it too. You'll feel lighter. More grounded. More centered. The things that used to rattle you won't hold the same power anymore. You'll navigate life with more grace, more clarity, and more peace. You'll find yourself responding to challenges in a completely different way—more conscious, more empowered, more attuned.

And no, this doesn't mean you'll never face challenges again. Life will still happen. But you'll know how to move through it. You'll have the tools to shift the energy. You'll respond, rather than react. You'll alchemize whatever comes your way instead of letting it define you.

This is the real power of Soul Alchemy. It's not about perfection. It's not about fixing yourself. It's about coming home to yourself. It's about becoming who you were always meant to be.

When you live from this place of alignment, everything changes— not because life suddenly becomes perfect, but because you've changed. You've returned to your truth. You've remembered your power. And now you're living it.

You become the conscious creator of your life.

And that's not just spiritual poetry—that's embodiment. That's frequency. That's the reality you're stepping into now.

Becoming the Guardian of Your Frequency

There comes a point in your journey when alignment is no longer something you seek only during the chaos or turn to in moments of crisis. It becomes a way of being. A living, breathing embodiment of who you are at your core. This is where you step into the sacred role of becoming the guardian of your frequency.

To be a Soul Alchemist is to know that your energy is not random. It is not something you leave to chance or allow to be shaped by your outer world. It is yours to tend to. Yours to align with. Yours to claim as the foundational element of the life you are consciously creating.

Becoming the guardian of your frequency is an act of radical self-responsibility. It means you no longer hand your power over to circumstances, emotions, or the energy of those around you. You become aware of how you feel, what you are holding, and what you are emitting at all times. You understand that your outer world is always reflecting back to you the energy you are carrying within. So rather than blaming, avoiding, or bypassing, you choose to meet yourself where you are, and you do the inner work to shift.

This level of energetic sovereignty isn't about being high vibe all the time or pretending everything is perfect. Quite the opposite. It's about being honest with yourself when you feel off, when something's not quite right, and choosing to realign rather than spiral. It's about cultivating the inner strength to hold your alignment even when the world around you is loud, chaotic, or heavy. And when you do slip—which you will, because you're human—you meet yourself with compassion instead of criticism. You acknowledge the misalignment without judgment and make the conscious decision to return to center.

As a Soul Alchemist, you learn to move with the flows of life without being consumed by them. You witness the energies that swirl around you, but you don't absorb them unconsciously. You set energetic boundaries, not just to protect your time and space, but to honor your nervous system, your inner clarity, and your path. You decide what you are available for and what you are no longer willing to carry.

You stop leaking your energy into relationships, responsibilities, and routines that drain you, and instead choose to channel that energy into your healing, your expansion, and your joy.

Living as the guardian of your frequency also means you become more discerning with your thoughts, your intentions, and the environments you expose yourself to. You begin to notice how certain conversations, spaces, or even forms of entertainment affect your energy. You feel the shifts in your body, in your field, and you no longer ignore the signs. This is not about living in fear or avoidance—it's about honoring your inner compass and trusting that your energetic well-being must come first.

And perhaps most importantly, this path invites you into a sacred level of self-devotion. You begin to treat your inner world as something sacred, worthy of care, worthy of presence. You understand that tending to your frequency is not just a spiritual practice—it is a daily act of love. It is a commitment to your truth, your power, and your evolution.

So what does it truly mean to become the guardian of your frequency?

It means that you stop waiting for life to shift from the outside in, and instead become the one who shapes reality from the inside out. It means that you recognize your frequency as your most valuable currency, and you protect it as such. It means that you embody your power as the Soul Alchemist you came here to be—one who transmutes, realigns, chooses, and creates from energetic clarity.

This is not a temporary phase. This is a lifelong devotion. To your truth. To your sovereignty. To your light.

And from this anchored, empowered state of being, you will find that life begins to move with you. Manifestations arrive with greater ease. Clarity comes more quickly. Relationships feel more authentic.

And your path, once fogged by doubt or distortion, becomes illuminated by the brilliance of your own alignment.

This is the power of soul alchemy. This is what becomes possible when you choose to rise. And you are more than ready.

Closing Incantation: The Power of Energetic Alignment

As you've discovered in this chapter, frequency is everything. It is the silent architect behind your experiences, your manifestations, and the reality you find yourself in. But unlike fate, it's not fixed. It is something you can shape, calibrate, and consciously embody each and every day.

Energetic alignment is not a one-time decision. It is a devotion—a practice that invites you to come back to yourself again and again, no matter how far you may have wandered. And each time you do, you become more sovereign, more whole, more *you*.

So take a breath now. Let your energy settle. Let this truth land in your body as you speak the words that follow. Speak them aloud. Speak them with intention. Speak them as the Soul Alchemist you are becoming.

Incantation:

I now choose to become the guardian of my frequency.
With every breath, I return to my truth.
With every choice, I reclaim my alignment.
I transmute what no longer serves me.
I embody the vibration of my highest self.
I honor my energy as sacred.
I hold boundaries that protect my peace.
I move through life with awareness, grace, and power.
I rise, anchored in my sovereignty.
I rise, attuned to my inner light.
I rise, aligned with all that I am becoming.
And so it is.

Chapter 11: Transmutation Practices That Work

---

*Embodied rituals and energetic recalibration tools for
lasting inner shifts and quantum level transformation.*

Inner healing isn't just a mental exercise. It's not something you think your way through or talk your way around. Healing is something you *feel* in your body—because the body is where it lives. The imprints, the tension, the patterns, the wounding—it's all stored in the body. Even the mental blocks that seem purely intellectual have been wired into your nervous system, into your tissues, into your cells. That's why healing must be embodied. It's not enough to understand the process intellectually; it must be lived and integrated into your entire being—body, mind, energy, and soul.

It's easy to collect knowledge, to read all the right books, to understand what's *supposed* to happen on the healing journey. But knowing what to do and actually *doing it* are two entirely different things. True transformation only occurs when you embody what you've learned—when the insights move from the mind into your lived experience. When your cells recognize the shift. When your energy recalibrates to the new frequency.

I've seen many people claim they've done the work—they've cleared their blocks, they've worked through their wounds—and yet they still feel stuck, unfulfilled, or disconnected from their purpose. That doesn't mean they didn't try or that their efforts weren't real. But what often happens is that they didn't go deep enough into the body. They may have stopped at the mental level. They may have skimmed the surface instead of dropping into the depths where real, lasting change takes place.

This is why embodiment matters. If you want to remember who you truly are—your essence, your truth, your authentic self—you must drop out of the head and into the heart. Into the body. Into your inner knowing. You cannot think your way into wholeness. You *feel* your way into it. You embody it. That's why they call it *heart-centered living*—because you speak, move, love, and heal from the heart. The mind can guide, but the heart is where your soul lives. And when you heal from that space, everything begins to change.

Throughout my own journey, I had to learn this the hard way. My path has not been easy. I've had to walk through the fire, time and time again. There were many times I wondered why it seemed like others could move through things so effortlessly while I felt like I was being dragged through the depths. But I understand now that I was never meant to just study transformation—I was meant to *embody* it so I could *transmit* it. I had to live it, breathe it, become it. Every word in this book comes from that place of embodied knowing, not from regurgitated teachings I read in someone else's book. This is lived wisdom.

And that's why I want you to go deep with this. I don't just want you to learn *about* these practices—I want you to *experience* them. To integrate them. To *become* them. Because that's when you shift timelines. That's when your frequency elevates. That's when you awaken into a version of yourself you've never met before—but who's been inside you all along.

Every time you release a limiting belief, clear an emotional wound, or move energy that's been stuck for years, you create space for something new. You create space for a higher frequency to take root in your body. But here's the thing—just clearing or releasing isn't enough. You have to *integrate* the shift. And that's the step so many people skip. They jump from one activation to the next, one healing modality to another, constantly trying to fix something they believe is broken. But nothing about you is broken.

The real transformation happens in the **integration**.

When you allow what you've released to fully leave your system—and then consciously anchor in a new energy, a new pattern, a new frequency—that's when your being recalibrates. That's when your nervous system upgrades. That's when your reality begins to reflect the shift.

Think of a time you went through a deep healing session. Maybe it was through energy work, breathwork, light language, or simply sitting with your emotions. You may have felt something move in your body, a lightness, a release. And maybe a few days later, you noticed something subtle had shifted. Your reactions were different. Your inner dialogue was softer. Life started to respond to you in a new way. That wasn't just a coincidence—that was *embodiment* in action.

I've seen this with my own work. I've had people write to me after listening to one of my light language activations on money or abundance, telling me they received unexpected financial blessings or felt completely different about their relationship with wealth. That's not just mindset work—that's embodied energetic work. The vibration shifted in their body and field, and their outer world followed.

This is why this chapter is so important. Here, I'll guide you through the practices that will help you integrate your healing, embody your growth, and anchor your transformation into your lived experience. Because that's what makes the change last.

We're not here to float in the clouds, detached from reality. We're here to bring our soul's frequency *into* our bodies, *into* our energy fields, *into* our daily lives. That's what embodiment means. It's not a concept. It's a lived reality.

When you learn to *live* your healing—when your actions reflect your inner transformation, when your choices align with your soul, when your energy radiates from a grounded, aligned place—that's when you know you've embodied the shift. That's when you become a walking transmission of your own light.

And that's what I want for you.

Your Body Is the Altar of Transformation

When we speak about alchemy, we often think of it as something mystical, intangible, even otherworldly. But here's what most people miss: the body is the anchor of alchemy. It's where the transmutation happens. It's the sacred vessel that holds the codes, the tension, the trauma—and ultimately, the transformation.

You cannot bypass the body on this journey.

It's through your breath, your movement, your posture, your voice—every physical expression—that your energy flows, recalibrates, and alchemizes. Your body is not just a bystander to your healing; it is the *container* for it. The body remembers everything the mind forgets. It holds the frozen moments, the suppressed emotions, the inherited imprints—and it also holds the key to releasing them.

Your breath is one of the most powerful tools for alchemy. With each conscious inhale and exhale, you're not just oxygenating your body—you're moving energy. You're creating space. You're signaling safety to your nervous system and presence to your soul. And when you pair breath with intention, you initiate quantum shifts.

Movement, too, is a language of energy. The way you carry yourself, the way you stretch or sway or dance—it all speaks to your energetic field. Sometimes the blocks you can't seem to shift through mindset work alone begin to dissolve the moment you *move*. Even subtle shifts in posture can either support or suppress your frequency. Standing tall, heart open, feet grounded sends a completely different signal to the Universe than slumping forward in defeat. Your body posture tells the story of who you believe yourself to be.

Sound is another powerful portal. Whether it's through your voice, chanting, light language, or even toning, sound vibrates through your cells, clearing stagnation and awakening dormant frequencies. And voice is especially alchemical because it not only vibrates through your own field—it cuts through energetic clutter in the field around you. It declares. It reclaims. It transmits.

This is why embodiment is so much more than just *thinking high-vibe thoughts*. You can't fake a frequency. You can't pretend your way into healing by reciting affirmations if the energy behind them isn't resonant. If your body still holds contraction, if your breath is shallow, if your nervous system is in survival mode—then your frequency will reflect that, no matter how positive your thoughts may be.

In the last section, I shared why inner healing must be embodied and not just understood intellectually. It's the same with frequency work. You cannot simply *think* yourself into a new reality. You *become* the frequency. And becoming is a full-body experience.

Embodiment means you don't just understand the teachings—you live them. You speak them. You breathe them. You move them through your body. You give them space to integrate, to settle into your bones, your cells, your aura.

The most profound shifts in my own life didn't come from reading more or understanding another concept—they came from those moments when I allowed my body to *lead*. When I wept on the floor in surrender. When I danced wildly to shake loose an old timeline. When I sat in stillness and let the energy move without needing to control it. When I used my voice to declare what I was no longer available for.

That's when the healing took root. That's when the timeline shifted. That's when I embodied the transformation, not just understood it.

So if you're doing the work but still not seeing the results—drop deeper into your body. Ask yourself: *Have I felt this all the way through? Have I given this energy permission to move? Have I integrated the shift, or am I still looping in the mind?*

Your body is the portal. It's not in your way—it *is* the way.

Let this be your invitation to partner with your body as your greatest ally in your alchemical journey. It's the part of you that's been holding the wounds, yes—but it also holds your power. When you breathe with it, move with it, and speak through it, you activate the codes that have been dormant, waiting for your permission to rise.

And from that embodied place, everything begins to change.

The Power Behind the Practice

Intention is the invisible thread that weaves through every practice, every ritual, every energetic shift you desire to make. Without intention, even the most powerful technique can fall flat. It might look right on the outside—you're saying the right words, moving your body just so, lighting the candles, doing the breathwork—but if the energy behind it isn't aligned, it's like trying to steer a boat with no wind in your sails. Intention is the current that directs the flow of energy, and in this work, energy is everything.

You can do all the right things and still not get the results you want—not because you did something wrong, but because your energetic signature wasn't aligned with your desire. It's your intention that directs the frequency you're vibrating at. And the frequency you hold is what the universe responds to. You don't receive what you say you want—you receive what you energetically match.

That's why just "thinking positive" or saying affirmations without feeling them often doesn't move the needle. The real shift happens when your intention comes from the core of your being—not from wishful thinking, but from deep embodiment. When you feel your intention in your body, when every cell says *yes*, the energy begins to reorganize itself. That's when you become magnetic to what you desire.

And I've lived this. For years, I said I wanted to be a teacher, to impact millions with my message, to truly make a difference in the world. I said it. I believed it—at least on the surface. But deep down, I didn't *feel* it yet. I didn't see myself as someone who could truly create that kind of impact. There was still a disconnect between what I said and what I believed about myself. And so, despite all the actions I took, despite having the strategy, the structure, the know-how—it wasn't working.

Now here's the thing most people don't know about me: alongside my spiritual work, I've built a marketing agency where I support physical therapists in growing their online businesses. I've helped clients go from zero to multiple six figures online. So I *knew* how to grow a business. I knew how to build offers, create funnels, write emails, run ads. Logically, there was no reason why my own business shouldn't have taken off in the same way.

But energetically—I hadn't yet embodied my intention. That was the missing piece. Until one day, something shifted. I stopped *saying* I wanted to be a teacher, and I started *being* one. I embodied it. I felt it in my body. I dropped into the energy of, "I *am* a teacher. I *am* an activator. I *am* a guide." And when that clicked—everything started to shift.

I started hosting challenges and to my amazement, people actually signed up—and showed up. I remember starting a Zoom call and seeing people already waiting in the room for me. That moment hit me so deeply. It wasn't just that I finally had an audience—it was the realization that *I* had changed. My energy had caught up to my vision. I wasn't striving anymore. I was *being* it. That was the power of embodied intention.

So when you step into your own practices—whether it's breathwork, light language, journaling, or simply speaking your truth—I want you to remember: it's not about doing it "right." It's about the energy you bring. You could sit in silence with one clear, pure intention and shift more than an hour-long ritual done without alignment. The energy behind your intention shapes the outcome. Always.

Let your practices be fueled by soul, not performance. Feel into the intention before you begin. Ask yourself: *What am I anchoring here? What energy am I choosing to embody?* That clarity—that devotion—is what transforms your rituals from empty motions into alchemical acts.

Because intention is not just a mental decision. It is a full-body declaration. It's the essence of soul alchemy—and it's what makes everything else come alive.

Tools of the Inner Alchemist

Now that we've explored the importance of embodiment and intention, I want to share with you some of my most beloved transmutation tools—techniques I use regularly to move energy, dissolve blocks, and realign with my highest frequency. These are practices that help me shift quickly when I feel stuck, disconnected, or energetically heavy. They are not just techniques; they are invitations into presence, into truth, into sovereignty.

Let's begin with the one I've already introduced to you throughout this book—the foundation of everything I teach.

1. The Clearing Statement

"I now clear and transmute this (name the emotion) across all times, space, realities, lifetimes, and dimensions."

This is your go-to technique for releasing lower-density energy and returning to center. It's simple, powerful, and accessible in any moment.

How it works: You begin by tuning into what you're feeling—fear, doubt, shame, frustration, anxiety—whatever is present. You drop out of the story and into the feeling. This part is important. We're not analyzing or replaying what caused the emotion—we're simply meeting the emotion itself with love and awareness. Once you've identified the core feeling, you speak the clearing statement out loud (or silently, if needed), and repeat it with intention.

The key here is **intention**. You are commanding the release—not forcing it, but inviting it with authority and love. Repeat the statement until you feel a shift. Sometimes it's subtle—a softening, a sense of spaciousness. Other times it's more obvious—an exhale, a wave of emotion, a flood of tears, or even a spontaneous insight. The goal is always the same: to dissolve the emotional or energetic density back into the nothingness it came from.

You can use this technique anytime you feel off, overwhelmed, anxious, or just "not OK." It's my anchor in chaotic moments, and I promise you—it works.

2. Light Language

If you've never heard of Light Language, let me briefly explain. Light Language is a multidimensional form of communication—beyond words, logic, and language. It's the language of the soul, expressed through sound, movement, or symbols. It carries encoded frequencies that speak directly to your energy body and higher consciousness. You can explore Light Language activations on my YouTube Channel https://www.youtube.com/@kaysanders

How I use it: I channel Light Language in much the same way I use the clearing statement. When I feel stuck or energetically tangled, I drop in, set an intention, and allow the frequencies to flow through me. Sometimes I use Light Language for clearing, other times for activation—calling in ease, flow, abundance, expansion, healing, divine remembrance, or alignment. I often pair it with the clearing statement or with intention setting to amplify the shift.

Light Language works on the cellular and DNA level. It bypasses the mind and speaks directly to your energetic and quantum field. It recalibrates you in a way that's often felt more than understood. I also use it to soothe my nervous system, regulate my energy, and upgrade my consciousness.

If you want to explore this modality more deeply, I created a free mini-course to help you get started: Discovering Light Language – A Beginner's Journey https://www.kaysanders.com/discovering-light-language

3. Shadow Work

Shadow work is truly the foundation of Soul Alchemy. It's not a technique—it's a devotion. It's the willingness to look at what has been hidden, disowned, or rejected within yourself. It's about meeting the parts of you that carry pain, resistance, fear, or shame with compassion and presence—not to fix or get rid of them, but to alchemize them.

I work with my shadows by identifying the emotion or trigger, using the clearing statement to release the charge, and then often bringing in Light Language to soothe and transmute. The shadows show us what's ready to be healed. They are doorways, not roadblocks. When approached with love, they become the fuel for our elevation.

4. Breathwork

Breath is life force—it's the bridge between your conscious mind and your subconscious body. Breathwork is one of the most direct ways to shift your energetic state. When you work with intentional breath patterns, you can release stuck emotion, activate dormant energy, and enter altered states of awareness.

Breath also calms the nervous system, grounds your energy, and helps regulate your emotions. You can use simple breath techniques like box breathing, circular breath, or just long, slow exhales when you're feeling anxious or overwhelmed. I also love combining breath with movement and sound for deeper integration.

When to use it:

- During or after emotionally intense moments
- When you need to reset your nervous system
- To ground yourself or prepare for ritual or energy work

5. Embodied Movement

Your body holds memories—emotional, energetic, ancestral. Movement can help you unlock and release them. I don't mean structured workouts (though those can be great too). I'm talking about **intuitive movement**—allowing your body to move in ways that express and free stuck energy. This might look like shaking, swaying, stretching, dancing, or undulating. There are no rules. Just tune in and let your body guide you.

How it works: Movement bypasses the mind and lets your body speak. It's especially powerful after healing work or energy clearing. Moving the body helps you integrate the shift, rewire your nervous system, and embody the new frequency.

6. Vocal Release

Your voice is a tool for liberation. Vocal release is the practice of using your voice—moaning, sighing, humming, toning, or even yelling—to move energy. There is something deeply primal and powerful about letting sound move through your body without censorship.

When to use it:

- When you feel tightness in your chest or throat

- When you're overwhelmed with emotion

- When you feel like you need to let something OUT

Even a simple sigh with intention can move volumes of stagnant energy.

These tools are not just techniques—they are sacred invitations into deeper embodiment. They are here to support you in transmuting dense energy, integrating your healing, and embodying the aligned, empowered frequency of your true self. Choose what resonates, adapt them to your flow, and let your inner alchemist guide the way.

Daily Rituals for an Aligned Life

Transmutation isn't something that happens once during a healing session or only when you hit rock bottom—it's something you live. It becomes a way of being. And one of the most powerful ways to anchor this into your life is through simple, intentional daily rituals.

You don't need hours. You don't need a spiritual toolbox full of complicated practices. What matters is that you create space in your day to tune in, clear what needs to be cleared, and align with the frequency of the version of you that you are becoming.

Let me share a few practices that can be used as anchors—one for the morning, one for emotional release during the day, and one to support quantum alignment. These are just examples. They are not prescriptions. My invitation is always the same: try what resonates, leave what doesn't, and most importantly, **listen to your inner guidance.** This is about energetic sovereignty—not doing what someone else tells you, but learning how to navigate your own frequency with presence and discernment.

Morning: Cleanse, Clear & Calibrate

Mornings are sacred. They hold the frequency of new beginnings and give you a chance to reset your energy before the outside world begins to pull on you. Here's a simple morning ritual to ground, clear, and align:

1. **Waterfall of White Light:**
   Visualize a radiant white-gold waterfall of light cascading down from above, washing through your body, dissolving and cleansing anything you may have picked up during the night or are still holding onto from the day before.

2. **Inner Fire Clearing:**
   Next, activate the fire within your solar plexus or heart space and imagine it burning away any stuck energy, fear, doubt, or heaviness. Use the **clearing statement** to transmute anything that surfaces: *"I now clear and transmute this (name the energy) across all times, space, reality, lifetimes, and dimensions."*

3. **Nervous System Calibration:**
   Attune to your nervous system—notice if you're tense, activated, anxious. If you are, breathe deeply, hold your heart, and invite a softening. Speak calming words to your system: *"I am safe. I am supported. I am grounded."*

4. **Step Into Your Aligned Self:**
   Consciously embody the version of you who is empowered, abundant, successful, and free. Visualize her. Feel her energy. Ask, *"How would she move through today?"* and begin your day from that place.

Midday: Emotional Release & Energy Reset

Even if your day started aligned, life happens. You may absorb someone else's energy, face a trigger, or notice an old pattern surfacing. Instead of pushing through, use this moment to pause and shift:

1. **Tune In:**
   Close your eyes. Ask yourself, *What am I feeling right now?* Drop into the emotion without judgment.

2. **Use the Clearing Statement:**
   Say it with intention as many times as needed. Focus on the feeling, not the story:
   "I now clear and transmute this…"

3. **Movement or Vocal Release:**
   Let your body move. Shake, stretch, dance, stomp—whatever feels natural. Or, make sound—sigh, hum, moan, tone. Let the energy move through and out of you.

4. **Return to Center:**
   After the release, take a few grounding breaths. Place a

hand on your heart or belly. Remind yourself: *I am back in my body. I am whole. I am aligned.*

Evening: Quantum Alignment & Frequency Embodiment

Evenings are powerful for integration and manifestation. As your mind begins to slow and your body prepares to rest, your subconscious becomes more receptive. Here's how to close your day in energetic alignment:

1. **Script Your Future:**
    Write from the perspective of your future self who is already living your desired life. Not "I will have" but *"I am… I feel… I experience…"* Let it flow from a place of embodiment.

2. **Tune into High-Frequency Words:**
    Choose words like love, joy, radiance, peace, power. Say each one slowly and feel it in your body. Turn up the dial of intensity. Anchor the feeling into your being.

3. **Meditate or Visualize:**
    Spend a few minutes in stillness, letting your nervous system settle. You can also visualize your future self or your desired timeline and allow yourself to drift into sleep from that elevated frequency.

There are many tools and practices available to you, but none of them will work if you're not energetically present. The key isn't which practice you choose, it's how deeply you show up for it. Let your intention be your guide.

And remember—there is no right or wrong way to do this. You don't need a rigid schedule or a long checklist. Some days you'll need movement, other days you'll need stillness. Sometimes you'll feel called to light language, other times journaling will bring the breakthrough.

Let this be a journey of discovery. Try these rituals. Adapt them. Make them your own. This is how you reclaim your sovereignty— by tuning into your energy and choosing what aligns. The more you live this way, the more natural it becomes. Eventually, these practices won't be something you *do*, they will become part of who you *are*.

Alchemizing Emotion Into Power

One of the most profound ways to alchemize emotion is through embodied practices—because emotions are energy in motion, and that motion must be honored, felt, and released *through* the body. When you try to process emotional tension only in the mind, you stay in the realm of thought—looping, analyzing, trying to "figure it out." But the body holds the imprints. The body is where emotions lodge themselves, and the body is where transformation must happen.

This is where practices like breathwork, movement, vocal release, and light language come in. Each one creates a bridge between your internal experience and your energetic field, helping you shift from dense, stuck emotions into higher states of resonance.

Breath connects you to life force. It's one of the simplest yet most powerful tools to calm your nervous system and regulate your frequency. Conscious, intentional breathing helps you move emotional energy—especially if it feels overwhelming or locked inside your chest, belly, or throat. Movement adds a somatic release. When you stretch, dance, shake, or even just walk with intention, you're inviting stored energy to move out. Movement clears stagnation and opens flow.

Voice is also a powerful tool. Whether it's sounding, toning, speaking a clearing statement, or channeling light language—your voice gives form to energy. It gives permission for what's inside to come up and out. Think of all the times you swallowed your truth or choked back tears. Letting your voice express without needing to "make sense" is one of the most direct ways to transmute emotion into higher frequencies like truth, power, and clarity.

When you work with these practices regularly, you begin to feel the shifts more quickly. You notice the difference between "thinking about healing" and *actually healing*. The shifts become embodied. You're not just managing your emotions anymore—you're transmuting them. You're dissolving the weight of old stories and reclaiming your light.

And that's the heart of emotional alchemy. It's not about controlling what you feel or pretending everything is fine. It's about *meeting* your emotions as sacred messengers, honoring the energy beneath them, and using your body as the vessel through which that energy is transmuted. It's an act of devotion to yourself, to your soul, and to the highest version of who you came here to be.

Trusting Your Inner Alchemist

When it comes to finding the right practices for your spiritual journey, there's no one-size-fits-all approach. Yes, I've shared several tools throughout this book—my clearing statement, light language, shadow work, energy rituals, and more—but ultimately, my deepest desire is not for you to follow my path step by step. I want you to *find your own*.

You are a trailblazer. Anyone who felt drawn to this book is not here to fit into someone else's mold—you're here to forge your own way. That's what being a Soul Alchemist is truly about: honoring your inner truth above all else and letting it guide your steps.

It's helpful to experiment. Try different techniques. Feel into what resonates. Some tools may work powerfully for you, others may not do much at all—and that's perfectly okay. If the clearing statement didn't give you the shift you hoped for, it doesn't mean you're doing something wrong. It just means your soul is calling for something else—and that's where your own intuitive rituals are born.

This journey is about listening deeply—listening to your body, your energy field, your emotions, and your soul. You'll start to feel what aligns and what doesn't. And once you begin to trust that inner guidance, you'll naturally start building your own way of transmuting, healing, and reconnecting.

For example, some people say you *should* meditate daily. And for a while, I tried to stick to that. But eventually, it felt like something I had to do rather than something that expanded me. So I stopped. I found what felt better for me—and now I meditate only when I feel called to. That's the freedom that embodiment gives you.

I don't follow rigid routines. I like variety. I listen in. Some days I'll channel light language. Some days I'll use my clearing statement. Other days I'll take a walk, move energy through dance, or simply journal. But I *always* do something to support myself—to return to center, to stay aligned. The difference now is that I no longer "do the work"—I *live it*. It's become part of me. That's embodiment.

And when you reach that level of integration, you no longer need to rely on daily rituals in the same way. You don't *have to* do anything— you simply *become* the energy. And from there, you choose intuitively what to do, when to do it, and why.

So if you're still building your connection with your inner alchemist, that's okay. Start where you are. Play with the tools. Follow your resonance. Let your intuition lead. In time, your daily rituals will become sacred moments of remembrance—not because you're trying to "fix" something, but because they bring you back to *you*.

That is the power of intuitive practice. It's not about perfection. It's not about sticking to a set of rules. It's about honoring your inner knowing, trusting your energy, and choosing what serves your expansion.

Devotion Without Pressure

One of the most important things I want you to take from this chapter is this: you do *not* need to do your practices perfectly. You don't need to force yourself into rigid routines, or follow someone else's structure just because it worked for them. Perfection is not the goal here—**devotion is.**

Spiritual growth isn't about checking off a to-do list. It's about *showing up for yourself*—every day, in whatever way your soul is calling for. It's about staying present with your energy, honoring your inner world, and choosing to work with what arises... without pressure or guilt.

I've said this before, but it's worth repeating: whenever a practice starts to feel like something you *have to* do, it becomes a burden. It no longer brings the shift or joy it once did. And when that happens, do yourself a favor—stop. Pause. Listen in. Ask: *What do I need right now? What would feel nourishing, supportive, activating?*

There's no right or wrong. Today you may feel called to meditate. Tomorrow, you might want to move your body, journal, sit in silence, or listen to a light language activation. The path of the Soul Alchemist is not linear—it's *intuitive*. You follow what resonates, and you trust that your soul knows the way.

That said, I *do* invite you to commit to doing something each day—not out of obligation, but out of love. Do something that helps you stay connected, aligned, and embodied. Because even though you don't need perfection, you *do* need presence. The consistency of choosing yourself, tuning in, and staying in relationship with your inner world is what creates true transformation.

Some days that might look like a full-blown ritual. Other days, it might just be taking a deep breath, using your clearing statement, or choosing a different perspective when a trigger arises. That counts. It all counts.

This is how you build a sacred relationship with your energy. You don't treat it like a chore—you treat it like a living, breathing connection. Something you tend to with love and respect. And in return, it shapes your entire experience of life.

So release the pressure. Let go of the "shoulds." You are not failing if you skip a day. You are not falling behind. You are simply being invited to go deeper into trust—trust that your soul knows when and how to guide you. Trust that your energy will speak, and that you have the wisdom to respond.

That is the essence of freedom. That is the essence of being a Soul Alchemist.

The Power That Becomes You

When you begin to work with energy consciously—intuitively, ritualistically, and with deep presence—something begins to shift on a fundamental level. You no longer feel like a victim of your circumstances. You stop trying to force change from the outside. Instead, you become the source. You become the one who holds the power, who sets the frequency, who chooses what gets to stay and what no longer belongs.

You've already seen how practices like clearing statements, shadow work, embodiment work, and energetic rituals can create profound internal shifts. You've felt how intention alone can activate timelines. And as you keep showing up for this work—not out of obligation, but with devotion—you start to witness the *alchemy* in real time.

Breakthroughs begin to happen—not because you pushed for them, but because you aligned with them.

You find yourself responding to challenges differently. You feel calmer in your body, more present with your emotions, more grounded in the truth of who you are. Life stops feeling like something you're trying to control or figure out, and starts feeling like something you're co-creating moment by moment, from the inside out.

The people around you notice. Your relationships shift. New opportunities begin to appear—often unexpectedly. The energy in your field becomes magnetic. You start to embody your own medicine, your own light, your own soul's wisdom. And it *radiates*.

This is what energetic empowerment looks like. It's not about doing the "right" things—it's about becoming someone who *knows* how to move through life with energetic integrity. Someone who can self-regulate, self-resource, and self-activate. Someone who doesn't just "know" the path... but *lives* it.

When you reach this level of inner alchemy, you no longer need to chase transformation—it becomes who you are. You no longer wait for permission—you *move* when your soul says move. You no longer search for the answers out there—you drop in, and the knowing rises.

This is the space where quantum shifts are born. Where timelines collapse. Where desires manifest. Where your soul leads, and life flows.

And this... this is the beginning of real freedom.

Closing Incantation: A Devotion to the Path of Alchemy

You've journeyed through many layers in this chapter—from the power of intention to the embodiment of transformation. These practices are not meant to become another list of things you "have to do." They are invitations—pathways—into deeper alignment, deeper presence, and deeper self-trust.

This work is about remembering your own medicine, and daring to live it. It's about honoring the cycles within you, and choosing to walk as the Soul Alchemist that you are. Let this incantation seal your devotion—not to perfection, but to presence. Not to pressure, but to power.

Let it call you home.

Incantation:

I now honor the sacred within me.
I choose to walk in devotion to my energy, my truth, and my becoming.
I open myself to the rituals, practices, and movements that align with my soul.
I release pressure, obligation, and the need to get it "right."
I embody the medicine that is mine to carry,
and I allow it to flow through my words, my presence, my choices.
With breath, with intention, with love—I now rise.
I am the alchemist of my own soul.
And I choose to walk as her, every single day.

✧ Part III: The Embodiment — Living as the Soul Alchemist ✧

"Embodiment is not a performance—it's a remembrance. It's the sacred act of living your truth, not just knowing it."

Y ou've cleared the noise. You've felt the fire. You've moved through the sacred discomfort of releasing what no longer serves. Now, it's time to rise into the frequency of your becoming.

This part of the journey is about embodiment—not as a concept, but as a way of being. It's where you begin to walk as your higher self. Not someday. Not once you've healed everything. But now. In this breath. In this moment. It's about aligning with the version of you who already lives in the timeline you desire—and letting her lead.

This is where quantum identity comes alive. Where manifestation isn't a technique but a natural extension of your embodied frequency. Where you stop waiting for permission or proof, and instead claim your life as the conscious creator you came here to be.

This is the essence of Soul Alchemy: **To feel. To transmute. To rise. To live it.**

Welcome to the embodiment. Let's begin.

Chapter 12: Embodied Alignment: Becoming the Frequency

How to anchor into the energy of your future self now—
before anything shifts externally, so you can attract from
resonance rather than force.

We often look outside of ourselves to experience something we believe will fulfill us on the inside. We chase the thing, the relationship, the outcome— believing that once we have it, we'll finally feel peace, joy, abundance, or validation. We get caught in the hustle of doing: creating, working, thinking, strategizing—all in hopes that it will lead to what we want. And yes, the action has its place, but there is something far more powerful that we often overlook.

That power is embodiment.

Do you remember my story from earlier about wanting to be a teacher? I was doing everything I could to grow my spiritual business. I was working hard, trying all the right things, pushing myself, but the return was minimal. I used to say, "I'm putting in all this effort and getting peanuts in return." No matter how much I hustled, nothing seemed to truly move.

It wasn't until I fully embodied the essence of the teacher I wanted to be—a teacher who makes a meaningful impact in the world—that everything began to shift. My YouTube channel started growing. My spiritual business started blossoming. Inspired ideas began flowing in, like this very book. But those ideas didn't just come from thin air—they were aligned ideas, high-frequency visions that matched the new energy I had anchored. Why? Because I had become the frequency.

When you're chasing something, it often stays just out of reach. Think about it like a puppy: if you run after it, it runs away. It's the same with your desires. The energy of chasing is actually the energy of *not having*. It's an energy of lack, and lack repels what you want. But when you become the version of you who already has it—when you embody that essence and live from that place—everything begins to align. You're no longer chasing. You're being. You've stepped into the frequency of "I already am."

This is embodiment. It's a shift out of wanting and into being. You stop wishing and start living as the version of you who already holds the desire. That version doesn't need to want—it simply is. And when you embody that energy, your outer world will eventually rise to meet it.

Wayne Dyer said, "Believe it and you will see it." I want to take that further: *Feel* it, *embody* it, and then you'll see it. Because your reality is not shaped by your wishes—it's shaped by your essence. You create from the inside out. Your external reality is nothing more than a mirror reflecting your inner energetic signature.

This understanding is powerful beyond measure. When you truly integrate this truth, nothing is out of reach. Anything—*everything*—becomes possible for you. The only missing piece is divine timing. Your job is to hold the frequency and trust the unfolding.

Now let's talk about change—maybe you're desiring more financial freedom, a new career path, or you want to start or grow a business. But you feel stuck. Scarcity surrounds you. The job market feels impossible. Business feels daunting. And even when you try to move forward, you feel resistance, blocks, or fear. So you stay in the energy of "I want."

But here's what "I want" actually says on an energetic level: "I don't have. It's not possible. It's too hard. I'm not enough." That's the frequency of lack. And so, you continue to create more of that in your external reality—more frustration, more limitation, more reasons to stay stuck.

But what if you stopped wanting and started *being*?

What if you chose to embody the essence of the you who already has overflowing wealth—so much money you don't even know what to do with it? You feel supported, abundant, generous, free.

Or you envision the version of you who wakes up excited to go to work in your dream job. You're doing what you love. Or maybe your business is thriving, your time is your own, and you're spending more of it doing what matters—with your family, your passions, and your purpose.

Sounds incredible, doesn't it?

But then that ache creeps in. That ache in your chest that screams: *I want this so badly! Why can't I have it? It feels so far away!*

Let's pause there. I want to guide you through something. Take a moment, close your eyes, and drop into your heart. Let go of that feeling of wanting but not having. Let it dissolve. Breathe.

Now visualize your dream life. See it as if it's already here. Feel yourself *living it*. Set aside the ache and allow joy, abundance, peace to fill you instead. As you hold that vision, I want you to call that version of you—the one who already lives this life—toward you.

Imagine stepping into them, or them stepping into you. Or perhaps you meet in the middle. Either way, *merge with that version of you.* Feel the essence of that identity settle into your being.

This is the version of you that already has what you're seeking. And this is who you must *become*—not someday, but now. Embody that frequency daily. Show up from that essence. Speak from that place. Think, feel, and act from that reality. Because the moment you do, the outer world starts to shift to meet the frequency you're now living from.

When you're aligned with your desired reality, you're not in lack. You're not in "maybe someday." You're in *certainty.* You no longer wonder if it's going to happen—you know it already is. You've become it.

Even though I haven't yet reached millions with my message, I've already embodied the version of me who does. I see her. I feel her. I *am* her. This book will touch hundreds, maybe even thousands of souls. My spiritual business is expanding with grace and ease. I can feel it all because I've already become it. And now, I simply wait for the physical world to catch up with the energetic reality I've already anchored.

This is how you shift from striving to becoming. From chasing to creating. From wanting to *embodying.* And once you do, life moves in ways that seem magical—because it's finally matching the frequency you've chosen to live from.

Feel It Before You See It

If you've ever dabbled in manifestation practices, you've probably had moments where something wonderful came through... and other times where it felt like the exact opposite happened—or worse, nothing at all. You visualized. You scripted. You journaled your desires over and over again. You practiced gratitude, made vision boards, followed all the steps… but the thing you wanted never materialized—or it arrived in a distorted or limited form that left you disappointed and confused.

Can you relate?

You're not alone. And no, it's not because you did something wrong or weren't spiritual enough or didn't "want it badly enough." The missing piece that no one really talks about—at least not in the depth that it deserves—is *embodiment*.

Most manifestation practices are wonderful tools to help you *touch* the frequency of your desires. They help you connect for a few moments to the essence of what you want. Visualization, scripting, gratitude—they all serve a purpose. But here's the truth: if you only *touch* the frequency and don't *live* from it, you'll always find yourself chasing. The frequency never stabilizes in your field long enough to shift your reality.

The real work begins when you stop making your practices just moments and instead turn them into a way of being. That's the embodiment piece.

Without embodiment, even the most powerful manifestation technique will leave you spinning your wheels. You can say all the affirmations and write all the intentions in the world, but if you're still energetically anchored in lack—if you're still holding onto "I don't have it yet"—then your outer world will keep reflecting that back to you.

Manifestation isn't about pursuing your desires. It's about *becoming* them.

When you embody the version of yourself who already has the thing you desire, you become magnetic. You no longer run after your dreams—you call them in. Think of yourself like a lighthouse: you don't chase the ships, you simply stand in your frequency, your truth, your light—and the ships (your desires) find you.

That's the frequency you want to hold.

Embodied manifestation is empowering. It lifts you up. It doesn't require chasing, proving, or begging the Universe. It frees you from the frustration and burnout of doing all the things but seeing no real results. Because that's another layer of pain, right? Watching manifestation gurus show off their luxurious homes, fancy cars, or $100K months, making it all look effortless—while you're sitting there doing all the inner work and still wondering, *why isn't it working for me?*

I've been there. I've felt that frustration. I've done the waiting, the hoping, the searching for signs, checking for proof. And every time I waited for that outer evidence to give me certainty, I stayed stuck. Because the truth is—*waiting for proof keeps you in lack*. It holds you in the energy of "I don't have it yet," which reinforces exactly that.

You don't manifest your desires by waiting for proof. You manifest them by becoming the living embodiment of your vision now.

Feel it first. Believe it first. Know it's already yours—not someday, but now. You don't need external validation when you're anchored in your inner knowing. You no longer ask, *when will it happen?* Instead, you live from the truth: *it already is*.

That's the shift that changed everything for me. I stopped waiting and started *being*. I stopped chasing and started *embodying*. And as I did, my reality began to align—not because I forced it to, but because I became someone who no longer needed it to. I *was* it.

That's what I want for you, too.

When Life Pulls You Out of Alignment (And How to Get Back)

I've talked quite a bit about embodiment and the power of becoming the frequency of your desires—but I also want to be honest with you: it's not always easy. Life happens. Emotions get stirred. Doubts creep in. And before you know it, you've slipped right out of that embodied state and landed back in the version of you who's striving, worrying, or feeling like nothing is working.

It's easy to embody the essence of your desires when things are going well—when money is flowing in, you feel aligned, and synchronicities keep showing up like magic. But what about those other moments? The ones where things go sideways, when the car breaks down, or a surprise bill arrives, and suddenly you're snapped back into fear, frustration, or survival mode?

Let's say you've been working on manifesting financial overflow. You've been doing the inner work—you've connected with the version of yourself who feels deeply abundant, held, and supported. You've felt her frequency. You've started to show up like her. It's felt good. And then… reality throws you a curveball. A big expense lands in your lap. You start to panic. Your nervous system gets activated. That energy of overflow? Gone. Now you're spiraling in lack again, wondering why this keeps happening and why, after all the inner work you've done, the universe still hasn't delivered.

Sound familiar?

This is one of the biggest challenges in the embodiment journey—and one of the most human. Because the truth is: it will happen. Not just once. Not just occasionally. It may happen *often*, especially at the beginning. Even now, after all the work I've done, I still catch myself slipping into old states—moments where I forget who I am, where I buy into fear, where I momentarily lose sight of my power.

And that's okay.

This path is not about perfection. It's about awareness and choice.

When you notice that you've slipped out of alignment, you don't need to judge yourself. You don't need to spiral into shame or try to "fix" anything. What you need is awareness. Because awareness gives you the power of choice.

You can recognize, "Okay, I'm feeling fear right now. I feel squeezed. My mind is spinning, and I want to panic." And in that awareness, you have a choice: do I keep feeding this state? Or do I pause, take a breath, and realign?

That moment of choice is everything.

Maybe you step outside. Maybe you put on music and move your body. Maybe you speak your clearing statement. Maybe you drop into your heart and remember the future version of you who is already living in overflow, who wouldn't flinch at a surprise bill, who always finds a way. That version of you exists, and the more you return to her—even when it's hard—the more she becomes your default.

Realignment is not about ignoring your reality. It's not bypassing. It's reclaiming your energetic sovereignty. It's remembering that *you* are the one who chooses which frequency you hold. Not the bill. Not the circumstance. *You.*

The other piece I want to highlight here is that getting thrown off doesn't mean you're doing it wrong. It just means you're human. This work is not about never slipping—it's about learning how to come back home to yourself faster each time.

So yes, you will drift. But with practice, the time between "I've lost alignment" and "I've returned to my center" gets shorter. You build that muscle. You train your system to come back to truth, over and over again.

This is the daily work. It's not glamorous. It's not flashy. It's subtle and deeply personal. But it's where the magic lives.

Because every time you choose to re-align—every time you anchor back into your truth instead of feeding fear—you are becoming the frequency of the life you're here to live. You are becoming the Soul Alchemist.

Making It Your New Normal — Stabilizing High-Frequency Living

In order to hold the energy of your desires long enough for them to materialize, you need to stabilize that energy within your body and field. You need to make it your *new normal*.

Let's say your current baseline income is $5,000 a month, but your soul is calling you toward an experience of doubling that—$10,000 or more. You're doing the inner work, embodying the version of you who already lives in that reality, and you begin to feel the essence of it: the spaciousness, the freedom, the overflow. But here's where most people sabotage themselves without realizing it—when they start to experience even small glimpses of what they've been calling in, they become *so* activated by the novelty of it that their nervous system registers it as unsafe.

Let's say a check for $10,000 shows up. You're over-the-top excited, shouting, dancing, jumping up and down, telling everyone: "I manifested this!" That reaction, while human and joyful, also sends a signal to your energy field that this is something unusual, unexpected, and *not normal*. And when your system perceives something as *not normal*, it often works subconsciously to bring you back to your old energetic baseline—back to the version of you who *wasn't* receiving windfalls like this.

This is where energetic stabilization comes in.

Instead of riding an emotional rollercoaster between *manifestation highs* and *old-default lows,* you want to train your system to respond to miracles with calm certainty. You want to feel deeply grateful—yes—but also energetically steady. You want to *normalize the extraordinary.*

It's the difference between, "Oh my god, I can't believe this happened!" and "Of course. This is who I am now."

When you begin to stabilize these new energetic set points, you send a powerful signal to your field: "This is safe. This is aligned. This is sustainable. And this is *my new normal.*"

So how do you actually *live* from that frequency?

You start by attuning to the energy you *want* to embody—and then practicing it every day. Not as a performance, but as a devotion. You start showing up as the version of you who already feels whole, already lives in ease, already walks in abundance and love. You carry yourself differently. You speak differently. You make decisions from a place of trust rather than fear. You interact with your world as someone who already has what she desires—not someone still trying to get there.

Living from the frequency of abundance means you don't micromanage every dollar or panic at the sight of an unexpected expense. You trust that money flows and always finds its way to you. Living from the frequency of wholeness means you stop trying to fix or improve yourself—you embody the truth that *you are already enough.* Living from the frequency of love means you soften your edges, let people in, and move through life with an open heart even when it feels vulnerable.

The more you *live* as this version of you—not just imagine her in meditation or write about her in your journal—the more solid that frequency becomes. Eventually, it stabilizes. It becomes familiar. And when it becomes familiar, it becomes *your new reality.*

And yes, you'll still feel grateful. You'll still feel joy. But it won't send your system into overdrive—it will feel like, *of course this is happening.* That's the key.

Because once your body, mind, and energy field believe this is your new normal… the universe has no choice but to meet you there.

Living From the End — The Identity of "Already Having"

To live from the end means to *become* the version of yourself who already has what you desire—and then live your life from that embodied identity. It's not about pretending or hoping or acting "as if." It's about full energetic embodiment. You don't just *think* about what you want—you *become* the version of you who has it, and you move through life aligned to her frequency.

When you live from the end, you no longer question whether it's going to happen. You don't wonder *how* it will come about. You *know* it's already done. You've already aligned to that future reality internally, and the external just hasn't caught up yet. But it will—because it must.

This shows up in how you think, how you feel, how you walk, how you speak, and how you make decisions. For example, if your desire is to have a thriving business, you begin to think like a thriving business owner. You speak with clarity and confidence. You make empowered choices. You no longer second-guess your ideas or hesitate to be seen. You act in integrity with the frequency of success—not just the hope of one day getting there.

Or let's say you desire financial overflow. Living from the end doesn't mean you suddenly become careless or go on a wild spending spree—but it *does* mean you start handling money the way someone with overflow would. You stop letting fear or guilt dictate how you interact with your finances. If an unexpected bill arrives, instead of

212

spiraling into lack or panic, you anchor into your abundant self and say, "This is handled. I've got this." You train your nervous system to stay regulated, steady, and secure—no matter what. That's living from the end.

You also stop making decisions from your current limitations. You no longer ask, "What can I afford?" or "What makes sense based on what I've done before?" Instead, you begin asking, "What would my aligned self choose?" "What feels expansive, true, and guided?"

You start living in alignment with the future you *now*. You adopt her habits. You embody her frequency. You stabilize your field to match what she already lives—and in doing so, you collapse timelines.

Because the truth is, the more you stay in the energy of hoping and chasing, the more you push your desires away. That chasing energy broadcasts lack. But when you fully embody the frequency of already having it—when you become the version of you who doesn't *need* the desire to arrive because she *already is it*—then reality reorganizes itself to match your vibration.

This is how quantum shifts happen.

It's not about striving harder. It's about *being* differently. When you walk as her, breathe as her, speak as her, and choose as her… your outer reality begins to match who you've become on the inside.

You feel more calm. More grounded. You stop looking over your shoulder for proof. You stop asking if it's working. You stop waiting for something to finally click. Because you know it already has. You're not chasing. You're not hoping. You *are*.

That's the power of living from the end.

The Identity You Hold — Becoming Who You Believe You Are

Your self-concept—how you see yourself, what you believe to be true about who you are—is one of the most powerful determinants of what you allow into your life. It's not just about what you want. It's about who you believe yourself to be in relation to that desire.

Do you remember the story I shared earlier about not seeing myself as a teacher? That internal narrative—*I'm not someone who can lead, teach, or guide others on a larger scale*—shaped everything in my spiritual business. It didn't matter how hard I worked, how many ideas I had, or how deeply I wanted it. I couldn't grow because I didn't believe in the identity of the one creating it. My self-concept was out of alignment with the vision I was trying to manifest.

For the longest time, I wanted to be someone who enjoys going to the gym. I admired people who had that level of dedication—who made fitness a lifestyle, who looked forward to working out. I wanted that for myself, but for years, I just couldn't get there. I had signed up for gyms before, but I'd go a few times, then stop, then cancel the membership. It always felt like something I couldn't stick with, no matter how much I wanted to be "that kind of person."

But eventually, something clicked. I realized that if I wanted to create a different reality, I had to become someone different—I had to shift how I saw myself. I stopped trying to force the habit from a place of willpower, and instead I focused on becoming the version of me who *is* that woman—the one who craves the gym, who thrives in the discipline, who feels strong, capable, and committed to her health and vitality.

And now? I go to the gym almost every single day. Not because I have to, but because I genuinely want to. It's become part of who I am. On the rare occasions I can't go—because of injury or illness— I feel it in my whole body. I get antsy. I miss it. It's not something I'm trying to do anymore. It's just *who I am.*

That's the power of shifting your self-concept.

Your internal identity shapes everything. And most of us hold identities rooted in lack or limitation. These identities can sound like: *I'm not good with money. I'm not tech-savvy. I'm not attractive enough. I'm not confident enough. I'm not meant to be big. I'm not that kind of person.* But these are just *stories*—stories you've picked up along the way, often without even realizing it. And as long as you keep aligning with these limited identities, your life will keep reflecting them back to you.

Even embodiment practices will only get you so far if your underlying self-concept is still built on shaky ground. You might visualize the future you, script about her, meditate on her essence—but if deep down you don't believe you *can* be her, or *deserve* to be her, or *are capable* of becoming her, then your nervous system will keep rejecting the vision. You'll keep hitting walls.

This is why aligning your self-concept is essential. You need to *become* the version of you who believes she can be, do, and have what she desires. Not someday. Not when you've "proven yourself." Right now.

Because when you shift your identity to match your soul's highest truth—when you adopt the frequency of *already being* that version of you—you no longer have to chase. You are already it.

And since your outer world is always a mirror of your inner world, once your identity stabilizes into wholeness, abundance, and truth, your outer world will naturally rearrange to reflect that. That's not just manifestation. That's *alchemy*. That's soul-aligned creation.

So if you want to call in a new reality, don't just look at what you want. Look at *who* you think you are. Ask yourself: *Does my current self-concept match the version of me who lives that life?* If not, it's time to update the internal blueprint. Reclaim the truth of who you really are—not who the world told you to be, not who your past conditioned you to become, but the expansive, powerful, radiant essence of your soul.

This is how you bridge the gap between where you are and where you want to be—not through effort, but through *identity*. When you change how you see yourself, you change everything.

Returning to Center — Resetting with Compassion and Power

Life happens. Energy shifts. Emotions surface. And even after all your inner work, all your embodiment, all your intention… you'll still wobble sometimes. You'll still have moments where you slip out of alignment, where you forget who you are, where the outer world shakes you enough to throw you off-center. That's not failure. That's being human.

As I mentioned earlier, slipping out of your embodied frequency will happen—and likely more often than you expect, especially in the beginning. It's not a sign that you're doing it wrong. It's part of the process. The key is not whether you stay perfectly aligned at all times. The key is what you do when you notice that you've slipped.

The first step is awareness. Simply acknowledge: *"Okay, I've fallen out of alignment."* Do so gently, without judgment, without spiraling into guilt or shame. You don't need to fix yourself—you're not broken. You're in the midst of building a new energetic foundation, one that requires time, practice, and deep compassion.

Once you've acknowledged the slip, bring your awareness back into your body. Drop into your heart. Come back to the essence of your desire. Not the need or the lack of it—but the feeling of *already having it*. Visualize your aligned self. Feel her energy. Remember how she walks, how she speaks, how she chooses. Breathe her in. Let her essence rise back up through you and gently re-center your field.

The more you practice this kind of energetic reset, the faster and more natural it becomes. And over time, you'll notice that you bounce back with more grace. That the slips become shorter. That you catch yourself sooner. This is energetic maturity. This is soul leadership.

But here's the most important part: you must hold compassion for yourself in these moments. Always. You are undoing years—sometimes lifetimes—of programming, beliefs, conditioning, trauma, and misaligned identities. You're re-patterning your nervous system, shifting your paradigm, stepping into a completely new frequency of being.

Of course there will be resistance. Of course old thoughts will creep back in. Of course fear, doubt, or fatigue will sneak in sometimes and pull you out of alignment. That's normal. That's expected. What matters is that you meet yourself with grace, not pressure. With presence, not punishment.

I still have moments where I slip. I still have days where my energy dips or my fears get loud. But I no longer make it mean something about me. I no longer spiral into shame. I've learned that the quicker I can love myself through it, the faster I can return to my center.

That is the work of the Soul Alchemist. Not chasing perfection, but committing to presence. Not controlling every outcome, but choosing again and again to return to truth. You don't need to get it all right. You just need to stay in relationship with your energy, your essence, and your inner alignment. That is more than enough.

You Are the Manifestation

When you embody the frequency of your soul's truth—when you let yourself become the living, breathing expression of your most aligned self—you no longer shrink back. You no longer dim your light to make others comfortable or talk yourself out of what you know you're meant to do. You don't second-guess your gifts or question whether you're "too much" or "not enough."

You simply **are**.

You show up fully. You speak from clarity. You walk into rooms—not to be seen, but because you know you bring a presence that shifts the energy. You radiate from the inside out. And that radiance, that deep alignment, becomes a frequency others can feel. It's not performative. It's not forced. It's not curated. It's embodied. It's your truth made visible.

When you move through life from this space, the universe responds differently. Opportunities begin to flow with more ease. People show up who are aligned with your frequency. You stop chasing, forcing, striving—and instead start magnetizing. You create from overflow, from your essence, from deep soul alignment.

This is where manifestation becomes natural. It's no longer about scripting the same thing over and over or micromanaging the how. It's about becoming the vibrational match for your desires *now*—and then allowing life to respond to who you are.

Nothing becomes out of reach anymore, because you're no longer trying to "get" what you don't have. You are already living as the one who *has it*. And from this space, your manifestations unfold more freely, because they're no longer driven by lack or proof-seeking... but by resonance.

Now, I want to briefly name something important here: the difference between **ego wants** and **soul desires.**

Ego wants are often rooted in external validation—they want the car, the house, the money, the fame—not necessarily because of the thing itself, but because of what it *proves*. Ego wants are often attached to recognition, approval, and status. There's nothing wrong with having material desires. The problem arises when those desires are rooted in lack, compensation, or trying to "fix" a wound.

Soul desires, on the other hand, speak from a different place. They are often quieter, but far more potent. The soul doesn't crave the thing—it craves the **state of being** the thing represents. The freedom. The spaciousness. The creative flow. The safety. The aliveness. The peace. When your desires come from this level, they're not about fixing or proving—they're about expressing, expanding, and remembering who you truly are.

And here's the truth: when you manifest from soul, life opens in ways you couldn't even plan for. Because soul-aligned desires are encoded with your highest timeline. They're not always flashy, but they're always fulfilling. And the beautiful paradox is this—when you follow your soul, the ego often gets its desires met, too... but without the struggle.

That is what becomes possible when you embody the frequency of your soul's truth. You stop striving. You stop proving. You stop waiting. You start emanating. You start aligning. And you start receiving—not because you finally earned it, but because you *became it*.

Closing Incantation: Living as the Embodied Truth of Who You Are

You are no longer the seeker, the striver, or the one who waits for permission from the outside world. You are the embodiment. You are the frequency. You are the manifestation.

This chapter wasn't just about learning a new technique—it was an invitation to shift how you *exist*. From this point forward, you're not just imagining the life you want or chasing it from a distance. You're becoming it. You're walking as your future self now. You're showing up in alignment with the version of you who already *knows*, who already *has*, and who already *is*.

This is the essence of embodied alignment. It's not something you do. It's something you live. Every time you wobble, you return.

Every time doubt creeps in, you choose truth. You anchor. You align. You become.

Let these words seal in the frequency you're now holding:

Incantation

I no longer chase—I become.
I embody the energy of all that I desire.
I hold it in my field. I breathe it into my bones.
I live it now, in this moment—not someday, but today.

I am aligned with my highest truth.
I remember who I am.
I remember what I came here to do.
And I now walk as her—unapologetically, unwaveringly,
with certainty and grace.

This is my truth.
This is my timeline.
And so it is.

Chapter 13: Nervous System Alchemy

Rewiring your body's capacity to receive,
regulate, and expand—so you can hold the
energy of the life you're calling in without
contraction or collapse.

Your nervous system is the gatekeeper of your embodiment. It determines what you allow yourself to feel, receive, hold, and sustain. You can do all the energetic work in the world, but if your nervous system doesn't feel safe holding that new frequency, it will quietly sabotage your efforts—pulling you back into the familiar, the known, the safe.

That's why regulating and expanding your nervous system is one of the most essential steps in spiritual embodiment. When your system is dysregulated—when it constantly swings between stress, shutdown, or overstimulation—anything outside your comfort zone will feel threatening. That includes visibility, money, love, success, attention, intimacy, joy, or simply being seen in your truth.

It's not that you're not capable of holding more—it's that your nervous system hasn't yet learned how to feel safe *while* holding more.

Remember what we talked about earlier: when you manifest something bigger than what you're used to—whether it's a financial windfall, a big leap in your business, or a major spiritual activation—your system can get thrown into chaos. That surge of "too much" energy can feel overwhelming, even if it's what you *wanted*. And if your body isn't prepared to normalize that new level, it will contract. It will unconsciously push the success away or sabotage it just to get back to what feels familiar.

This is why so many people feel like they "crash" after breakthroughs or start doubting themselves just after a big up-level. The nervous system doesn't yet know how to stabilize that new level of expansion.

So what do you do?

You train your nervous system to expand with you. You consciously build capacity to hold more love, more visibility, more power, more money, more joy. You normalize the things you're calling in—*before* they arrive—and create a sense of safety within your body to hold them.

This is where the idea of becoming a safe space for your own energy comes in.

To become a safe space for your own energy means that your body and field are no longer resisting who you are becoming. Your essence has room to anchor. There is no war between your soul's truth and your body's tolerance.

When you are a safe space for your own energy:

- You don't second-guess your intuitive nudges.

- You feel grounded even in expansion.

- You can hold joy without waiting for the other shoe to drop.

- You can be visible without shrinking.

- You allow abundance without guilt or panic.

Becoming this safe space is what allows your soul essence to fully root into your human experience. It's not about bypassing discomfort. It's about regulating through it. Grounding through it. Expanding anyway.

Because the truth is, your soul is infinite—but your body needs time to catch up. And it's your nervous system that decides how fast you can safely expand.

Uncovering Hidden Resistance in the Energy Field

Sometimes, even when you're doing "all the right things" — meditating, journaling, visualizing, staying consistent with your healing work — it still feels like nothing's changing. You're stuck, blocked, or like life is just not responding the way you hoped. The truth is, it might not be your mindset or your actions that are the problem — it might be your nervous system.

Old wounds like trauma, chronic stress, or survival patterns don't just affect your thoughts and emotions. They embed themselves deep into your energetic body and your nervous system. Somewhere in the past, you might have internalized the belief that you don't deserve abundance, that you're not good enough, or that you have to earn love or safety. These beliefs become energetic imprints. And when they're left unaddressed, your system unconsciously resists what you say you want.

It's like your field is still broadcasting an old frequency of "not safe," "too much," or "I can't handle that" — even as your conscious mind is saying, "I want more." This mismatch creates energetic

223

interference. Opportunities may be all around you, but you can't fully see or receive them because your system isn't attuned to them. It's not that the Universe isn't responding — it's that your body is pushing things away to protect you.

This is why I took the time to guide you through how to calm and regulate your nervous system back in Part II. Because your nervous system isn't just a biological system — it's also an energetic one. People don't just read your words or your actions. They read your field. Your nervous system is what others respond to, consciously or unconsciously. You've probably had moments where you met someone and something just felt "off." That's because your system was picking up on their energetic signature — the unresolved imprints in their field. The same happens in reverse.

Your body will tell you when it's overwhelmed or overstimulated. Sometimes the signs are subtle. You might feel edgy, anxious, overly tired, or strangely unmotivated. You might experience tightness in your chest, a sense of urgency, or mental fog. Or you might notice yourself procrastinating on the very things you say you want. These are all nervous system cues that say: "This is too much." Even expansion — the very thing you've prayed for — can trigger these signals if your system isn't ready to hold more.

Think of it like trying to pour a gallon of water into a small cup. If your system hasn't been expanded to hold the energy of your next level, it will feel like pressure, chaos, or even burnout. And not burnout from just overworking — but from overstimulation, from energetic overload, from pushing without recalibrating.

This is why regulating your nervous system is non-negotiable. You need daily or regular check-ins with your body and your field. Not just when things feel bad, but even when things are going well — especially when they're going well. Excitement, success, windfalls, big growth — all of that can activate your system just as much as fear or stress. You want to normalize the feeling of things going right. Make it safe to feel good. Make it familiar to receive more. That's how you open yourself to expansion without the crash.

You become a safe space for your own energy when you create internal spaciousness — when you pause, breathe, notice, recalibrate, and anchor back into presence. That safety radiates outward. And that is what allows life to meet you fully.

Alchemizing the Nervous System with Grace

Regulating your nervous system doesn't have to be a dramatic process. In fact, the most powerful nervous system alchemy often happens in the most subtle, gentle moments. It's not about doing more. It's about becoming attuned to your energy and learning how to bring yourself back into harmony — slowly, safely, intuitively.

One way to begin is by simply tuning into your field and setting the intention to calm your system. You've already practiced this in Part II of this journey — using awareness and breath to bring yourself back into presence. When your nervous system is activated, your energy becomes scattered. It may feel like you're floating outside of yourself, disconnected from your body, from safety, from clarity. But when you bring your awareness into your field and breathe intentionally, you begin to anchor back into your center.

In those moments, you can imagine pulling your energy back into your body — calling your scattered energy home. One helpful practice is to visualize the white light of Mother Earth rising up from deep below, entering your feet, moving slowly up your legs, into your hips, your belly, your heart, and all the way up through the crown of your head. At the same time, invite the light of the heavens — Father Sky — to pour down through your crown, moving through your body and down into the earth. Let both streams run in unison, meeting at your heart and flowing through your spine like a river of light. You are the center point — the channel that connects heaven and earth. Just sit with this energy. Let it recalibrate you. Let it stabilize your field. Let it restore harmony.

This simple practice is powerful. It harmonizes the nervous system, clears energetic noise, and allows you to feel deeply grounded while also connected to higher realms. You may feel calmer, clearer, and more energized afterward — not from doing more, but from remembering your own center.

Other gentle practices include:

- **Breathwork**, especially slow rhythmic breathing (inhale for 4, hold for 4, exhale for 6) to signal safety to the body

- **Touch-based anchoring**, such as placing one hand over your heart and one on your belly while repeating a calming phrase or affirmation

- **Laying flat on the ground** to discharge excess energy into the earth

- **Vocal toning or humming** to vibrate the vagus nerve and soothe the system

- **Slowing down your movement** to match the frequency of calm — walking slowly, speaking slowly, eating slowly

- **Closing your eyes** and simply feeling the weight of your body on the surface beneath you, bringing yourself fully into the here and now

What all of these have in common is that they bring you back into the body. They remind your system that it's safe to be here. Because embodiment is the gateway to expansion. You cannot hold more light, more abundance, or more spiritual insight if your nervous system doesn't feel safe enough to receive it.

Anchoring in the body is what allows you to stretch without snapping. It's what makes your growth sustainable. If you try to expand without being grounded, your system will contract — not because you're doing anything wrong, but because it's trying to protect you. But when you're anchored, when you've created safety in your body, then your field can open. You can hold more. You can become more. You can embody more of your light without burning out or collapsing under the weight of your evolution.

This is the path of nervous system alchemy — not to push your way into becoming, but to *receive* your expansion by creating space for it in the body. You regulate not to calm down your power, but to prepare yourself to hold more of it.

The Cost of Leaping Without Grounding

Have you ever experienced a massive high — a breakthrough, a success, a moment of feeling so deeply connected to possibility — only to crash days later and wonder what happened? One moment, you're elevated, expanded, unstoppable. And then... it all collapses. You're fatigued, unmotivated, scattered, maybe even doubting yourself again.

That energetic crash is not a sign that you weren't ready. It's a sign that your nervous system couldn't hold the expansion — because it hadn't been brought along for the ride.

This is one of the most overlooked aspects of quantum leaping.

We all want to go higher, faster, farther. And yes, you *can* collapse timelines. You *can* shift realities in an instant. But if you leap into a higher frequency without having the energetic capacity to *hold* that new state — your system will snap back, just like a rubber band stretched too far. It's not because you're not meant to expand. It's because your nervous system is doing what it's designed to do: protect you from what it perceives as a threat.

When you jump into new levels of visibility, abundance, love, or power without stabilizing your nervous system, your body says, "This isn't safe," even if your mind and soul are saying, "Let's go!" And the result is contraction. Your field constricts. The very things you were manifesting begin to fade or feel out of reach again. You doubt yourself. You pull back. You may even sabotage.

This is why integration is *everything*.

Integration is not just downtime. It's the phase where you normalize your expansion. Where your system gets to digest the growth. Where you become the new version of yourself *safely*.

When you take the time to integrate, you're saying to your body: "This is safe. We're not in danger. It's okay to let this in." You recalibrate your field to match your new timeline, not just visit it briefly and fall back.

You see, it's not just about going higher — it's about going *deeper*. Deeper into your body. Deeper into your safety. Deeper into your trust.

You want the success, the abundance, the transformation — *and* the ability to hold it with ease. That's what true embodiment is. Not just touching your desires, but living inside of them as your new baseline.

So when you manifest a windfall, reach a big goal, experience a spiritual breakthrough — pause. Breathe. Ground. Normalize. Let the nervous system feel the truth of this new reality. Let it become your new normal. Because when your nervous system feels safe at this higher frequency, then there's no contraction, no snapback — only expansion that sticks.

Quantum leaping becomes sustainable *only* when your body feels safe to go with you.

And that's what you're learning to master — not just the art of rising, but the grace of staying risen.

Expanding Your Capacity to Receive and Hold the Life You Desire

When we talk about abundance, love, visibility, or power, most people focus on how to *get* more — how to manifest more, call in more, attract more. But very few talk about how to *hold* it once it arrives.

Because you can only receive what your nervous system and energetic field feel safe holding.

Think of it like a cup filled with water. Once it's full, any additional water will spill over. You can't receive more until you either *make room* by emptying some out — or you *get a bigger cup*. Most people unconsciously make room by settling, sabotaging, or shrinking. But there's another way — a more powerful way. You can *expand your cup*. You can widen your energetic container so that you're capable of receiving and holding more without fear, overwhelm, or shutdown.

This is what it means to widen your window of tolerance. To build the capacity to hold more love without pushing it away. More money without freaking out or going into lack. More visibility without contracting or hiding. More power without self-doubt or guilt.

You do this gently — by meeting your current edge and stretching it, a little at a time, with presence and care.

One way to do this is through energetic field expansion:

1. **Tune into your body and your energetic field.** Close your eyes and notice: how far does your field reach? How close is it to your body? Does it feel rigid or soft, expansive or tight? Just become aware of your current baseline without judgment.

2. **Now, begin to stretch your field outward.** Imagine your energy moving beyond your skin, your room, your home —

radiating outward in all directions. See it filling with white or golden light. Let it expand until you notice the first signs of resistance, discomfort, or nervous system activation.

3. **Pause and breathe.** Let your body catch up with your energy. Anchor yourself in this new expanded space. Let it *normalize*. This is key. Breathe deeply and say to yourself, "It's safe to hold more. This is my new normal."

4. **Expand again.** When you feel ready, stretch your field even farther. Go slowly. Breathe deeply. If resistance or fear arises, don't push through — simply meet it with compassion and allow your body to acclimate. Normalize again. Breathe again.

5. **Then gently bring your field back in, but with the *intention* to keep it flexible.** You're not reversing your growth — you're simply coming back into your body while maintaining the energetic capacity you've just expanded into.

This practice not only rewires your nervous system to feel safe holding more — it builds a more spacious, resilient, and flexible energetic field that can stretch with your desires instead of snapping back or shutting down.

You can do this anytime you feel constricted, overwhelmed, or ready to rise to the next level.

Other gentle daily or weekly practices that help build this capacity over time include:

- **Somatic grounding** — placing your hand over your heart or womb space and breathing until you feel your body soften.

- **Body scanning with breath** — slowly scanning your body from head to toe, noticing where tension lives, and breathing presence into those spaces.

- **Movement** — dancing, stretching, walking barefoot on the earth. Anything that gets you out of your head and into your body helps regulate and expand.

- **Heart coherence** — breathing in and out through the heart, anchoring in love and gratitude until your system relaxes into coherence.

- **Journaling through activation** — when you feel fear or tension, ask yourself, "What part of me feels unsafe here?" and offer it compassion instead of pushing it away.

The goal is not to force your way into more. It's to *become* the version of you who can hold more with grace, calm, and capacity.

Because when your nervous system and energy field say *yes* to more — not from hype, but from embodied readiness — then life meets you with more.

Not as a fluke. But as your new normal.

Embodiment Begins Where Safety Lives

True embodiment doesn't come from forcing a visualization, saying affirmations, or trying to feel your way into a desired state. Embodiment only begins when the body says *yes* — *w*hen your nervous system is no longer bracing, resisting, or performing, but softening into presence, receptivity, and stillness. That is where embodiment truly lives.

There's a distinct difference between doing a practice and being in the experience of it. You might sit in meditation, visualize wealth or light or expansion, and go through all the motions — but if your jaw is clenched, your breath is shallow, or your belly is tight, your body is telling a different story. Your nervous system isn't on board, and that misalignment matters.

Embodiment without safety becomes performance. You can say the right words, breathe the right way, even channel powerful energy — but if your system doesn't feel safe, you're not being the frequency. You're trying to override your body's truth. And eventually, that dissonance between what you're doing and what your body is actually experiencing catches up with you.

But when safety is present, everything shifts. Regulated and grounded, your nervous system allows the body to become a clear, open channel — not just for energy, but for truth. That's when you feel a real shift. Your breath naturally deepens. Your belly softens. Your chest opens. You're not trying to be present… you are. You're not saying you trust… you actually do.

True embodiment doesn't always feel like bliss or euphoria. Sometimes, it's a quiet sense of stability, a grounded awareness in your bones, a subtle inner spaciousness. It's not loud — but it's undeniable. It's the moment your body stops resisting and starts receiving. That's when your energy practices become portals rather than performance.

So if you ever find yourself wondering why a ritual feels flat, or why you can't seem to drop in — pause. Don't push. Ask yourself, "Do I feel safe here?" If the answer is no, that's where you go first. You breathe. You ground. You soothe. You open gently.

Because when your body feels safe, the energy flows. And when the energy flows, embodiment happens naturally.

Your Nervous System: Ally of Your Expansion

When your nervous system becomes your ally rather than your obstacle, everything changes. You no longer move through life bracing for impact, managing emotional volatility, or swinging between brief moments of inspiration and waves of contraction. Instead, you feel grounded, present, and steady in your own body. You become a clear, open channel for all that wants to move through you — your light, your vision, your power, your truth.

A regulated, flexible nervous system allows you to receive without resistance, to grow without crashing, and to expand without collapsing. You begin to hold more love without the fear of abandonment, more money without the panic of losing it, more success without the dread of being seen or judged, and more energy without overwhelming your system. This is the magic of a nervous system that's aligned with your soul.

You also start recognizing the subtle signs — when tension creeps in, when your breath shortens, or when your mind begins to spiral. Instead of letting these moments derail you, you pause. You regulate. You anchor back into your body and recalibrate your frequency. You no longer mistake activation for truth. You meet it with compassion and power.

You become someone who can hold more. Not just wish for more or try to manifest more — but truly hold it in your body, in your field, and in your nervous system. Because abundance without safety will always slip through your fingers. Love without safety becomes neediness. Visibility without safety feels like exposure. Power without safety leads to burnout.

But when your body is on board — when your nervous system is attuned, grounded, and harmonized — then you become limitless in what you can receive and embody. This is what you've been building all along: a nervous system that doesn't fight your desires, but expands with them. A body that doesn't resist your light, but becomes a home for it. A frequency that doesn't collapse under pressure, but roots even deeper into truth.

Your nervous system is not your enemy. It's your sacred ally — the bridge between your energy and your physical reality. And when it's aligned... so are you.

Closing Incantation: The Body Remembers Safety

You were never meant to carry so much tension. So much urgency. So much internalized pressure to hold it all together. Your body has always known the way back to harmony—it simply needed you to listen.

Regulating your nervous system isn't about eliminating stress or forcing calm. It's about widening your capacity to hold more: more sensation, more aliveness, more truth, more abundance. It's about creating enough inner safety for your soul to expand. It's about teaching your body that it's safe to soften, safe to shine, safe to receive.

The more you honor your body's signals, the more it opens. The more you choose presence over pressure, the more your energy stabilizes. And the more you attune to your inner rhythm, the more your outer reality begins to reflect the peace and power you now embody.

Let this be your moment to reset. To return. To remember.

Incantation

"I now release all energetic tension, survival programming, and stored fear from my body and field.
I regulate my nervous system with love and intention.
I choose to feel safe in my expansion, grounded in my light, and at home in my body.
I now anchor the frequency of peace, safety, and receptivity—so my soul can fully live through me."

Chapter 14: From Ritual to Reality

Making your embodiment a lifestyle, not just a morning practice

---

Have you ever noticed how good it feels to meditate, journal, or drop into an embodiment practice — only to lose that sense of connection and alignment as soon as your day begins? You might feel grounded, open, and inspired during your morning rituals... but then life starts to happen. Emails flood in, your to-do list takes over, and suddenly that beautiful energy you cultivated starts to dissolve. It's not that the practice didn't work — it's that you were still relying on the *practice* itself to hold the energy for you.

This is something so many on the spiritual path experience. You start to compartmentalize your connection. You're "in it" when you're on the mat, in ceremony, or journaling at your altar... but once you close the journal or leave the room, you slip back into old patterns, default habits, or the familiar 3D grind.

But embodiment isn't about what you do in your sacred space. It's about how you *live* outside of it.

Throughout this book, we've returned again and again to the idea that embodiment is not a performance — it's a way of being. The goal isn't to rely on practices forever. The goal is to become the frequency so fully that you *are* the embodiment, whether you're sitting in meditation or standing in line at the grocery store. That's the moment when your practices shift from a *need* to a *choice* — not something you reach for to fix yourself or get back into alignment, but something you genuinely *enjoy* because they deepen your relationship to your soul.

In the beginning of my journey, I was the same. I used to meditate every morning, sometimes twice a day — and on challenging days, even a third time. I had my journal, my gratitude lists, my visualizations... and they worked. They helped me feel better. But the effects were often temporary. I still found myself thrown off by unexpected triggers or slipping back into old thought loops as the day unfolded. I was doing all the "right" things, but I hadn't yet become the embodiment of them.

Over time, something shifted. As I deepened into this work, especially the practices of soul alchemy I now teach, those rituals became less about *getting* into alignment and more about *staying* in alignment. I no longer needed to reach for a practice to "fix" how I felt. Instead, I started *living* from the frequency I used to only access during ritual. My energy became more stable. My connection more constant. My nervous system more regulated. And the practices I once depended on became something I now turn to for joy, expansion, or deepening — not rescue.

Let this be your north star: your practices are sacred, and they will continue to support you in beautiful ways. But they are not the goal. The goal is to become the embodiment of what those practices point you toward. The goal is to blur the lines between your sacred time and your everyday life so that your entire *life* becomes the ceremony.

And when that happens — when you live from the frequency rather than visiting it — you become the embodiment of your soul's truth not just for a moment, but for a lifetime.

Turning the Mundane into the Miraculous

Every task, no matter how small or ordinary, holds the potential to become sacred — not because of what you're doing, but because of how you show up for it. Washing the dishes. Walking the dog. Folding laundry. Answering emails. These aren't just chores or obligations — they can become moments of deep presence when you bring your full awareness into the here and now.

This is the essence of sacred living: presence.

When you stop multitasking and instead immerse yourself fully in what you're doing — when your attention is not scattered in ten different directions, but anchored in the now — you bring a sacred stillness into your body, into your field, into the act itself. You create space. You become aware. And in that awareness, the ordinary becomes extraordinary.

But when you rush through your day, juggling tasks while your mind races from one thought to another, you're no longer present in your body. You're no longer connected to the moment. You're no longer anchored in your energy. And without realizing it, you slip out of alignment.

This is something most people don't even notice. The distraction becomes so normalized that you don't realize how far you've drifted until something feels "off" — anxiety creeps in, your energy feels scattered, your breath becomes shallow. That's not just mental overwhelm — that's your body calling you back to yourself.

This is why cultivating awareness — and especially learning to *pause* — is so powerful. The pause is the portal. It's what helps you reconnect to your breath, your body, and your energy. It's what allows you to bring yourself back into alignment gently, without judgment. In that moment of stillness, you reclaim your presence. And when you reclaim your presence, everything shifts.

Even the simplest acts can become rituals of alignment when you approach them with reverence and attention. Pouring tea can be a ceremony. Brushing your hair can be a grounding practice. Watering your plants can be an invitation to breathe deeper. Sacredness isn't reserved for the meditation cushion or your altar space — it lives in your body, in your awareness, in the way you move through your day.

This is what it means to bring the sacred into the ordinary. You don't need more rituals. You need more presence.

And the more you practice this — noticing where you tend to "turn off" your alignment during daily tasks and choosing to return to yourself instead — the more your entire life becomes the ceremony.

Becoming the You Who Already Has It All

When do you feel most connected to your future self — the version of you who already has it all? Is it during a meditation, a visualization, or an embodiment practice? Or does it sometimes happen spontaneously — in a quiet moment, a breath of stillness, or a flash of deep knowing that floods your body without effort?

You've learned how to connect with your future self throughout this journey. But now the real invitation is this: can you hold on to that essence *after* the practice ends?

That's the key.

It's one thing to feel deeply aligned in the moment — to tap into the energy of your future self during a practice. But if you leave that energy behind when the ritual ends, you return to your default setting. The shift remains temporary. The outer reality doesn't have time to respond to a fleeting glimpse — it responds to what you *sustain*.

So when you find yourself in those moments of deep connection, when you feel fully aligned with your future self — pause. Soak it in. Memorize it. Instruct your body to remember this frequency, to hold it, to normalize it. Breathe it into your cells. Anchor it in your bones. Let that feeling become familiar, so familiar that it no longer feels like a stretch — it simply becomes who you are.

In the beginning, you may slip in and out of it often. That's normal. Embodiment is a practice, not a perfection. But over time, the more you return to it, the easier it becomes. You're rewiring your nervous system. You're reconditioning your energy field. You're teaching your entire being that *this* — this version of you — is safe, natural, and available now.

And here's what you can learn from those powerful moments of alignment: they are your roadmap.

Pay attention to *when* and *how* those moments happen. What were you doing? What were you thinking or feeling? What did your body feel like? What shifted in your energy? The more you study those moments, the more insight you gain into what supports your alignment — and what pulls you out of it. That awareness helps you recreate those conditions more often. You can start weaving that energy into more of your day, into more areas of your life, until your entire reality becomes an extension of your future self — lived now.

This is how you collapse timelines. This is how you become the embodiment.

Living from Alignment as the Embodied You

What would your life look like if alignment wasn't something you *did* — but something you *lived?* How would you wake up? Move through the day? Speak to others? Rest your body at night? What subtle shifts would ripple through your entire life if your embodiment became your default?

This question is more than just reflection — it's a roadmap.

Because when you can begin to imagine the life that flows from your fully embodied state, you also begin to see what's out of alignment with that vision. You start noticing where you're still efforting, controlling, or depending on rituals to access what could instead be your natural state of being.

Just think about how it would feel to wake up each day already aligned — already grounded in your truth, already anchored in your frequency. You wouldn't need to do five different practices to shift your energy because your energy would *already be there.* You might still choose to meditate or journal, but not because you *need* to — simply because it feels good.

And when challenges arise — because they will — you wouldn't spiral or crash the way you used to. You'd respond with grace, self-trust, and a deeper inner stability. You'd pause, realign, and move forward — all from a place of embodiment.

Maybe you'd speak more intentionally, with softness and power. Maybe you'd move through your day with more calm presence and ease. Maybe your rest would deepen because your body no longer carries the tension of misalignment. Even the most mundane moments — washing dishes, checking emails, sitting in traffic — could feel like a continuation of your sacred inner world.

When embodiment becomes your way of life, you no longer chase alignment — you *are* alignment. You walk through your day as the version of you who already has it all, because that essence is no longer something you access… it's something you *are*.

And that's when life begins to shift around you — not because you're forcing it, but because the frequency you carry speaks for you.

Holding Your Embodiment When Life Presses In

Where do you tend to fall out of alignment? Is it when you're around certain people? In particular environments? Under pressure? In moments when old patterns sneak in unnoticed?

This is where awareness becomes your greatest ally. The first step in maintaining your embodied state is understanding what pulls you out of it. What are the triggers — the specific scenarios, people, or energy patterns — that tend to knock you off-center? How do you feel just before it happens? Does your body tense? Does your breath become shallow? Do you start people-pleasing, shrinking, or second-guessing yourself?

When you can identify the *where*, *when*, and *how* of disconnection, you gain the power to make a different choice in the moment. That's what true embodiment is — not perfection, but presence. The ability to pause, feel what's happening, and *consciously* return to alignment.

Being a Soul Alchemist doesn't mean you never get triggered — it means you recognize the trigger in real-time and alchemize it. You notice the energetic shift and choose again. You stop mid-pattern, mid-reaction, mid-meltdown, and breathe yourself back into your truth. You don't abandon yourself to keep the peace, fit in, or perform. You honor yourself by staying rooted in who you've become — even when the world tries to pull you back into who you were.

This is why boundaries matter. Not just physical ones, but mental, emotional, spiritual, and energetic boundaries. It's not about keeping others out — it's about keeping yourself aligned. When your energy is constantly leaking, being compromised, or spread too thin, staying embodied becomes almost impossible. But when you honor your limits, your flows, your capacity — you remain a sovereign field.

Embodiment isn't just about feeling good in your morning practice — it's about holding that energy in real-world moments. It's saying no when you mean no. It's not over-explaining or shrinking to make others comfortable. It's standing in your truth with softness and strength.

So ask yourself: What practices help me return to center quickly? What boundaries protect my energy and keep me rooted in my truth? And am I willing to honor those boundaries even when it's uncomfortable?

Because the more you honor yourself, the easier it becomes to hold your alignment — not as a temporary state, but as the way you live.

The Power of the Pause

Awareness is always the first doorway back into alignment. The moment you notice that something feels off — that subtle tightness in your chest, the heaviness in your mood, the irritation bubbling beneath the surface — that's your cue. It's the early warning signal that something has nudged you out of alignment. You may not know what it is just yet, but your body knows. It always knows. That feeling of *NOT OK* is your signal to pause, pay attention, and recalibrate.

And the beautiful thing is, you don't need a 30-minute ritual or a full morning routine to shift your energy. You just need intention, presence, and a few powerful tools you can use anytime, anywhere.

Start by tuning into your field. Feel into your nervous system. Is it activated? Do you sense a buzzing, pressure, or static in your energy? If so, close your eyes for a moment and intend to calm it down.

Breathe white light through your system. Let it wash over your field, dissolving any interference, tension, or energetic noise. Invite your nervous system to soften, regulate, and return to center.

You can also come back into your breath — not just to breathe, but to *feel* the breath. Notice the space between each inhale and exhale. That sacred pause is a portal to the present moment. And within that pause, you can return to who you are. The real you. The you who is grounded, steady, connected, and whole.

Another way to anchor yourself is by reconnecting with the essence of your future self. Just a moment of feeling her presence, calling in her energy, and remembering what it's like to walk as her — that's embodiment. And it doesn't take long. You simply need to *feel* it again.

You can also tune into empowering frequencies like love, joy, peace, abundance — not just thinking the words, but letting them move through your body. Say them internally or out loud and then turn up the intensity. Let your field expand and attune to that vibration. You are the amplifier.

And when heavier emotions or blocks come up, use your clearing statement. Let the fears, doubts, and attachments dissolve into the nothingness they came from. Say it with conviction: *I now clear and transmute this (emotion or energy) across all times, space, reality, lifetimes, and dimensions.* Let it go. Let it dissolve into the nothingness it came from.

These are not "extras" — these are your anchors. These simple, sacred micro-practices can shift your entire state in a matter of moments. You can do them individually or combine them as needed. What matters most is that you remember to *use* them. To interrupt the momentum of misalignment and reclaim your center again and again.

Because every moment you choose to realign, you become more of the version of you who lives in truth, presence, and power — not just in the morning, but all day long.

The Sacred Power Within You

There comes a point in your journey where the tools are no longer the source — they're simply mirrors. They reflect the energy that already lives within you.

Think about the way we sometimes place our power outside of ourselves. We light the candle, hold the crystal, pull the cards, and hope they'll somehow "activate" us — as if the energy is out there. But the truth is, you are the sacred space. You are the altar. You are the ritual. Everything else is just a bridge to help you remember what already lives inside you.

There's nothing wrong with using tools or practices. They can be beautiful allies, especially in the beginning. But over time, the invitation is to stop seeing them as the *thing* that holds the power — and start recognizing that they only amplify the energy you already carry.

As you continue to embody the teachings, rituals begin to evolve. They stop being something you *do* to get into alignment... and become something you do simply because you love them. Not to shift, but to savor. Not to access power, but to express it.

Because your power is no longer something you reach for — it's something you live from.

You begin to walk as the ritual. Your presence becomes the transmission. You no longer "enter" sacred space... you *are* the sacred space. Your breath, your body, your frequency — all of it is already attuned to the divine. And that changes everything.

When you walk through the world as the embodiment of your soul — grounded, steady, aware — you no longer need to chase signs or cling to practices to feel safe, powerful, or connected. You become the source. You become the embodiment of the sacred in every moment.

This is the real alchemy: when you stop searching for the divine and start *being* it.

Closing Incantation: I Am the Living Temple

You've come so far. Through every chapter, every insight, every activation, you've remembered more and more of who you truly are. And now, the journey becomes less about doing and more about being. This is where the practices begin to dissolve into presence, and the rituals become woven into the flow of your everyday life.

This chapter is not about abandoning the sacred tools that have supported you. It's about realizing that they were always reflecting *you*. The crystal is not the source of your clarity — you are.

The altar is not the space of transformation — you are. The breath, the ritual, the invocation — all of it has led you back to the one holding the energy: your embodied self.

This is the invitation to dissolve the separation between your spiritual practice and your lived experience. To stop compartmentalizing the sacred as something you visit and start living as the sacred space itself. You don't need to light a candle to access your power. You don't need to sit in meditation to meet your soul. You are already connected. You are already whole.

When your embodiment becomes your baseline — not just a morning ritual or something you reach for when things feel hard — you begin to live in harmony with your truth. You become the energy you once tried so hard to attain. Your presence begins to speak louder than your practice. And your life itself becomes the altar.

And so we anchor it now.

Incantation

I no longer chase alignment —
I live it.
I no longer reach for the sacred —
I remember I am it.

I breathe as my future self.
I walk as my higher truth.
I bring presence into the ordinary
and devotion into the mundane.

Every breath is a blessing.
Every step is a ceremony.
Every word is a vibration of who I've chosen to become.

I now embody the essence of my soul
not only in ritual, but in flow —
the flow of my life,
the flow of my becoming.

I am the sacred space.
I am the living temple.
I am the embodiment.

Chapter 15: Walking Through the World in Your Truth

Authentic expression, aligned action, and energetic congruence

---

So often we move through the world wearing masks, hiding behind versions of ourselves we've crafted to be accepted, to be liked, to feel safe. We soften our edges, dim our light, filter our words, and try to be what we think others want us to be. We fear judgment, rejection, and being misunderstood, so we hold ourselves back in ways we've long normalized — yet deep down, we know something is off. We feel the disconnect between who we truly are and how we're showing up. That's the energetic misalignment — and you can't fake your way out of it.

As a Soul Alchemist, walking in your truth is not about performing. It's about embodying. It means you no longer abandon yourself to be pleasant. You stop playing small, stop silencing your soul, and stop apologizing for your presence. You begin to move in the world with integrity to your essence — not just in private moments, but in how you live, lead, and relate to others.

When you walk in your truth, you stop worrying whether others like you or resonate with you. You no longer crave validation or try to squeeze yourself into places that were never meant to hold your full light. You accept yourself so fully that the need to be accepted by others fades away. And in that space of self-honoring, something powerful happens — your energy aligns. There's no more inner conflict. No more spiritual static. You become congruent. Clean. Clear.

I used to hold back because I believed I was "too much." Too loud. Too intense. Too different. My energy felt too big for the spaces I was in — so I dimmed it. I softened it. I shrank. I didn't realize then that I was fragmenting myself to survive, to avoid discomfort, to make others comfortable. But what it cost me was far greater than their approval — it cost me my alignment. I wasn't showing up as the real me. And I could feel it. Others could feel it too, even if they couldn't name it.

When you are not in energetic congruence, there is a subtle friction in your field. You might feel uneasy, anxious, out of sorts, or drained — especially in social settings. Others might perceive you as being "off" without knowing why. Those who are energetically sensitive can pick it up immediately, but even those who aren't will feel the dissonance on some level. That's what happens when your inner and outer worlds don't match.

And let's be honest — aren't you tired of it? Tired of holding back, tired of shrinking, tired of trying to fit into places you were never meant to belong? It's exhausting to constantly monitor your light. But when you stop hiding — when you finally allow yourself to be all of you — it's like breaking out of a cage you forgot you were in. The freedom is undeniable. The energy is magnetic. And the sense of alignment, that deep soul click, is something you'll never want to trade again.

The truth is, you're doing yourself and others a disservice when you hold back. Your light is needed. Your energy — in its raw, unfiltered form — carries codes, healing, and permission for others to do the same. Even if they don't understand it, even if they resist it, they still need it. And the world becomes more coherent, more alive, when each of us dares to live from that place of full-spectrum authenticity.

Being in energetic congruence means that who you are on the inside matches how you show up on the outside. It's not about perfection, it's about integrity — energetic integrity. Your words, actions, energy, and presence all speak the same language. There's no more efforting, no more pretending, no more distortion. Just truth, embodied.

And that's my deepest hope for you. That through this book, through your own reflection and integration, you'll find the strength and the courage to let go of who the world told you to be — and become who you've always been. Fully. Unapologetically. Powerfully. You.

Reclaiming the Voice You Silenced to Survive

On this path, we all go through phases. In the beginning, it's incredibly common to hold back — especially if your family, friends, or community don't understand the spiritual path. You may soften your voice, keep your practices private, or avoid expressing the depth of your truth because you fear being judged, misunderstood, or labeled as "too much" or "too out there." The fear isn't irrational — it's rooted in lifetimes of persecution, rejection, and energetic imprinting. But staying small eventually becomes more painful than being seen.

The more you heal, the more you shed, the more you awaken to the truth of who you are, the harder it becomes to keep hiding. There comes a moment — or many — when something inside of you starts stirring. It might feel like an ache, a pull, or even a burst of wild frustration that says: *Enough*. Enough shrinking. Enough editing. Enough hiding the sacred fire that burns inside of you. Your ego may protest. It may try to keep you safe by reminding you of all the ways you've been rejected or misunderstood in the past. But your soul will feel the call. And once that call rises within you, it's impossible to ignore.

This is the moment when the blinders begin to fall away. You start to see more clearly who you are — and who you've been pretending to be just to survive. You begin to embrace your inner vibrancy, your authenticity, your multidimensionality. And it's not a performance. It's not about being loud or visible just for the sake of being seen. It's about alignment. It's about congruence. It's about your outer expression finally reflecting your inner truth.

I want to gently invite you into an honest reflection: Where in your life are you still holding back? Where are you dimming your light, silencing your voice, or softening your truth to make others comfortable? This requires deep honesty and self-compassion — because realizing how much of yourself you've hidden can feel heartbreaking. But awareness is not defeat. Awareness is power. With awareness comes the power of choice. And once you see where you've been shrinking, you can choose to expand.

That choice — to stop hiding — is one of the most empowering things you can do for yourself. It's not always easy, and it may feel unfamiliar at first. You might be tempted to slip back into the shadows, to quiet your truth out of habit. But every time that happens, you have an opportunity to choose differently. You can say, *No. I've hidden long enough. I'm no longer willing to abandon myself for the comfort of others.* And then you dig deep — into your body, your breath, your inner fire — and you rise.

Reclaiming your voice doesn't happen all at once. It's a process. It begins with giving yourself permission to speak, even if your voice shakes. It begins with acknowledging that your truth is worthy of being expressed, even if others don't understand it. It helps to create safe spaces — even just with yourself at first — where your nervous system can begin to relax into the experience of being seen. Journaling. Speaking aloud. Standing in front of a mirror and saying the words you've never said. These are all powerful entry points.

But ultimately, reclaiming your voice happens through *embodiment*. You don't find your voice by thinking about it. You find it by using it. By allowing it to move through you. By staying with yourself when the discomfort arises and choosing to speak anyway. Every time you honor your truth — even in the smallest way — you build trust with yourself. You rewire your system to feel safe in your full expression. And that safety becomes the foundation for deeper liberation.

My hope is that this book has stirred something within you — a remembering, a rising, a reclaiming. That something in your being is saying, *I'm ready to be all of me.* Because when you reclaim your authenticity, you also reclaim your voice, your power, and your radiance. You no longer apologize for your essence. You no longer seek permission to shine. You become the most vibrant, empowered version of yourself — not because you're trying to be anything, but because you've stopped pretending to be anything less.

And the beauty is, it doesn't just liberate you. It liberates everyone around you. You become the permission slip, the activator, the living embodiment of what's possible. And that, dear Soul Alchemist, is the real work.

The Difference Between Soul-Led and Fear-Led Action

One of the most important shifts on the path of the Soul Alchemist is learning how to take action from alignment rather than fear — from soul rather than ego. It means no longer moving through life based solely on logic, pressure, or perceived obligation. Instead, it becomes a way of living where your steps are guided by the quiet knowing within. Soul-led action isn't forced. It doesn't rush. It moves from a deep sense of inner clarity — a feeling that says, *this is mine to do.*

Most people are conditioned to act from the mind. We do what we think we *should* do, what seems logical, what others expect of us. Decisions are made from fear of missing out, fear of failure, fear of judgment — or the need to prove, perform, or be accepted. And while those actions may look reasonable on the surface, they often lead to friction, burnout, and misalignment. When you're moving from the mind alone, you may take action that's technically "right," but it doesn't *feel* right. There's a disconnect. And that dissonance often shows up as energetic resistance, unnecessary struggle, or the feeling of always taking one step forward and three steps back.

The Soul Alchemist learns to approach action differently. Instead of asking, "What makes the most sense?" or "What do others expect from me?" you drop into your heart and ask, *What feels aligned? What feels expansive? What feels true — even if it doesn't make sense on paper?* You pause, connect inward, and let your soul — that wise, grounded essence within you — show you the next step. Soul-led action is guided by energy, not logic. It's intuitive. It's vibrational. It doesn't always offer a linear explanation, but it always brings you closer to your highest path.

Here's how you can often tell the difference: fear-based action feels constricted, heavy, flat, or driven by urgency. It may sound like, *I have to do this now or I'll fall behind,* or *If I don't act, I'll miss my chance.* It's reactive. It pushes from the outside in. Soul-led action, on the other hand, feels light, spacious, sometimes even exhilarating — even when it's unfamiliar. It doesn't mean you won't feel fear. In fact, aligned action often *does* stretch you outside your comfort zone. But even if it scares you, there's a calmness underneath the fear — a sense that says, *this is mine to do,* and it feels *true.*

Trust is the bridge that allows you to act on that guidance, especially when the path ahead isn't fully visible. There will be times when the soul's guidance seems strange, uncertain, or even inconvenient. You might question whether it was "just your imagination" or second-guess yourself when the outcome doesn't unfold immediately. But trust isn't about always being certain — it's about staying connected to that inner feeling of truth, even when the outer world hasn't caught up yet.

Building trust with your soul takes practice. It means being willing to pause and check in before acting. It means noticing the subtle difference between the mind's urgency and the soul's stillness. It means giving yourself space to listen — not for answers, but for resonance. Soul guidance doesn't come with long explanations or endless logic. It's simple. It's clear. And it lands in the body like a *yes*, even if your ego has questions.

And when in doubt, you can always tune in again. Ask: *Does this feel light or heavy? Expansive or tight? True or performative?* Your body will tell you. Your energy will tell you. Soul guidance feels alive. It resonates in your field. Ego chatter feels off — like a performance, a push, or a slight disconnect from yourself. When something doesn't feel quite right, that's often your soul nudging you to pause, to listen more deeply, to realign.

This way of living may not be the norm — but for the Soul Alchemist, it becomes everything. Because when you act from soul, you move in harmony with life. You co-create with the unseen. And every step you take becomes an act of devotion to the truth of who you are.

The World Responds to Your Alignment

When you're in full alignment — when your inner truth matches your outer expression — the world can feel it. You emanate an energetic coherence that is magnetic, grounded, and radiant. There's no static, no distortion, no confusion in your field. You carry yourself with a sense of authenticity and embodied presence that people naturally respond to. You don't have to explain it, justify it, or prove anything. Your energy speaks first, and it speaks with clarity.

This is the power of energetic congruence: when your inner and outer worlds align, your presence becomes undeniable. People might not know why they feel drawn to you, but they will sense the integrity in your energy. You'll notice more ease in conversations, more opportunities unfolding, and a deeper sense of flow in your relationships and business. You won't need to chase or convince, because your frequency does the inviting for you.

On the flip side, when you're misaligned — when you're pretending, performing, or holding back — people sense that too. Even if they can't articulate it, there's a subtle feeling that something doesn't quite add up. That's because energy doesn't lie. And everything is energy. So whether or not someone is consciously aware of it, they are constantly responding to what your field is broadcasting.

I learned this firsthand in my business. For a long time, I tried to present myself as a successful entrepreneur. I had the polished website, the offers, the YouTube channel — all the outward markers of someone who had it together. But behind the scenes, I was barely getting by. I was struggling financially and energetically, but I kept pushing forward with the idea that I had to "fake it until I made it." The problem was, my energy was saying something completely different than my brand. What I projected on the outside was confidence and success, but inside, I was operating from lack and desperation. And that disconnect created resistance — not just within me, but in how others responded to me. I could never understand why potential clients weren't saying yes. But now I know: they were picking up on the incongruence. My energy wasn't aligned with my message.

Everything shifted when I started showing up in full alignment. When I stopped pretending. When I stopped trying to be what I thought others needed me to be and started being *me*. The real me. Authentically. Fully. Without filters. And that's when clients started flowing in. My marketing agency began to grow effortlessly. And my spiritual business started to shift too — my YouTube channel gained momentum, people responded to me differently, and I began to attract aligned opportunities that I had previously struggled to reach. Why? Because my energy and my words were finally speaking the same language.

When you show up as your full self — unfiltered, honest, empowered — the outer world will mirror that back to you. People can feel the difference between someone who is *trying* to be something and someone who *is* that something. Authenticity has a frequency. And it's irresistible.

Of course, there will be moments when refusing to shrink or conform creates friction. When you stop playing by the rules that once kept you safe, not everyone will understand. Some may push back. Others may fall away. But those moments are invitations — not setbacks. They're asking you: *Will you shrink to be accepted, or will you rise as your true self?*

The truth is, people respond to authenticity. They respect it. They're drawn to it. And they instinctively retreat from what feels inauthentic, even if they don't consciously know why. So when you choose to walk through the world in full alignment — when you no longer shrink, conform, or hold back — you become a beacon. Not just for others, but for yourself. You show your system, your soul, and the universe that you're no longer willing to live a fragmented life.

You are a Soul Alchemist. You don't dim your light. You don't silence your voice. You don't fake your way through life. You *become* the embodiment of your truth. And when you do, the world doesn't just respond — it rises to meet you.

Holding Your Truth When Others Don't Understand

There comes a point on your path when you're fully in your power — deeply aligned, vibrant, and unapologetically walking in your truth. It feels expansive, liberating, and unshakable. Until... you're around people who don't get it. Who look at you sideways when you talk about energy or intuition. Who subtly — or not so subtly — try to pull you back down into their comfort zone. That's when the real test begins: not of your worth, but of your *anchoring*. Can you hold your truth even when others don't see it? Can you stand firm in who you are without needing their approval?

Here's something important to remember: you never have to lower yourself to meet others where they are. You are not here to shrink, to conform, or to dim your light for anyone's comfort. But you *can* extend your hand — energetically — to those around you. You can invite them to rise without pushing, without preaching, and without needing them to join you. And if they're ready, they will. But if they're not, it's not your job to convince them. Everyone awakens in their own time, and no amount of explaining or pleading will open a door they're not ready to walk through.

This is where discernment becomes sacred. When you're around others who aren't on the same frequency, it's not about shutting down or hiding who you are. It's about honoring what they're able to receive without compromising your own alignment. You don't have to share everything. You don't have to pour your soul out in every conversation. You simply meet people where *they* are, without lowering where *you* are.

For example, where I live, I don't often come across many people who are consciously on the spiritual path. At the gym, in the store, in everyday life — most people I meet are still asleep to much of what I do or speak about. So when someone asks what I do, I don't immediately launch into channeling, activations, light language, and the multidimensional path of soul alchemy. Instead, I offer a simple entry point: *I'm a spiritual life coach.* That's it. Just enough to test the waters. If they're curious or open, I share more. But if they're not, I don't push. I don't force. And I don't take it personally.

This isn't about shrinking. This is about sharing from an empowered place, where you're rooted in your truth but also attuned to the people around you. You're not holding back out of fear. You're choosing discernment out of love — for yourself, and for them. It's not about hiding your light. It's about shining it in a way others can actually receive, rather than blinding them with something they're not ready to understand.

So how do you hold your ground in those moments when you feel the pull to collapse or shrink? First, you anchor back into *your* truth. You remember who you are, what you've walked through, and how far you've come. You take a deep breath and reconnect with your body — your presence. You ground into the energy of *I don't need to be understood to be valid. I don't need to be seen to be real.*

Then, you give yourself permission to share only what feels aligned. Not from fear, but from inner sovereignty. You don't owe anyone full access to your soul. You get to choose how much you share, when, and with whom. That's not hiding — that's honoring. That's mastery.

It also helps to have *your own safe spaces* — people, communities, or even private practices where you can fully express yourself without filtering. Not everyone is meant to be your mirror. Some people are simply passing through. And some will never understand what you're here to do. That doesn't mean you're wrong. It just means you're different. And different isn't a problem — it's your power.

So when the world doesn't get you, when people look confused, dismissive, or even critical, hold steady. Speak only what is aligned to speak. Let your energy do the rest. Your frequency is doing more than your words ever could. And your job isn't to convince — your job is to embody.

You are the Soul Alchemist. You don't collapse into old versions of yourself to make others comfortable. You don't conform to avoid discomfort. You stand in your truth with grace, discernment, and unwavering self-respect. And in doing so, you become the very thing others didn't know they needed — not a teacher, not a savior, but a living, breathing invitation to rise.

The Ripple Effect of Embodied Truth

When you fully embody your soul self — the truest, most aligned version of who you are — something powerful happens. Not only does your inner world shift, but your outer world begins to reflect that alignment. You stop emanating distorted or fragmented energy. You stop sending out confusing signals. And instead, you begin radiating a clear, coherent, and elevated frequency that affects everyone around you — whether they realize it or not.

Because energy doesn't lie. When you're out of alignment, when you're hiding behind masks or holding back your truth, you can feel it in your body — and others can feel it in your presence. You might show up frustrated, irritated, reactive, or drained. Not because anything external is necessarily wrong, but because internally, you're constricting your energy. It's like trying to squeeze into clothes two sizes too small. You *can* do it, but it doesn't feel good. It's uncomfortable. It's unnatural. And it takes an enormous amount of effort to maintain.

Authenticity, on the other hand, is easeful. It's not performative. It doesn't require constant vigilance. You're not trying to manage how others perceive you. You're simply being who you are — in your fullness, in your joy, in your truth. And when you do that, your mood lifts, your energy softens, your nervous system relaxes, and your presence becomes magnetic. People feel better around you, not because you're trying to fix or teach them, but because your field is clear and your embodiment is real.

And that's the ripple effect: when you stop pretending, you unconsciously give others permission to do the same. Without saying a word. Without preaching or persuading. Just by *being* who you are, you serve as a mirror — reflecting what it looks like to live without apology, without distortion, and without energetic masks.

Think about it: if you've been pretending, playing a role, or hiding parts of yourself, chances are most of the people around you have been doing the same. We're conditioned from an early age to conform, to be "good," to fit in and not rock the boat. So when you show up in your raw, unfiltered truth, it can be shocking at first — but it's also deeply refreshing. It touches something inside others. It activates a memory of freedom. And even if they resist it at first, a part of them will start to whisper, *I want that too.*

This is what it means to uplift others energetically. Not by telling them what to do or trying to change them — but by modeling what it looks like to be free. You extend an invisible invitation every time you embody your truth. You become a living transmission that calls others higher, not through force or persuasion, but through resonance.

And perhaps most importantly, you no longer feel the need to manage others' discomfort or hold yourself back for their sake. You understand that your embodiment is enough. That your light is a service. And that authenticity is the most generous thing you can offer the world.

So let yourself be the mirror. Let your life be the teaching. You are not here to convince — you are here to *be*. And in that being, you will awaken something in others far more powerful than anything you could ever say.

Closing Incantation: I Walk in My Truth

Walking through the world in your truth is not a one-time choice — it's a daily devotion. It's a path of presence, power, and deep energetic responsibility. You're not just expressing your truth through your words or your work — you're radiating it through your energy, your boundaries, your actions, and your being.

Some days, it will feel effortless. Other days, it will challenge everything in you not to collapse back into the familiar. But this is the path of the Soul Alchemist — not one of perfection, but of *continual remembering*. You will forget, and then remember. You will fall out of alignment, and then rise again — each time stronger, clearer, more you.

Let this chapter be a reminder that your embodiment *is* the teaching. That your alignment *is* the magnetism. You don't have to prove yourself. You don't have to convince anyone. All you have to do is keep returning to the frequency of your truth and let that truth ripple through your life.

You were never meant to fit in. You were meant to activate. To disrupt. To liberate. And to lead — simply by being who you are.

Incantation

I no longer shrink to make others comfortable.
I no longer hide the fire that burns within me.
I no longer wear the masks that once kept me safe.

I choose to walk through this world in full alignment.
I choose to let my truth speak louder than my fear.
I choose to let my presence be a mirror for what's possible.

I speak when my soul has something to say.
I rest when my body asks to soften.
I move only in ways that honor my energy.

I release the need to be understood.
I release the temptation to perform.
I release the fear of being too much.

My light is not too much.
My power is not too much.
My truth is not too much.

I am the Soul Alchemist.
And I walk in my truth — unapologetically, unfiltered, and free.

Chapter 16: Let it Be Easy, Let it Be True

Embodying your soul essence in everyday life through
conscious words, actions, and presence

So many of us grow up believing that our worth is directly tied to what we do, how hard we work, and how much we achieve. That belief doesn't come out of nowhere—it's deeply ingrained through early experiences, societal expectations, and even spiritual teachings that subtly perpetuate the same cycle.

From the time you were young, you may have learned that love, attention, or approval had to be earned. You were praised when you did something "good" and possibly punished or ignored when you didn't meet expectations. These early dynamics teach the nervous system to associate safety and worthiness with performance. Over time, that wiring runs so deep, you don't even question it—you just keep pushing forward, trying to prove you're good enough, worthy enough, deserving enough.

Even in spiritual spaces, this pattern can quietly persist. You may hear phrases like "you have to raise your vibration," "do the work," or "clear your karma"—which, while well-intended, can still trigger the subconscious belief that you have to fix something about yourself to be worthy of what you desire. That you're not there yet. That you're not enough until you've reached some elusive state of perfection or purity.

This subtle message creates an invisible finish line that keeps moving. And the more you chase it, the more exhausted and disconnected you feel. You try harder, work more, tweak your affirmations, meditate longer—but still come up short. And each time, that reinforces the idea that maybe you're just not doing enough.

But here's the truth: you're not here to prove anything. You're not here to earn your worth. You're here to remember it.

All that pushing, grinding, and proving energy often masks a much deeper wound—the fear that you won't be loved, accepted, or safe unless you perform. That unless you do everything right, you'll be left behind. But when you keep trying to manifest from that place, you're creating from lack. From misalignment. And that energetic state creates resistance, no matter how hard you try.

The soul doesn't operate like that. Soul moves from alignment, not effort. When you follow soul, things often unfold in surprising, easeful, even playful ways. You may be guided to slow down, do less, or let go of what you thought you needed to make it happen. Soul-aligned action doesn't come from proving—it comes from presence. It comes from resonance. And it always feels right, even when it's uncomfortable.

This is your invitation to stop pushing. To stop proving. To stop hustling for what already belongs to you.

Because when you're truly aligned, you don't need to chase. You allow. You receive. You trust. And from that place, things begin to flow—not because you worked harder, but because you finally stopped trying so hard to be worthy of what you already are.

The Quiet Ways Performance Still Creeps In

Even after awakening to the spiritual path, many still find themselves caught in old performance-driven patterns—pushing, proving, and comparing—because these habits are so deeply rooted in societal and childhood conditioning. For years, we were taught that value is earned through effort. Praise came when we achieved something. Love and attention often felt conditional. So even when we've begun doing the inner work, these subconscious imprints linger.

In work or career, this might look like constantly overdelivering, overworking, or taking on more than you should in an effort to be seen, valued, or promoted. In your business, it could manifest as blurred boundaries with clients, people-pleasing tendencies, or overextending yourself to prove that you're "worth it." You might even struggle to say no because a part of you still believes that success requires sacrifice.

When it comes to money, many unconsciously feel the need to "earn" their abundance. There's often guilt around ease or effortless receiving. If someone handed you a $10,000 check with no strings attached, would you be able to receive it fully—or would you feel uncomfortable, wondering what you did to deserve it? The same goes for small things—like someone buying your dinner or offering to help you. Do you allow yourself to receive with grace, or do you feel the need to immediately give something in return?

This pressure also shows up in relationships. You may give and give, but struggle to receive in equal measure. You may feel frustrated that others don't meet you halfway, but unknowingly you might be blocking their ability to do so because of your own discomfort with receiving or your unconscious need to earn love, approval, or validation. It's not always that others aren't willing—it's often that your energetic field hasn't made space to allow it in.

These cycles are exhausting. They drain your nervous system and fray your energy. Over time, this overextension creates tension in the body, anxiety, burnout, and a subtle sense of unworthiness that lingers even as you try to stay on your spiritual path. You can't force alignment. And you can't override the inner programming with willpower alone.

Comparison is another sneaky expression of this pattern. You might look at others in your field or on a similar path and feel discouraged—wondering why things seem to flow for them while you're still struggling. But here's the truth: no two people have the same energetic blueprint. No two people carry the same wounds, imprints, or karmic threads. On the surface you might share a career or a lifestyle, but the inner terrain is vastly different.

When you compare yourself to others, you collapse into lack. You see in them what you feel is missing in you. But what if those triggers are actually mirrors? What if the envy or longing you feel is a spotlight revealing the exact places where healing or integration is needed?

That's the gift. These moments of performance, pressure, or comparison are invitations to look deeper—not to judge yourself, but to bring loving awareness to what's still playing out beneath the surface. When you can recognize the pattern, you reclaim the power to choose something new.

The Subtle Energy of Misalignment

The way you recognize when you're in force versus flow is actually quite simple—your body and energy will always tell you the truth. It comes down to how it *feels*. When you're in force, life feels heavy, effortful, and frustrating. There's tension in your body. Things move slowly or not at all. You feel like you're pushing a boulder uphill or swimming against the current with a weighted backpack strapped to your back.

On the other hand, when you're in flow, life opens. Things just *work*. You don't have to overthink or overdo. Ideas drop in, aligned opportunities show up, synchronicities unfold, and it feels like you're swimming with the current—supported, carried, held. You feel light, expanded, even excited. There's a sense of ease and inner spaciousness, even if your circumstances haven't fully shifted yet. Deep down, you just *know* everything is working out.

This contrast between force and flow is rooted in alignment. Force often comes from the mind—trying to figure things out, chasing outcomes, doing what others say you "should" do, or taking action from fear or scarcity. It creates restriction, resistance, and energetic misalignment. And when you're out of alignment, you'll feel it: a lack of clarity, frustration, anxiety, mental fog, exhaustion, or even irritability with the people around you. There's friction in your life and within yourself.

Flow, on the other hand, is born from alignment. It doesn't mean you don't take action—it means the action is guided, inspired, and rooted in your soul's truth. You're not forcing outcomes or proving your worth. You're simply following what feels light and aligned. You're doing just enough—and it's enough. And when you operate from that place, things often unfold in better ways than your mind could have planned.

There are signs that tell you when you're trying too hard: You overthink every move. You feel pressured to "make something happen." You second-guess yourself or rely on others to tell you what's best, even when it doesn't feel right. You feel off—but you do it anyway because it seems like the "right" thing to do.

That's how you know you're in force—not flow.

Now think back to a time in your life when things unfolded effortlessly. You weren't grinding or hustling—you were simply following the thread of what felt aligned. You felt calm, energized, even fulfilled. That's flow. That's your natural state. That's what happens when you stop trying to prove yourself and start trusting your inner guidance.

And that's the energy you want to spend more time in—not because it's some idealized spiritual state, but because it actually works. It honors your nervous system. It keeps you grounded. It allows you to receive. It feels *good*. And from that space, everything becomes easier—because you're no longer in your own way.

The Lie of the Struggle

The belief that success, abundance, or growth must come through struggle is one of the deepest and most limiting programs we carry— and it's not even ours. It's inherited. We've been conditioned for generations to believe that the only path to prosperity is through hard work, sacrifice, and proving ourselves.

Your parents may have told you to work hard. Their parents told them the same. This isn't just personal conditioning—it's ancestral. Layered into your DNA is the lived experience of survival, war, poverty, hardship, and striving. Many of our ancestors didn't have the luxury of letting life be easy. So they passed on the tools they had: grit, endurance, and sacrifice. Not because they didn't love us— but because that's what kept *them* alive.

But what if you're not here to survive anymore? What if you're here to *create*?

You've probably internalized the idea that ease is lazy or undeserved. The "no pain, no gain" mentality is everywhere. Hustle culture, grind mindset, spiritual over-efforting—it's all wrapped in the illusion that the more you suffer, the more worthy you become. That if something comes too easily, you didn't earn it. That unless you push, it won't happen. These beliefs aren't just outdated—they're energetically misaligned.

And I get it. These ideas don't just live in your head—they live in your body. You may feel resistance, even guilt, when you try to rest or slow down. Taking a nap, watching a show, or simply *being* instead of doing can trigger anxiety. There's a voice that says, "If I don't work, it won't work." But that's not your truth—it's your programming.

The truth is: your soul does not need you to sacrifice, push, or prove. The truth is: you *can* have what you desire simply because it's aligned with who you are becoming. You don't have to trade one thing to get another. You don't have to earn your worth. You *are* worthy.

And here's what I've learned the hard way: forcing and grinding doesn't speed up the process—it slows it down. I used to work 14-hour days, burning myself out trying to force success. I thought if I just did more, pushed harder, I'd finally arrive. But it only left me exhausted, frustrated, and questioning everything.

That's not alignment. That's survival programming masquerading as ambition.

As you step into the path of the Soul Alchemist, I want to invite you to unhook from the old paradigm of "more effort = more results." That equation doesn't work in the quantum. In truth, the less resistance you hold, the more easily things flow. The more you align your energy, the more life organizes around that frequency.

And that doesn't mean you don't take action. It means the actions come from a deeper place—from soul, not fear. You don't push to make it happen. You open to *receive* what's already on its way.

This shift requires trust. Trust that when you follow your inspiration, when you take aligned steps, when you honor your inner guidance— things will unfold. Often in ways you couldn't have orchestrated from the mind.

When you stop forcing, you soften. Your energy becomes receptive. You open space. And in that space, life rushes in. Let go of the guilt around rest. Let go of the fear that ease means you're not doing enough. Let go of the ancestral weight that says you must prove your worth through suffering. Let it be easy. Let it be true. Because it can be.

The Frequency of Ease

True ease is not laziness. It's not bypassing. And it's certainly not avoidance. Ease is an elevated frequency. It's a state of openness— of energetic receptivity—that allows life to move through you without resistance. When you stop gripping, controlling, or forcing outcomes, you create space for clarity, synchronicity, and divine guidance to come in. You become more attuned to the present moment, more available to inspiration, and more capable of recognizing what's truly aligned for you.

When you're tapped into ease, you expand.

Your nervous system relaxes. Your energy field softens. Your awareness sharpens. Suddenly, things begin to make sense. You receive insights you couldn't find when you were stuck in the mental loop of problem-solving. Ease invites flow. And in that flow, clarity becomes accessible—not because you tried harder, but because you surrendered deeper.

Think about a time when you were obsessively trying to solve a problem. You thought about it from every angle, exhausted yourself with contemplation, and still found no solution. Then you stepped away—maybe you took a walk, played with your kids, watched your favorite show, or just rested—and suddenly, without trying, the answer arrived. Why? Because you let go. You moved into alignment. You created space for the soul to speak.

That is the power of ease.

Now, let's be honest: ease is often misunderstood. Some people confuse it with bypassing—spiritually detaching or avoiding uncomfortable truths in the name of "flow." But bypassing feels different in the body. It's a form of denial, a numbing of the truth. Ease is presence, not avoidance. It asks you to *feel* fully, not ignore what's hard. It requires deep inner trust, not disconnection.

Bypassing avoids the discomfort. Ease *moves through* it.

There's also a fine line between ease and resistance masked as rest. Sometimes we convince ourselves we're "choosing ease" when in truth we're avoiding the next aligned action out of fear, overwhelm, or self-doubt. The difference lies in awareness. Are you choosing ease from a place of inner alignment—or avoiding movement out of fear of failure, judgment, or expansion?

This is why attuning to your body, your energy, and your truth is so important. Ease isn't passive—it's powerfully receptive. It's an intentional shift from the head to the heart. From proving to allowing. But let's not pretend it's easy to choose ease.

I remember moments when I was so spiritually and energetically drained, all I wanted to do was lie on the couch and rest. My body was begging for stillness. But the clock said 1pm. My to-do list was still long. And as I sank into the cushions, TV playing, soul finally exhaling—the guilt crept in. That inner taskmaster whispered, *You should be working. You're wasting time. You're being lazy.*

This is what so many of us face when we try to live differently. We feel guilty for resting. We resist the inner nudge to soften. The monkey mind—conditioned for productivity, praise, and performance—fights against the quiet voice of soul that says, *Slow down. It's safe to trust. Let it be easy.*

And that's where your work is. To become aware of the voice that shames you for resting. To recognize the part of you that panics when you pause. And to choose, again and again, to listen to the deeper guidance—the one that honors your capacity, your energy, and your intuitive knowing.

Ease doesn't mean doing nothing. It means doing only what is truly aligned—and doing it from a place of clarity, not urgency. It means giving yourself full permission to relax without guilt. To receive without earning. To move through life with grace rather than tension. This is what it means to live as a Soul Alchemist. Let it be easy. Let it be sacred. Let it be true.

When You Let Life Reorganize Around Truth

Beautiful things begin to unfold when you release the need to perform, prove, or push—and instead move in resonance with your soul. You begin to feel different in your body. There's more spaciousness. More calm. You stop running an invisible marathon every day, and instead find yourself moving with the flow of life. You don't feel so rushed, so behind, so gripped by urgency. You're no longer chasing worthiness. You're simply allowing yourself to *be*—and that's enough.

From that space, life shifts. Your relationships become more authentic, grounded, and fulfilling. You're no longer giving from a place of depletion or performing to be liked. You're giving from overflow, and receiving with openness. You start attracting people who resonate with the real you—not the masked version who tried to fit in or be everything to everyone.

Money begins to flow with more ease. Not because you're hustling harder, but because you're aligned with your soul's essence. Inspired ideas come through more clearly. You take action from a place of excitement, not pressure. And somehow, those small aligned actions create bigger momentum than all the forcing and striving ever did.

Your energy field softens. Your nervous system regulates. Your frequency rises. And when that happens, your spiritual connection deepens. You receive more light. You're open to higher levels of guidance. You access your spiritual gifts more easily—not because you worked for them, but because you *made space* for them. Alignment opens you to higher consciousness. Ease invites embodiment. You become magnetic—not through effort, but through presence.

As you live in this way, something else begins to happen. The world around you responds. Life reorganizes itself around your authenticity. Opportunities that once felt like hard-won battles now find their way to you. People treat you differently because your energy is different. You're no longer unconsciously broadcasting fear, self-doubt, or lack. You're emanating trust, wholeness, and ease. And that ripple extends outward.

Your presence becomes a transmission. Just by being in your energy, others feel more grounded, more safe, more at peace. Your calm creates calm. Your alignment gives others permission to slow down, too. To be who they really are. To soften. This is how you shift the collective—not by preaching, but by *being*.

Of course, the opposite is also true. When you're living from performance and pressure, you emanate unease. That energy is contagious. It creates friction, tension, and disconnection in those around you. But when you live in resonance—with soul, with truth, with trust—you become a steady, grounded force. And the world feels that.

Let yourself be that steady force. Let your life become the proof that alignment works. Let ease become your way of being—not just for your own joy, but as an offering to the world.

Closing Incantation: Returning to Ease

You were never meant to force your way forward. You were never meant to sacrifice your peace to earn your worth. The path of the Soul Alchemist is not one of pushing—it is one of presence.

There is a power that lives in ease. A wisdom that flows when you stop performing and start listening. A resonance that guides your next step—not because you're striving, but because you're aligned.

Let this be the moment you drop the old ways of proving and pushing. Let this be where you choose to let it be easy, and let it be true.

Incantation:

I now release the need to prove, push, or perform.
I dissolve every imprint that told me I must earn my worth through struggle.
I reclaim my right to ease, alignment, and soul-led creation.
I allow spaciousness to guide me, truth to lead me, and resonance to carry me forward.
I trust that my path unfolds not through pressure—but through presence.
It is safe to let it be easy. It is safe to let it be true.
And so it is.

Chapter 17: Embodying Boundaries, Discernment, and Devotion

Protecting your frequency without disconnecting from others

As you continue to embody the essence of the Soul Alchemist, we must now turn our attention to a vital aspect of energetic sovereignty—boundaries. While we've touched on this throughout the journey, it's too important to remain in the background. Boundaries are often where power is lost, energy is drained, and self-betrayal takes root. And not because we're weak, but because we care. We want to help. We want to be there for others. We want to feel needed. But unchecked generosity becomes depletion when it comes at the expense of our own well-being.

A Soul Alchemist understands that boundaries are not about walls— they are acts of sacred devotion. They are energetic agreements that say: *I honor myself enough to protect what is sacred within me.* These aren't just physical boundaries, though that's part of it. There are four dimensions of boundaries that must be honored—physical, emotional, energetic, and spiritual.

Physical boundaries relate to your time, space, and physical body. Saying no. Not overcommitting. Not letting people violate your personal space or physical comfort. If someone's presence feels invasive—whether they touch you without permission or assume access to your time—you are allowed to draw a firm line. You are not here to operate from obligation. That energy is dense, draining, and rooted in the belief that you owe others something. You do not. Your "no" is just as sacred as your "yes."

Emotional boundaries protect your internal stability. If someone talks down to you, gaslights you, or emotionally manipulates you, you have every right to stand tall in your truth. That doesn't mean lashing out or meeting aggression with aggression. It means speaking clearly and calmly from your center: *I will not tolerate being treated this way. I am not available for this dynamic.* The goal is not to dominate the other person—but to refuse to abandon yourself in the presence of their discomfort.

Energetic boundaries are crucial for those walking the spiritual path—especially if you're highly sensitive or tend to absorb others' emotions. Whether you're in a crowded room or around energy-draining individuals, you get to decide what enters your field. You are not a fuel station for others' unprocessed emotions. You can set the intention: *Any energy others need from me flows through me, not from me.* You are the transmitter—not the source. When you do this consistently, you stay energized, centered, and sovereign.

Spiritual boundaries become essential when you open your intuitive channels or work with spirit guides and unseen realms. If you're doing mediumship or channeling work, you must establish clear "business hours." Just because you're spiritually open doesn't mean all energies are welcome to drop in uninvited. Let your field know: *I only allow in beings of light who have been invited. I am not available for interference outside of sacred time.* And above all, discernment is key. Not every being claiming to be of the light is. You have the authority to close the door to anything misaligned.

When your boundaries are in place—respected and enforced—you conserve your power. You protect your frequency. You reclaim your sense of safety, clarity, and sovereignty. You stop leaking energy into places where it's not respected or reciprocated.

And how do most people leak energy unconsciously?

- By saying yes when they want to say no

- By over-explaining or justifying their decisions

- By trying to fix others instead of holding space

- By tolerating disrespect in the name of "keeping the peace"

- By absorbing emotions that aren't theirs to carry

- By abandoning their needs to earn love, praise, or belonging

These patterns are subtle but powerful. They slowly chip away at your inner knowing, your energy reserves, your joy. But you can choose a different way.

Let's also acknowledge that the word "boundaries" can feel rigid or isolating. So here's a reframe: think of boundaries as *sacred devotion*. You're not building walls—you're tending to the temple of your being. You're honoring the vessel that holds your soul. And that devotion creates energetic strength. It communicates silently to the world: *I respect myself. You will too.*

People may not like your boundaries—especially if they benefited from you not having any—but they will respect them. Because self-respect is magnetic. It activates a quiet power. And when you enforce your boundaries from a grounded, self-honoring place—not out of spite or defense—you teach others how to treat you without saying a word.

This is how the Soul Alchemist protects their frequency: not by shutting out the world, but by choosing where their energy flows.

Not everyone and everything gets access. And that's not selfish—it's sacred.

Inner Knowing vs Inner Noise

As you deepen your embodiment as a Soul Alchemist, boundaries alone are not enough—you must also learn to trust your inner compass. Discernment becomes your sacred tool for navigating the world with clarity, grace, and integrity. It is what allows you to move through life in alignment with truth rather than being swayed by fear, obligation, or outside noise.

The deeper your connection to intuition, the more naturally discernment will rise within you. Your intuition is always speaking—through a sensation in your body, a nudge in your chest, a wave of unease, or a moment of quiet knowing. These signals are not to be dismissed or doubted. They are the whispers of your soul, gently nudging you toward your path or away from something misaligned.

A Soul Alchemist listens.

That means when something doesn't feel right, you don't override it. You don't gaslight yourself. You don't stay just because it looks good on paper or because someone told you it's the right thing. You honor that whisper of truth, even if it's inconvenient. Even if it stretches you. Even if it's hard.

But here's the thing: intuitive guidance doesn't always feel *comfortable*. Sometimes your intuition will lead you into the unknown, and that can bring up fear. That's where discernment becomes essential—so you can tell the difference between fear that protects and fear that restricts. Between a "no" that comes from truth and a "no" that comes from trauma. This is the difference between judgment and discernment.

Judgment is reactive. It's based on past pain, comparison, ego, or conditioning. It divides, limits, and closes your heart. Discernment, on the other hand, is grounded, clear, and centered. It sees what is true without needing to make anything or anyone wrong. It simply asks: *Is this aligned with who I'm becoming?*

You can use discernment in every area of life:

- In relationships, to sense who uplifts you and who drains you

- In environments, to feel what nourishes your energy and what contracts it

- In opportunities, to know what's truly aligned vs what's rooted in ego, pressure, or people-pleasing

And the more you use discernment, the more refined your intuition becomes—because you're showing your inner guidance that you're listening.

This is also where your nervous system plays a crucial role. When you make aligned choices, your body feels at ease. Your breath softens, your chest opens, your mind quiets. There's a felt sense of *rightness*, even if what you're choosing is unknown. Misaligned choices, on the other hand, trigger constriction. You may feel anxious, heavy, or exhausted. Your body knows before your mind does. The key is to pay attention.

But what happens when you feel like you don't have a choice?

Maybe you're in a job that drains you, but you need the income. Maybe someone in your life needs your help, and you don't want to let them down. It's easy to fall into the energy of resentment here— to feel stuck, powerless, or forced.

Here's how you reclaim your sovereignty:

Let's say you just got home from a long day at work. You're tired. You want to rest. But a family member needs a ride, and you're the only one available. Instead of forcing yourself through it, pause. Acknowledge your truth: *I don't want to do this right now. I'm tired. I wish I didn't have to.* Let yourself feel that. Then return to your heart. Ask yourself: *Why might I still choose to do this?* Maybe it's because this person is important to you. Maybe it's because it feels good to support them. When you shift from *I have to* to *I choose to*, you take your power back. You're no longer a victim of your circumstances—you're the conscious chooser of them.

Or take the example of staying in a job that no longer feels aligned. You wake up dreading it. But walking away right now isn't an option. So what do you do? Again, you acknowledge your truth: *I don't like this. I wish I could quit today.* Honor that. Then shift into choice: *I'm choosing to go to work because it supports me in building my future. It's the bridge to my passion.* That simple inner pivot changes everything. Your job may stay the same—but your relationship to it becomes empowered.

This is discernment in action. It's not just about saying yes or no—it's about saying yes with clarity, or no with peace. It's about making choices from devotion to your alignment, rather than fear of judgment, loss, or disruption.

And it's also about taking full responsibility for the energy you bring to your life. When you choose something—even something imperfect—you meet it with ownership. That's when your nervous system begins to regulate. That's when you start feeling safe in your own body. That's when ease becomes your default—not because life is easy, but because *you* are aligned.

Discernment isn't cold or distant—it's one of the most loving things you can practice. It doesn't separate you from others; it brings you closer to yourself. And the more deeply you know yourself, the more clearly you see everything else.

Devotion as a Way of Being

True embodiment is not something you achieve once and then maintain passively. It's a living, breathing commitment—a devotion to your soul that continues even when life feels heavy, messy, or uncertain. Devotion is what carries you through the moments when fear whispers louder than truth, when the path ahead seems unclear, or when everything in you wants to give up and retreat. In those moments, a Soul Alchemist doesn't abandon the path—they deepen into it.

Devotion is the heartbeat of embodiment.

It's not dramatic or grandiose. It's quiet and steady. It's the choice to stay aligned with soul even when doubt tries to take the wheel. It's the courage to keep moving forward when the mind screams for certainty but the soul nudges you into the unknown. It's what keeps you grounded in truth when the world around you feels noisy and chaotic.

This kind of devotion isn't about spiritual performance or chasing high vibes. It's about choosing again and again to be in relationship with your soul. To listen. To pause. To return.

Sometimes it looks like showing up for your practices—whether that's meditation, journaling, energy clearing, light language, movement, or simply sitting in stillness and feeling what's alive in you. Other times, it looks like recognizing when your nervous system is overstimulated and taking time to regulate and restore. It means honoring your capacity while staying committed to your growth. Devotion doesn't demand perfection—it invites presence.

And that presence is what allows you to *integrate*.

You can't truly embody what you haven't integrated. And yet, this is where many seekers get stuck. They chase the next breakthrough, the next healing, the next activation—without ever fully absorbing what came before. They touch the divine, but don't allow it to *change* them. Integration is where transformation becomes embodiment. And devotion is what makes integration possible.

It's devotion that keeps you in the work even when it's not glamorous. Even when you're not receiving visions or downloads. Even when you feel stretched, raw, or emotionally undone. Devotion reminds you that every experience—especially the hard ones—carries wisdom. It teaches you to lean in, to feel deeply, to ask: *What is this here to show me? What gift is waiting to be unearthed beneath this discomfort?*

When you live from this place, nothing becomes wasted. Every shadow becomes gold. Every trigger becomes a teacher. Every spiral becomes an opportunity to rise.

And something beautiful begins to happen: you stop being shaken by life in the way you used to. The very things that once knocked you into a spiral for days may still arise—but you move through them with grace, awareness, and trust. You recognize the pattern. You know how to meet it. You know how to alchemize it. This is the power of devotion. This is the power of soul alchemy embodied.

Because when you live this work, you don't just *remember* your power—you *become* it.

You bring it into your daily choices. Into your relationships. Into the way you respond to challenges. Into the way you lead, speak, rest, and create. Devotion weaves the sacred into the ordinary until there's no longer a divide between your spiritual path and your human life.

And that's the ultimate alchemy.

Anchored in Truth, Open in Heart

One of the most challenging arenas for a Soul Alchemist to stay embodied is within their closest relationships. Whether with family, partners, friends, or colleagues, relationships often become mirrors for where you are still abandoning yourself in order to belong. You may override your truth to keep the peace. You may suppress your needs to avoid conflict. You may soften your boundaries or downplay your desires to be liked, loved, or accepted. And at first glance, it can seem harmless—just being "kind," "flexible," or "easy to get along with." But beneath that surface often lives a deeper pattern of self-abandonment.

These patterns don't always start with malice. Often, they begin in childhood—when being attuned to others' needs helped you stay safe or receive love. But if left unchecked, they follow you into adulthood, where they quietly erode your self-trust and disconnect you from your authentic path. Every time you say yes when you mean no, every time you shrink so someone else can shine, every time you silence your truth to avoid discomfort, you chip away at your inner anchoring. You step out of alignment and into survival. And your energy begins to scatter.

This is why relationships can be such powerful activators for your spiritual growth—because they reveal exactly where you're still leaking energy or contorting yourself to feel safe. Not because others are wrong or toxic, but because your soul is calling you to remember who you are and to relate from that place. And the truth is: you can be open-hearted without abandoning yourself. You can hold compassion while honoring your own limits. You can love others without making yourself small for their comfort.

This is where discernment meets devotion—where you learn to stay rooted in your truth while still keeping your heart open. It means noticing when guilt, obligation, or emotional enmeshment try to pull you off-center, and lovingly choosing to return to yourself instead. Energetic cords often form in relationships where boundaries are unclear or where emotional dependence is masked as connection.

These cords can create a subtle pull on your field, making you feel drained, confused, or even responsible for someone else's emotions.

And unless you become aware of them, you may unconsciously keep giving your energy away, believing it's love—when in reality, it's a form of entanglement.

Clearing cords, releasing guilt, and disentangling emotionally isn't about cutting people out of your life. It's about reclaiming your energetic sovereignty so you can show up more authentically. So you can relate from fullness rather than depletion. From truth rather than fear.

Because in healthy, soul-aligned relationships, your wholeness is not a threat—it's a gift. And the more you honor your own needs, voice, and energy in your relationships, the more you invite others to meet you there. You become a mirror for what's possible. You model what it looks like to be deeply connected without self-abandonment. To be open without leaking. To love without losing yourself. That's what it means to embody sacred relating. That's what it means to be a Soul Alchemist in relationship.

Recognizing When It's Time to Step Back

There comes a time on your journey of awakening and coming home to yourself when people in your life will begin to fade away. Friendships may dissolve, relationships may come to an end, and some connections may evolve into something different, making space for new ones to enter. This is not something to fear or resist— it is part of the natural cycle of soul evolution. Every person you encounter is in your life for a reason, and once that reason has been fulfilled—once the growth, lesson, or purpose has been served—the bond may begin to dissolve. This might happen suddenly, or slowly over time. Sometimes they walk away. Other times, it's you who feels called to step back.

Of course, this can be deeply uncomfortable, even painful. It can bring up feelings of sadness, confusion, or grief—especially if the connection once felt so close, supportive, or meaningful. But when you allow yourself to recognize the signs of misalignment, when you acknowledge the quiet knowing that the spark is gone or that the resonance is no longer there, you begin to free yourself from the energetic toll of forcing what no longer fits. Sometimes you'll notice the connection begins to feel heavy. Conversations feel strained. You feel as though you're speaking two different languages, or like you're constantly explaining yourself and still not being understood. The closeness you once shared begins to fade.

And when you ignore these signs—when you try to force a connection to continue out of habit, fear, guilt, or loyalty—you begin to create a disruption to your inner harmony. This affects you on all levels: physically, emotionally, energetically, and spiritually. You may feel more tension in your body when you're around that person. You might feel anxious, agitated, or depleted after spending time with them. Emotionally, there may be a growing sense of resentment, frustration, or even dread. Energetically, your field begins to constrict—you feel squeezed, disconnected from your truth, or ungrounded without fully understanding why.

These are signs that something is no longer in alignment. They are not punishments or failures—they are invitations. They are reminders from your soul to come back into integrity with yourself.

The key here is to honor what is. To trust that when something begins to feel off, when the connection no longer nourishes or expands you, it is safe—and sacred—to let go. You don't need to create drama or force a confrontation. You don't need to blame or explain. You can step back with love, grace, and compassion. Not from a place of resentment or judgment, but from a place of honoring your energy and your evolution.

Letting go doesn't make you a bad person. It doesn't mean you didn't care or that the relationship wasn't meaningful. It simply means that your paths are no longer meant to be intertwined in the same way.

By honoring this truth, you create space—for yourself and for the other—to grow, expand, and align with what is next.

And the beautiful thing is: when you create space, life responds. As you release what no longer resonates, you become more energetically available to the people who are meant to meet you where you are now—those who match your current frequency, who honor your truth, and who uplift and support your continued evolution. These soul-aligned connections feel different. You don't need to perform, explain, or shrink. You are met fully as you are. But those connections can only enter when you're willing to let go of what is no longer aligned.

So trust the signs. Listen to the whispers. And honor your sacred path—even when that path asks you to walk away from what was, in order to fully receive what's meant to be.

Embodying Boundaries as a Frequency, Not Just a Practice

By now, you've come to understand that boundaries are far more than just words, actions, or external practices—they are a frequency you carry. When you truly honor your needs, when you embody your truth, when you are devoted to your energy and well-being, that creates an unmistakable resonance that others feel. It communicates without words: *this is who I am, this is what I allow, and this is what I do not.*

You don't have to explain yourself, over-justify, or defend your decisions. When you're truly rooted in the energy of self-honoring, others can feel it. The frequency of sovereignty speaks louder than any declaration ever could. This is what it means to be the boundary, rather than needing to set one all the time.

The inner shift happens when you stop trying to manage other people's reactions or expectations, and instead turn inward to ask:

What do I need to feel safe, clear, and aligned right now? When you commit to honoring that—regardless of how others respond—you shift from performing to emanating. You are no longer outsourcing your worth or waiting for permission. You simply *are*, and that "beingness" sends a strong energetic signal that says, *I am not available for anything that violates my peace, my truth, or my path.*

And the beautiful thing is: when you hold this frequency consistently, you naturally begin to repel what isn't aligned—without needing to fight, explain, or push away. What once may have triggered you or drained you no longer enters your field. What used to demand your energy now dissolves before it can even touch you. You move through life as a clear, sovereign presence. And others respond accordingly.

People respect those who respect themselves. Even if they don't like it, even if it challenges them, something in them recognizes your strength and honors it. You no longer attract the same dynamics you once did—because your frequency won't allow it. And that is the true power of becoming energetically untouchable.

Closing Incantation: The Frequency of Sacred Sovereignty

Let this moment be a sacred seal— a return to your truth, your power, your sovereignty.

You have journeyed deep into the realm of energetic boundaries, discernment, and devotion. You've remembered that honoring yourself is not selfish—it is holy. And that your frequency speaks louder than any words ever could.

This incantation is here to help you integrate what you've embodied, to root it deeper into your cells, your field, and your life. Speak it out loud. Speak it with conviction. Let every word activate your inner authority.

Incantation

I now claim the frequency of sacred sovereignty.

I honor my energy, my truth, and my inner knowing.

I set boundaries not from fear, but from deep devotion to my soul.

I release guilt, shame, and obligation—and return to self-respect.

I no longer shrink, explain, or overextend.

I am a clear channel. I am a grounded force.

I walk with discernment, integrity, and grace.

I now clear and transmute all distortions around boundaries,
power, and self-abandonment

across all times, space, realities, lifetimes, and dimensions.

It is done. It is sealed. I am sovereign.

Chapter 18: Living from Your Future Self Now

Embody the energy of your future self and lead from the timeline you're calling in.

In this final chapter of Part Two—our journey through embodiment—we now arrive at what is perhaps the most powerful aspect of it all: living from your future self *now*. This is embodiment in its most activated form. This is where you no longer wish for your life to change—you become the change. You stop waiting for the outer world to catch up and instead begin *emanating* the version of yourself who already lives the life you desire.

Because here's what you must understand: you don't have to wait for your circumstances to shift in order to feel the way you want to feel. If what you desire is happiness, freedom, abundance, fulfillment, joy, or expansion—you don't have to wait until those things "arrive" to feel them. You can access those states right now. In fact, you must.

Nothing external can create lasting inner fulfillment if the inner self is still anchored in lack. You may experience temporary highs when something finally arrives or manifests, but if the internal frequency hasn't shifted, you'll quickly return to the baseline you were trying to escape. True transformation doesn't come from the outside in. It's an inside-out embodiment. That's what this chapter is about: becoming the embodiment of your desires before they arrive—so that your outer reality has no choice but to rise and match who you are *being*.

This is where we return to two powerful truths I've touched on earlier in this book. The first is the **Law of Reversibility**, which teaches us that if a particular state of being or experience can produce a feeling—then that feeling, when generated and embodied first, can also create the experience. In other words, if receiving a certain amount of money would make you feel secure and empowered, then feeling secure and empowered now can magnetize the experience of receiving that money.

The second truth is this: your external world is always a mirror of your internal world. The energy you carry, the identity you hold, the beliefs you embody—*that* is what gets reflected back to you. So when you shift your internal frequency, when you begin to live, think, feel, and act like the version of you who already *has* what you desire, life begins to rearrange itself to match that. The mirror responds to the source.

And this doesn't have to be complicated. You don't need to hustle or chase or prove. You don't have to say affirmations all day or spend hours in meditation. You simply need to embody the *essence* of your desire. Practices like scripting, visualization, gratitude, and affirmations can absolutely support that embodiment—but they are tools, not requirements. They are training wheels to help you enter the frequency of your future self until it becomes your natural state.

One of my favorite embodiment tools is **scripting**—writing from the identity of your future self as if it's already done. You drop into the frequency of the version of you who already lives your dream life, and you write in present tense, describing how amazing life is. Not as a future goal or hopeful vision, but as *now*. You don't say "I am going to create…"—you say, "I am so in love with the life I've created. Every day I wake up feeling free, joyful, and lit up by my purpose." You want to write as if you're already living it. But more importantly—you want to *feel* it. The emotion is what energizes and amplifies the frequency. Without the feeling, the words are empty.

Another powerful technique is Neville Goddard's **SATS**—State Akin To Sleep. This is a practice where you relax your body into a sleepy, twilight state, just before drifting off, and then impress your subconscious with scenes of your fulfilled desire. In this deeply receptive state, your mind is most open to suggestion, and you can imagine a scene that implies your desire is already fulfilled—like seeing yourself receive the call, sign the contract, step into the dream home. You play this scene over and over, until it becomes real in your emotional body. When you drift off with this energy imprinted, you begin to merge timelines in your sleep.

These embodiment practices help you train your energy to match your desires. Over time, you don't need the techniques anymore. They served their purpose by helping you shift your identity. Because once that version of you is no longer something you try to become— but who you *are*—you've collapsed the gap between where you are and where you want to be.

This is what it means to live from the end. You live *as if* it's already true. You stop hoping and wishing and start being. You take actions as the version of you who already has what she wants. You think her thoughts. You carry her essence. You show up in the world as *her*. And when that identity becomes your new normal, your external reality has no choice but to catch up.

So let's talk timelines. You're not stuck in one static life path. There are infinite timelines available to you. One where you have everything you've ever dreamed of. One where you're living a life beyond anything you can currently imagine. And yes, also timelines that are filled with limitation, scarcity, and struggle. You get to choose which one you align with—based on your identity and embodiment.

Every time you tune into your future self—the one who already has what you're calling in—you are *merging timelines*. You collapse the long, winding road of trial and error and leap into alignment with your desired future. Yes, your outer reality might still take a little time to adjust, but energetically, emotionally, spiritually—you're already living it. And that's what matters.

You've become the version of you who no longer *hopes* for change— you *embody* it. That is energetic leadership. That is Soul Alchemy in motion.

Collapsing Timelines Through Embodied Choice

Your beliefs, your energy, and your choices are shaping your timeline moment by moment. Every action you take—whether conscious or unconscious—is reinforcing a version of self. If you want to call in the future you've envisioned, it's not enough to simply want it or visualize it occasionally. You must *become* it. That means choosing the thoughts, actions, beliefs, and energetic states that match the version of you who already lives that future.

When you align with the essence of your future self—when you embody her identity, trust her choices, and live from her energy— you begin collapsing the space between where you are and where you want to be. That future timeline, the one where you're already living the life you've been calling in, merges with the now. It's not magic, although it may feel like it. It's physics. It's alignment. It's timeline convergence through embodiment.

The more consistently you live from the frequency of your future self, the more your external reality begins to reconfigure to reflect that shift. People, opportunities, and synchronicities begin to align with the version of you you've chosen to embody. Your current reality can't help but catch up with who you've become.

And yet, the opposite is also true. If you keep showing up the same way—thinking the same thoughts, believing the same limitations, staying in the same vibration—you continue reinforcing your current timeline. Not because you're wrong or broken, but because you haven't yet shifted your point of origin. That's why embodiment is everything. You must *be* the change—not wait for the change.

Of course, this process is not linear. There will be moments when you feel fully embodied, magnetic, and deeply aligned with the future you. And then—life happens. You get triggered, doubt creeps in, old emotions resurface, and suddenly you're pulled back into your former self. That doesn't mean you've failed. It means you're human.

What matters most is how you respond. Do you spiral into self-judgment? Or do you recognize what's happening, take a breath, and choose again? Returning to alignment is a skill, and like any skill, it becomes easier with practice. The more often you realign, the more natural it becomes to live from the embodiment of your future self—even in moments of stress, overwhelm, or uncertainty.

Eventually, the contrast becomes so clear that it's hard to stay misaligned. Once you've tasted the power and peace of your expanded self, slipping into the old version of you will feel like trying to wear clothes that no longer fit. You'll feel the energetic mismatch. And that awareness becomes your greatest ally. It pulls you forward. It sharpens your discernment. It invites you to keep choosing, again and again, the version of you who already lives what you desire.

And that is the true power of timeline merging: not just shifting your outer world, but transforming who you are at the core—so that your new reality is no longer a vision you're moving toward, but a truth you're living from.

Becoming an Energetic Leader in Your Own Life

As a Soul Alchemist and conscious creator, your role isn't to wait for external validation—it's to lead yourself first. This means becoming the energetic authority in your own life. It means attuning to your internal state and taking responsibility for your frequency. You begin to recognize when your energy feels off—when it's constricted, scattered, heavy, or simply not resonant with who you're becoming—and you know what to do about it. Whether through breathwork, light language, meditation, clearing, nervous system support, or intentional stillness, you learn how to restore alignment from the inside out.

You tend to your energy like a sacred garden. You prune what no longer serves, remove what's been draining you, and anchor yourself in expansion. You become the guardian of your field—honoring your needs, staying rooted in your truth, and making choices that support your highest timeline. You're not just reacting to life anymore—you're leading it. And that is the essence of energetic leadership.

Leading yourself first doesn't mean being perfect or having everything figured out. It means walking your path with integrity. It's not about preaching what you haven't lived—it's about embodying the work. You become the example, not through words alone, but through presence, action, and the way you hold your own frequency through both the highs and the unknowns. You live the truth you teach. You show others what's possible simply by being it.

But here's the part many struggle with: your external reality takes time to catch up. When you're becoming the next version of yourself—aligned, clear, sovereign—it can feel disheartening if the outside world doesn't immediately reflect that shift. This is when doubt creeps in. You may wonder, "Is it working? Will it ever come?" And this is where the deeper initiation happens.

This is the moment you're invited to trust—not blindly, but with the deep, embodied knowing that everything is already aligning. You've already shifted. The energetic dominoes are in motion. And while Divine Timing can feel like an annoying phrase when you're ready now, it simply means that the unfolding is occurring in the highest, most supportive way for your evolution. It means you are becoming energetically available for what you've asked for—not just desiring it, but capable of receiving and sustaining it.

Often what delays our manifestations is not the universe's hesitation, but our own unconscious resistance. Lingering doubts, buried fears, unintegrated patterns—they quietly distort the signal we're sending out. So the work continues. You stay curious. You observe the thoughts and emotions that rise when things don't move fast enough. You clear what no longer aligns. You choose to return, again and again, to trust.

Embodiment helps you hold steady through the gap. When you're grounded in clarity, aligned in your energy, and confident in who you're becoming, you no longer grasp or chase. You magnetize. You stay devoted to the essence of your desire—not the timeline, not the outcome, not the details. The how, the when, the form it takes— none of that is your job. Your only job is to stay in the embodiment of what you've chosen. To allow life to meet you there.

There's a powerful difference between chasing something and claiming it. When you chase, you affirm that it's outside of you. When you claim it energetically, you're saying, "It's already mine. I already am her. I'm just letting the physical rearrange itself." From this place of embodiment, you become receptive to infinite possibilities. You stop micromanaging how it has to come, and instead remain open to the path of least resistance—the path that may be far better than anything your mind could imagine.

Let's say you desire soul-aligned work that brings you deep fulfillment, financial freedom, and the flexibility to live life on your terms. You may assume that being an entrepreneur is the only path. But in your tunnel vision, you might miss another opportunity that delivers exactly what you want in a completely different form. That's why staying open is essential. When you're attached to the outcome

, you limit the flow. But when you align with the *essence*, you allow the universe to surprise you—in the best possible ways.

Energetic leadership is about embodying the vision, holding the vibration, trusting the process, and taking inspired aligned action. It's not passive. It's not wishful thinking. It's active surrender. Clear intention. And unwavering devotion to who you are becoming.

That's how you lead yourself. And when you do, life follows your lead.

The Vibration of Inevitability

There's a frequency that changes everything—not hope, not desire, not wishing—but *inevitability*. When you shift from "I hope it happens" to "It's already done," something profound clicks into place. You stop grasping. You stop second-guessing. You move differently. You breathe differently. You start showing up in the world with a quiet confidence that says, "Of course this is happening. Of course this is who I am." That is the vibration of inevitability.

Cultivating this frequency begins with the inner narrative. You stop questioning if you're worthy or if you're ready. You stop analyzing every delay as a sign of failure. Instead, you anchor into the knowing that the version of you who already has what you desire exists right now—and you are becoming her. You adopt the mindset that there is no Plan B. Not because you're forcing it, but because this vision is aligned with your soul's truth. And soul truth always finds a way.

To anchor this vibration into your body and energy field, practices become essential—not as effort or "doing," but as tools to help you *become*. One of the most powerful tools for this is **scripting**—writing from the perspective of your future self in present-tense detail, immersing yourself in the feelings, the identity, and the lived experience of the timeline you're now claiming. This practice, especially when done consistently, creates a neural and energetic imprint that begins to reshape your reality from the inside out.

Another potent technique comes from Neville Goddard: **SATS**—the State Akin To Sleep. This is a liminal state between waking and sleeping, where your conscious mind quiets and your subconscious becomes highly impressionable. In this deeply relaxed state, you can visualize scenes from your fulfilled desire—already lived, already embodied. You see it, feel it, breathe it as if it's your current reality. Because to the subconscious, there is no difference between what's imagined and what's real. And when the subconscious accepts something as real, life rearranges to make it so.

You can also amplify this frequency through my 90-Day **Soul Alchemist Manifestation Planner**, which was created to help you align with your desires energetically—not just with goals or tasks, but through conscious embodiment. Each prompt is designed to help you recalibrate your focus, clear energetic blocks, shift limiting narratives, and move through your day in full resonance with your vision. It becomes your daily devotion—an energetic alignment tool that reinforces the inevitability of your desires, every single day.

You can find the Manifestation Planner here:
(https://www.kaysanders.com/soul-alchemists-manifesting-planner

Another essential practice is the **Law of Assumption**, which teaches that if you want something, you must first assume it is already yours. This is not a mental trick—it's a shift in embodiment. You begin to speak, walk, act, and respond as the version of you who already has what they desire. It removes the question of *if* and replaces it with *when.* There's no more convincing or waiting. You become a living affirmation of the reality you've chosen.

For those ready to go even deeper, **Quantum Jumping** can support this frequency. This technique allows you to connect with a version of yourself who already lives the reality you want—whether that's the successful entrepreneur, the deeply fulfilled leader, the radiant version of you living in joy, wealth, and purpose. Through meditation or visualization, you merge with that version, adopt their energy, and embody their essence. It's a way of collapsing the gap between who you've been and who you're becoming.

Even something as simple as an **embodiment walk** can reinforce this shift. Go for a walk while holding the energy of your future self. Let your body language match her. Let your breathing, thoughts, and energy reflect her. Ten minutes a day of walking as her can be more powerful than hours of trying to "think positive."

You can also create a **future self altar**—a sacred space that reflects your embodied reality. Include symbols, objects, scents, or images that represent the life you're aligning with. This isn't about forcing a manifestation. It's about reinforcing your identity. Every time you see this space, your subconscious is reminded: *this is who I am now.*

And don't forget the foundational practices we've explored throughout this book—energetic clearing, nervous system regulation, emotional alchemy, and grounding into your truth. These are not random techniques—they're spiritual technologies. Each one contributes to your ability to hold the vibration of inevitability without collapsing under the pressure of the "not yet."

When you embody inevitability, your magnetism shifts. You no longer emit the frequency of "wanting" or "waiting," which can actually repel what you desire. Instead, you radiate the essence of "already done," which draws your desires to you like a magnet. Your field becomes clear, coherent, and powerful. Others feel your energy before you say a word. Opportunities begin to present themselves with less effort. The synchronicities increase. You start noticing how life mirrors your inner state with uncanny accuracy.

This is the true power of creative embodiment. You're not forcing. You're not hustling. You're aligning. You're becoming. And as you walk in this vibration, your outer world begins to take the shape of the inner certainty you've anchored. That's what makes the quantum leap possible—not more effort, but more alignment.

Dissolving the Illusion of Separation Between Now and the "One Day" Version of You

One of the greatest illusions that keeps you stuck in a loop of striving, waiting, and not-quite-there energy is the idea that your desired self, your future reality, your full embodiment — is "out there," somewhere in the distance. That someday, when you're more healed, more aligned, more confident, more successful... then you'll finally live the life you've been dreaming of.

But this separation is not real. It's a construct of the mind and the conditioning you've absorbed. It's the voice that says *"you're not ready yet,"* or *"it's not the right time,"* or *"once this thing happens, then you can step into it."* And yet, that future version of you already exists in the quantum. She's not waiting. She *is*. She's already whole, already clear, already living and breathing the reality you desire. And the only thing keeping you from her... is the illusion that she's separate from you.

The way to collapse that illusion is not by hustling harder or proving your worth — it's by *deciding* that the version of you who has it, lives it, feels it, embodies it... is already here. That you don't need to wait for your outer world to confirm it. You confirm it *first* with your energy, with your choices, with your presence.

This is what it means to walk as her, to speak as her, to make decisions as her — not someday, but now. Not when you feel 100%

certain, but when you choose to let your energy lead. Not when it's all mapped out, but when you claim it with your frequency.

The moment you stop chasing the future and *start being it*, your frequency shifts. That's when you stop living in a perpetual gap between now and "someday." That's when you collapse time. Because there's no more distance between you and the life you desire — you are the living embodiment of it, now. Not a performance. Not a trick. A choice. A frequency. A truth.

And the more you return to that truth — even when doubts arise, even when fear whispers that it's not safe to believe — the more solid your embodiment becomes. You stop leaking energy toward the "not yet" timeline, and instead anchor yourself into the now, where creation happens. This is where magic unfolds. This is where timelines bend. And this is where the soul alchemist within you finally rises — not someday, but today.

Living as a Conscious Embodiment of What You Desire

There comes a moment on this journey when the desire to *manifest* transforms into a devotion to *embody*. It's no longer about making vision boards, writing your goals 55 times in a row, or constantly thinking about what you want to call in. Those tools may have served you in the beginning. They helped shift your focus, open your imagination, and move energy—but they were never the point. The point was always to become the version of you who no longer *needs* to manifest in order to receive—because you already *are* the frequency of what you desire.

This is the essence of conscious embodiment. It's when your way of *being* is what activates your field. When you walk through life with the energetic posture of "it's already done." You don't have to try to convince the universe anymore. You're no longer performing, hoping, or proving. You're no longer in the energy of wanting. You've moved into the energy of becoming.

That shift—from doing manifestation techniques to *being* the embodiment—is where the real power lives. It's not that the practices are wrong or unnecessary. In fact, tools like scripting, SATS (State Akin to Sleep), or any of the other practices I have shared so far, are powerful gateways into alignment. They help regulate your nervous system, rewire your identity, and strengthen your energetic field. But at some point, they stop being something you *do* to get results—and they become sacred rituals that simply support who you already are.

Living this way doesn't mean you never have doubts or challenges. It means you meet those moments as the future version of you who already knows how to respond. You become anchored. Disciplined not by force, but by devotion. You choose to stay in resonance with your higher self, even when your reality hasn't caught up yet. You understand that your job isn't to chase the outcome—it's to hold the frequency and let life rise to meet you there.

This is where your magnetism becomes undeniable. Because you're no longer leaking energy through fear, impatience, or grasping. You're no longer trying to *get* something—you're allowing it to come *to you*, because you've already claimed it in your being. You've already become the one who receives. And that is an energetic signature the universe cannot ignore.

Conscious embodiment is a daily devotion. It's a moment-by-moment remembrance of who you truly are. It's trusting the deeper timeline of your soul and surrendering the timeline of your ego. It's no longer about needing proof—it's about choosing presence. You become the one who leads with energy. The one who moves with intention. The one who receives not by force, but by frequency.

And this changes everything.

Because when you live this way, you stop waiting for your future to arrive—you *become* it. You *live* it. You *radiate* it. Every step you take is infused with the essence of what you're calling in. And that is when reality has no choice but to rearrange itself around your embodiment.

This is the moment your desires are no longer outside of you.

They are you.

Closing Incantation - I Am the Living Embodiment of My Soul's Vision

As we come to the close of this chapter—and with it, the entire second part of this journey—you are no longer the same. You've remembered, reclaimed, and risen into deeper levels of embodiment. You've moved beyond techniques and tools and into the living frequency of your desires. This isn't just about manifesting outcomes anymore. It's about living as the one who no longer chases, who no longer doubts, who no longer waits.

Embodiment means you become the transmission of your vision. You live it, breathe it, speak it, and vibrate it—long before the evidence shows up in your external reality. This chapter wasn't meant to give you more to do, but rather to activate who you already are. The future is no longer a distant destination. It is a state of being you've now accessed, integrated, and begun to live.

Let this incantation be your anchor. Let it affirm your choice to walk forward no longer as the seeker, but as the embodiment. The one who has remembered that she was never waiting—only realigning.

Incantation

I now embody the essence of my highest timeline.
I no longer wait for the future—I walk as her now.
I release the illusion of delay, of not yet, of someday.
My energy speaks the truth of who I am becoming.
I align with the frequency of trust, clarity, and sovereignty.
Every cell in my body vibrates with the knowing: it is already done.
I dissolve resistance and open wide to receive.
I no longer need to prove, to chase, or to seek—
I simply choose to become.
In this moment, I claim my place as the living embodiment of my
soul's vision.

✧ Part IV: The Radiance — Becoming the Transmission ✧

"You no longer have to prove your light. You simply live it—fully, boldly, unapologetically. Who you are becomes the invitation, the activation, the spark that awakens something in others."

This final part is not about becoming more, doing more, or learning more. It is about the radiant expression of all that you've already remembered, reclaimed, and embodied. This is where your energy begins to speak louder than your words. Where your life becomes the living prayer. Where who you are *being* activates others without effort or intention—simply through presence.

You are no longer striving to heal or chasing your potential. You are now living it. Fully. Authentically. Unapologetically. This is the phase where embodiment becomes expression. Where devotion becomes leadership. Where soul alignment becomes the foundation for every creation, connection, and calling.

In this part of the journey, you stop searching for your purpose and realize—you *are* the purpose. Your soul work, your relationship with abundance, the way you lead, love, and serve—they are no longer external pursuits. They become the natural overflow of the frequency you carry. They *are* the evidence of your integration.

You don't need to push, prove, or perform. You simply become. The transmission moves through you—not because you're trying, but because you're aligned. You are the portal, the lighthouse, the sacred offering. This is the path of radiance—where your light is no longer hidden, and your presence alone opens the path for others to rise.

Chapter 19: Your Presence is the Message

The silent transmission of truth, embodiment, and impact

As you fully embody the truest, most authentic version of yourself, you become the message. Your frequency becomes the transmission that ripples outward, touching others in ways words never could. It is through your embodied presence that you uplift, activate, and inspire. When you are deeply rooted in your truth, there is a magnetic quality about you—a resonance that moves people, shifts energy, and opens new possibilities. You are no longer trying to become; you are.

You are the Soul Alchemist. You are the expression of your essence, your light, your knowing. And that radiance reaches others long before you speak, teach, or create. Your presence is what people feel. Your embodiment is what they respond to. In a world where so many are ungrounded, disconnected, and disoriented, your embodiment becomes the beacon that brings them home to themselves.

This is how you activate others: not by fixing them, convincing them, or trying to lead them somewhere they haven't asked to go, but by being so fully yourself that it stirs something within them. You become a living reminder of what's possible. Of authenticity. Of truth. Of freedom. And you do not have to start a business or share your message publicly for this to happen. If you feel called to, yes—you can step into a more visible role as a healer, mentor, guide, or teacher. But even without that, your presence alone is catalytic.

And if you do feel that inner nudge to share your message more boldly, the impact can be profound. You will help others remember their truth, return to their power, and rise in their own frequency. You may feel called to expand your current work, evolve your message, or serve in new ways. Or you may feel the pull to begin something completely new. Trust that when the time is right, the next step on your path will become unmistakably clear.

If you've been led to this book, and you are still reading now, I believe you will feel the truth of what I'm about to share. This is a message from my guides to you. Not for your logical mind, but for your soul. Let it activate you.

Channeled Message

"Beloved soul, you have arrived at your next destination of greater awakening and embodiment. Deep down you know there is a path you are meant to walk upon—a path that is least traveled by those not ready to embrace a higher path. But as you read these words, we wish to invite that inner knowing, that inner sense of trust, that your path is unfolding. You are already on the path to greater fulfillment and service—to yourself and to those you are here to support on their journey.

Do not fear, resist, or ignore the nudgings that have been present for some time. We understand that sometimes it is easier not to listen, not to pay attention—but through the words within these pages, you may have felt a stirring, an inner whisper that it's time to pay attention. It's time to stop hiding. It's time to embrace that which your soul came here to do, to be, to express.

So much is hidden beneath the surface of your awareness—and here we do not speak of the shadows, the limitations. We speak of your gifts, your powers, your essence, your knowing. So much is there for you to uncover, embrace, and fully embody.

The time to hide has come to an end. You have been activated through this book, through the words on these pages, and through this message we are sharing with you at this time. You have come here for a greater reason, and you have learned much through this book that we impressed onto Kay to write, to express, to share—because these words are potent, and they will assist you in your remembrance... remembering once again who you are deep within, hidden away—the essence of your divine self, the essence of your being.

Embrace that which lays dormant within you—now more easily accessible the more you embrace this work of embodiment. It's time to remember once again who you are—not the self you see in the mirror every day, but the you that resides deep within. Connect with that part. Let that authentic self, your soul self, lead you on your path. Because the path ahead is now opening up to you. It awaits your readiness—for you to claim your path, what your soul came here to do— and to embrace it all with an open heart, an open mind, and a readiness to stop hiding and instead be the light you came here to be.

Remember, beloved soul, the truth that is now available to you. The truth you are now ready to accept. The truth you are now ready to embody.

Be the light. Be the wayshower. Be the bridge that helps others find their way.

Blessed be, beloved soul. Blessed be."

***

I hope you feel these words stir something deep within you—a knowing, a remembering, a readiness. When you fully embrace who you are without holding back, that's when your inner light ignites. That's when you become the lighthouse.

And here I want to speak to that metaphor, because it matters. Especially if you feel called to start a business or share your message more publicly, you'll likely hear a lot about strategy, visibility, and how to "get out there." But I want you to remember the lighthouse. The lighthouse doesn't move. It doesn't chase ships. It stands steady, grounded in purpose. It shines its light unwaveringly so others can find their way.

This is your invitation. Be like the lighthouse. Let your light shine from a place of authenticity and alignment. You don't need to jump from one thing to the next, or chase visibility, or get swept up in the noise. Find what resonates. Follow the path that aligns with your soul. Then commit to that path with steady devotion.

Because it's not the strategy or the latest trend that magnetizes people to you—it's your essence. Your energy. Your presence. Energy precedes matter. And your energy speaks louder than any words ever could.

So focus there. Focus on your alignment. Focus on your embodiment. Because your presence *is* the message. And as we enter Part IV of this journey together, we will deepen into the quantum practices and energetic mastery that make you the magnet for everything your soul is here to receive and share.

Recognizing Your Quiet Power

You may not see yourself as anyone particularly special or impactful—but you'd be surprised just how powerful your presence already is. If you're here reading this, I know you've already done a great deal of inner work. You've likely been on your awakening journey for some time. And even just by making it to this part of the book, you've allowed your frequency to shift. You've explored the layers, looked at your patterns, and begun to reclaim parts of yourself that were once hidden or fragmented.

All of that inner work has changed you. It has elevated your field, deepened your essence, and amplified your energy in ways that may not be visible to you—but they are absolutely felt by others. You are already emanating a higher vibration than most of the people around you—your family, your friends, even strangers you cross paths with. And that alone makes you someone of energetic significance.

You leave an energetic footprint wherever you go. In every conversation. Every interaction. Every space you enter. You carry a presence that is different now—and people notice, even if they don't consciously understand why. And you didn't just stumble upon this book by accident. You were drawn here for a reason. My work tends to attract the trailblazers, the wayshowers, the energetic change-makers—the ones who don't just want to understand transformation but *become* the embodiment of it.

Yes, that includes you.

If you're still reading, then I want you to hear this clearly: you are not just someone with potential. You are already impacting the world through your beingness. Through your energy. Through your truth. Whether or not you have a platform, a title, or a public role, your frequency is affecting those around you—and beyond.

Maybe you've noticed that people naturally gravitate toward you. They ask for your perspective. They feel lighter after spending time with you. They feel seen, understood, heard. That's not random. It's a reflection of the frequency you hold. And that ripple effect goes much farther than you realize. Because when you uplift one person, that person goes back into their own life carrying that uplifted energy—and *they* begin to show up differently for their loved ones, their children, their co-workers. It spreads. You shift one moment, one heart—and that shift continues, quietly but powerfully, through every interaction they have.

That's energetic leadership. And you're already doing it.

Even if you don't have a business, a brand, or a platform, you're still transmitting energy in every moment. You're influencing others just by being yourself—*and especially* when you're grounded in your authenticity. You are the lighthouse, even if you're standing on a quiet shore right now. The world still feels your light.

Now, here's a deeper layer to this truth: You are a transmitter and receiver in every moment—what you hold, the quantum reflects.

You're not just putting energy out into the world—you're also tuning your frequency to what comes back to you. If you're holding lack, the quantum field mirrors that back. If you're holding unshakable self-worth, clarity, or joy—that too is amplified and returned. You're always co-creating through resonance. The quantum doesn't respond to words or wishes—it responds to the *embodied signal* you broadcast.

This is why energy work, inner alignment, and emotional regulation matter so much. They're not just self-help practices. They're tools for calibrating your field so that your entire life can rise to meet the frequency of who you truly are.

And if you're ready to take this even further, we'll go deeper into quantum co-creation practices in the final chapters of this book—so you can begin working with the quantum field not just passively, but intentionally, as the energetic leader you already are.

Let this truth land in your body: *You are already impacting the world. The only question now is—what will you choose to hold, to embody, to transmit next?*

The Power of Alignment Over Strategy

You've heard me mention aligned action many times before—because in the end, it's not just about *what* you do, but how energetically aligned you are with the strategies you choose, the steps you take, and the way you show up. As a Soul Alchemist, leadership doesn't begin with a to-do list. It begins with your soul leading the way.

Soul-aligned leadership is about only doing what you *feel* deeply called to do—regardless of what anyone else says you *should* do. Others may give you advice, they may have well-meaning suggestions, or they might even try to convince you that their way is the "right" way. But the truth is, no one knows what's truly right for you—except your soul. And as a Soul Alchemist, you've already built a strong connection with your soul. That's who you follow now. Not the fear-based voices. Not the noise of the world. Not the pressure to do more or be more. Just soul.

So if something doesn't resonate—don't do it. If it feels off, misaligned, or heavy—trust that and let it go. Do the things that feel joyful, easeful, flowing. That's your guidance system.

Now, I'll be honest—sometimes even aligned strategies include tasks you may not particularly love. For example, I love recording my videos. That's where I shine. But editing them? Not my favorite. Even though I do that kind of work for my marketing clients, when it comes to my own videos, editing feels tedious and time-consuming. And yet, for now, I still edit them myself. Why? Because the *overall* strategy—the YouTube channel, the content, the message—is deeply aligned. Eventually, I'll outsource that part. But until then, I continue, knowing that I'm still in alignment with the greater vision.

Compare that to something that's completely out of alignment for me—like social media. I've tried it before. I used to force myself to post all the time. But I hated it. It felt loud and attention-seeking, like I had to shout "Look at me!" to be seen. That's not how I'm meant to show up. That's not my energy. It's not how I magnetize my audience.

These days, I focus on what's aligned for me: my YouTube channel, my email list, my live challenges, running ads. All of these allow me to show up like a lighthouse—steady, grounded, radiant. I don't run around trying to be seen. I stand in my light, and those who are meant to find me will.

And even if you're not running a business or planning to, this still applies. Where and how you invest your energy matters. Your inner alignment creates coherence, and coherence is what magnetizes everything—opportunities, connections, resources, abundance, joy. The outer world responds to your state of being.

So don't be the frantic lighthouse running around trying to find the right spot. Be the steady one. Energetically aligned. Clear. Radiant. That's how you draw what you desire toward you.

Now let's talk about "figuring out the how"—because this is where so many people get stuck. And here's the truth: the how is not your job. Your job is alignment. Your job is coherence. Your job is to become the version of you who already has what you want—and to move through the world *as that version.*

That means doing the inner work to raise your frequency. That means aligning your thoughts, emotions, and energy with the essence of your desires. That means taking action from a place of inspiration and soul nudges—not from fear, lack, or pressure.

When you are energetically aligned, the "how" reveals itself. You'll get the nudge to reach out to someone, to say yes to an opportunity, to follow an unexpected idea. The steps will unfold naturally, and you'll *know* when it's right. You won't have to force or strategize your way into the next level—it will come through the field, as a reflection of who you've become.

When you try to "figure out the how" from a place of mental pressure or survival patterns, you often end up spinning. You overthink. You chase. You fall into actions that are out of alignment because they stem from fear or impatience. And then you wonder why it's not working.

But you know better now. You've already learned how to recognize when your energy is off. You've already practiced shifting back into alignment. You've already released the old programs and patterns that were keeping you in doubt and scarcity. So now, it's time to walk the path of the Soul Alchemist more fully than ever before.

Trust that energy always precedes matter. Trust that if you stay aligned, embodied, and coherent with the version of you who already has what you desire—then that reality must reflect itself in your external world. It's inevitable. It's just a matter of divine timing and how long it takes the outer world to catch up to your inner shift.

So don't waste time figuring out how. Just keep becoming the *who*. Keep choosing the frequency. Keep honoring what feels aligned. And let the rest unfold.

Leading from Soul, Not Ego

Let's talk about what it truly means to lead from the soul. A soul-led leader doesn't lead to be admired, followed, or praised. They don't need to convince anyone of their worth, expertise, or importance. They don't chase success, applause, or validation. Instead, they lead from depth. From stillness. From inner knowing. They lead because they *can't not*—because it would go against their nature not to share what's flowing through them.

Soul-led leadership is marked by certain unmistakable qualities—humility, devotion, authenticity, and trust.

Humility doesn't mean shrinking or playing small. It means being deeply rooted in the understanding that you are a vessel, not the source. It's the quiet confidence of knowing who you are *without* needing to prove it. You walk into a room and your energy speaks before you do—not because you planned it that way, but because you are anchored in truth.

Devotion is the heartbeat of your leadership. It's not about grind or hustle—it's about showing up for what matters most, day after day. It's a love that runs deeper than motivation. You're devoted to truth. To the people you serve. To the unfolding of your soul's work. You're not here to check off boxes—you're here to midwife transformation.

And authenticity—it's your frequency. It's not something you try to do; it's something you *are*. When you lead from soul, there are no masks. You don't package yourself to be palatable. You allow your truth to be seen, even when it's raw. Even when it's tender. You trust that your presence is enough, and that your unique energetic signature is exactly what the people you're meant to serve need to feel.

Now let's explore one of the most powerful—and most challenging—facets of soul-aligned leadership: surrender.

We've touched on surrender earlier in this book, but it deserves its own deeper look. Because surrender is at the very core of conscious creation—and it's often the very thing the ego resists the most.

Surrender means letting go and trusting, without a doubt, that what you desire is already on its way. It means releasing the grip of control. It means resisting the urge to micromanage the Universe, or to hustle and force things into existence just because your current reality isn't lining up fast enough.

Surrender asks you to *stay in alignment and stay in trust*—even when everything around you tells a different story. Your ego will try to convince you it's not working. It will shout that you need to do more, figure it out, work harder, and make it happen. But true surrender means you set down the busy chatter and drop back into your heart. You stay in presence. You stay open. You allow the quantum field and divine timing to bring things to fruition in ways your mind could never orchestrate.

Here's a metaphor I love: imagine going to a restaurant. You browse the menu, decide what you want, and place your order with the waiter. Once you've given your order, you don't panic. You don't go back to the kitchen to make sure the chef is doing it right. You don't second-guess your choice every five seconds. You trust your food is being prepared. You might even enjoy the wait, sip a drink, connect with the people around you. That's surrender.

You handed over your desire, and now you wait with trust, knowing your order is being fulfilled. That's how creation works. And yes, sometimes it takes longer than you'd hoped. Sometimes it looks like nothing is happening. But if you stay open, grounded, and faithful— it arrives.

Mastering the essence of surrender is what makes you a **clear vessel** for higher work. Because it's in surrender that you become the bridge. The channel. The messenger.

When we talk about being of service at a higher level—whether that's offering healing, channeling, teaching, or simply holding space—it's through surrender that you receive the messages, the codes, the wisdom. You open yourself to something greater than your mind can comprehend. And that only happens when you stop trying to control the outcome and start trusting the process.

This book you're reading is a living example of surrender. So much of what I've written has been channeled, guided, or inspired by a force far greater than myself. Yes, it's written in my voice. Yes, my stories are here. But I surrendered to what wanted to come through. I listened. I trusted. I followed the guidance. Even when it didn't make logical sense.

And that's what it means to lead from soul. To be a vessel. To be open. To surrender your own agenda so that something greater can move through you. You don't need to have all the answers. You don't need to plan it all out. You simply need to surrender who you *thought* you were, so you can become who you've always been underneath the conditioning, the striving, the noise.

You let go of the ego's agenda and make space for your soul to lead. You dissolve the old stories and make room for truth. You open your hands and say: "Use me. Guide me. Move through me." That is the path of the Soul Alchemist. That is how you become the vessel—not just for your desires, but for the greater work your soul came here to do.

Releasing the Pressure to Prove or Perform

On your path, there may be times when you feel the need to do more, learn more, or somehow become more before you allow yourself to lead. You might believe you need another certification, another program, another book, another healing before you're "ready." But let me remind you of something essential: you already have everything you need within you. You already carry the wisdom, the gifts, and the frequency that others are waiting for. You don't have to become someone else to lead—you just have to remember who you are and allow that to be enough.

This is what soul leadership truly means. It's not about standing on a stage or launching a massive movement—though it might look like that for some. Soul leadership is about leading yourself first, about showing up in alignment with your own truth and letting that embodied truth ripple out into the world. It's about trusting your energy more than your resume. It's about how you live, how you show up, how you serve—not because you're trying to be impressive, but because you're simply being yourself, anchored in integrity and essence.

Often, the drive for more is really a disguise for something deeper— a hidden fear that you're not enough. That fear might stem from old stories of unworthiness, rejection, or not being capable. But sometimes, it's even subtler than that. You may actually fear what will happen if you do succeed. Success brings consequences, and while some of them are beautiful—abundance, recognition, fulfillment—others can feel more confronting. What if your life changes? What if you outgrow people close to you? What if others judge you, ask more from you, or resent your expansion?

These inner fears can quietly hold you back from fully stepping in. But here's the thing: once you bring awareness to them, you have the power to clear them. You know the tools. You know the energetics. And you know the truth. Any fear, belief, or illusion that says you're not ready, not enough, or not allowed to shine—can now be cleared. Use the clearing tools you've already learned. Say it with me: *"I now clear and transmute this fear, this pressure, this belief that I am not enough, across all times, space, reality, lifetimes, and dimensions. I dissolve it into the nothingness it came from."*

Because that's where it belongs—in the nothingness.

These fears are often what keep you in the energy of doing instead of being. Performing instead of embodying. When you think you need to prove something, you dilute your essence. But when you trust that your presence is enough, your energy becomes a transmission. You stop striving and start radiating. You stop trying to be "more" and realize that your authenticity is the most powerful force you carry.

You don't need to have your life all figured out to lead. I certainly don't. And honestly, none of us ever will—because we're here to grow, not to perfect ourselves. If you waited until everything in your life was tidy and complete, you'd never show up. And the people you're meant to serve would miss out on your light. You are already qualified. Not because of what you've done, but because of who you are. And if you're a few steps ahead of those you're meant to guide, that's all that's required. You continue evolving, and with every step, you bring others along with you.

Remember, many people are still asleep. Others are just beginning to wake up. And they need someone like you—someone real, someone grounded, someone who walks their talk and leads with heart. Someone who doesn't pretend to have it all together but shows up anyway, with love and truth and devotion.

So let go of the idea that you're not ready. Let go of the belief that you need to do more or be more. Your essence is already potent. Your light is already making a difference. You are already transmitting something sacred.

As the title of this chapter reminds you: *Your presence is the message.* Not your accomplishments, not your strategies, not your perfection. It's your essence—your vibrational signature—that speaks louder than anything you could ever say or do. So let yourself be seen. Let yourself be felt. Let yourself lead.

Becoming the Living Transmission

As I just mentioned, your presence—your energy—is the message. It's not about what you do, what you create, or what you say on the surface. And yet, every one of those expressions can become a vehicle for your essence. Your creations, your words, your offerings—they can carry your energetic signature when they are birthed from a place of inner alignment and truth.

Let's say you feel called to write a book, build a course, share an idea, or start a business. When that impulse doesn't come from the mind trying to figure out what will sell, impress, or be accepted—but instead arises from an inner knowing, a sacred download, or a soul nudge—what you create carries your energetic imprint. That creation becomes a transmission. Your frequency, your light codes, your soul essence move through the thing you've created. That's what makes it magnetic. That's what makes it alive.

This book, for example, holds my essence. Not just because I channeled many of the words within it, but because as I'm writing these words, I'm deeply connected to Source. I'm not just writing with my intellect—I'm transmitting my energy. These words are not meant to fill your mind, they are meant to touch your soul. You may not know me personally, but you can feel me. Because I'm here with you, in the energy that lives between the lines.

That is what it means to infuse your work with soul. That is what it means to be the transmission.

And this doesn't only apply to tangible creations like books, courses, or offerings. It happens in everyday moments. It happens in conversations, eye contact, a listening ear. You don't need a business, a platform, or a grand mission to live as the transmission. Even in something as simple as a conversation, your essence speaks. Your presence becomes a gift. The way you listen, the way you hold space, the way you allow someone to feel safe, seen, and honored—*that* is the work. That is your radiance.

We live in a world that's often distracted and disconnected. Most people aren't fully present. They're half-listening, multitasking, worrying about the next thing. So imagine the impact it has when someone like you chooses to *be here*—to bring their whole self into a moment. That kind of presence is rare. And because it's rare, it's potent. When you offer that depth of presence, people feel it in their nervous system. They soften. They open. They remember something sacred.

So understand this: your energetic signature isn't confined to what you do—it emanates from who you are. Every space you enter, every word you speak, every action you take becomes an opportunity to transmit the truth of your soul.

And when you show up as the truest, most authentic version of yourself, you are honoring the sacredness of this work. You are saying yes to the divine intelligence that chose to express through *you*. You're not trying to be what others expect. You're not diluting or performing. You are letting the fullness of your essence be seen, felt, and experienced.

This is one of the highest forms of devotion—to be faithful to your truth in a world that constantly invites you to become someone else. To lead, to serve, and to love from your core—not because it's strategic, but because it's sacred.

When you live in this way, your life becomes the message. You don't need to explain yourself. You don't need to convince anyone. Your energy does the talking. Your alignment does the work. Your presence *is* the activation. And that is what it truly means to become a living transmission of your purpose.

Closing Incantation — You Are the Message

Your impact was never meant to come from trying harder, doing more, or striving to be something you're not. True leadership doesn't arise from pressure or performance—it emanates from your presence. The more you allow yourself to be fully seen in your truth, the more your energy becomes the activation. You don't need to force your way forward or craft a perfect message. When you're anchored in your soul and aligned with your essence, your frequency does the speaking for you.

This is what it means to lead from within. It's not about proving your worth or perfecting your path—it's about showing up with devotion, authenticity, and trust in the resonance you naturally hold. Because who you are, in your most honest and embodied expression, is what touches others the most.

Let the following words land in your body as an energetic recalibration—a remembrance of the sacred power of simply being yourself.

Incantation:

I now release the need to prove, to push, or to perform.
I no longer chase impact—I *become* it.
I lead with presence, not pressure.
I share my essence freely, trusting it is enough.
I dissolve all distortions, fears, and false expectations
into the nothingness they came from.
I allow my being to speak louder than my words.
I allow my frequency to pave the way.
I remember that my energy leads—
and that who I am is the message.
So it is.

Chapter 20: Purpose Without Pressure

Living your soul mission without burnout or over-efforting

L et's dive into purpose—purposeful living, living out your soul's higher calling of being of service. So many seek to understand and figure out their life's purpose, wondering what they're here to do. And that nudge often begins somewhere along your spiritual awakening journey. It's your soul's way of whispering that something more is available to you, that you didn't come here just to survive—you came to serve. So you begin your search. You're guided to take different courses, read books, learn modalities, and all of these become catalysts for awakening your higher calling.

Because your soul came here with a mission. To be of service. To be a guide, a teacher, a lighthouse, a channel, a healer. You came to be the change, to walk the path that uplifts not only you but those around you.

But what often happens on the journey is that, somewhere along the way, that sacred mission turns into striving. It becomes heavy. It shifts from inspired service into self-sacrifice. Somewhere along the path, you start to believe that living your purpose means giving all of yourself away. That in order to help others, you must suffer. That to stay spiritual, you must charge less—or not at all.

Let me be clear: that is a distortion. That is conditioning. That is not truth.

You are meant to be compensated for your work, your energy, your transmission, and your presence. Because the more money you make, the more impact you can create. The more resourced you are, the more you can give back, expand, and reach people in bigger ways. It's not about greed—it's about energetic reciprocity. It's about sustainability. It's about embodying what you teach.

You are here to make a big impact. Not a small one. Not a "just-get-by" one. Big. Transformational. World-changing. And that doesn't happen through martyrdom or depletion. It happens through energetic alignment and the willingness to honor what you're really here to do—without apologizing for it.

Now let's talk about the energy of "should."

"Should" is what pulls you out of alignment. It's what convinces you that the way everyone else is doing it must be the only way. That you need to post more. Be more visible. Hustle harder. Offer what's popular—even if it drains you.

This is how purpose becomes pressure. And pressure disconnects you from the soul of your mission.

Your soul's mission was never meant to feel like a job. It's meant to feel like joy. It's meant to fill you up as much as it uplifts others. And when you move into a space of constant doing—always working, fixing, launching, striving—you lose the essence of what actually makes your work powerful: your light.

Believe me, I know. I lived it.

There was a time when I started to feel negatively toward my spiritual business. I had done all the "right" things. Worked the long hours. Tried to make it happen. But the results never matched the effort. And I was exhausted. Frustrated. Disillusioned. I thought maybe it wasn't meant to be.

But what was really happening is that I was out of alignment. I was still doing what I thought I *should* do. Holding onto outdated offers. Avoiding live events because I was afraid of being seen unfiltered. Pushing offers I didn't even enjoy because they used to work—but no longer resonated.

And of course it didn't work.

Because your soul's mission can't thrive in a template that no longer fits. It needs space. It needs freedom. It needs *you*—the real you.

As soon as I listened, everything changed. I let go of the long-term coaching packages that no longer felt aligned. I realized I'm not here to hand-hold—I'm here to activate. I'm here to go deep, shift the energy, speak the truth, and allow transformation to happen in just a few potent sessions. That's how I work best. That's how my mission expresses through me now.

And that's what I mean when I say: when you don't let your soul's mission work *through* you, you start to lose parts of yourself. You become disconnected. Burnt out. Bitter. Resentful. But when you surrender to the way your soul wants to create, express, and serve—you become a channel for something far greater. You open to soul-led creation. You follow the nudges. You stop trying to control or plan every detail. And from that place, the work that's meant to come through you flows with ease.

This book is that for me. It's not coming from me—it's being expressed *through* me. That's what it means to live your soul's mission.

It's no longer something you do. It's something you *are*. And when you *are* your mission, everything you touch carries its essence. Your words. Your energy. Your presence. Your life becomes the embodiment of your highest calling.

"You don't live your mission. You *are* your mission."

Trusting That Your Soul Work Doesn't Require Burnout to Be Worthy

There's an outdated paradigm that tells us we have to work hard to be worthy. That value is only earned through effort, that success must be paid for in sweat, struggle, and sacrifice. But let's be honest—that's an illusion. A deeply ingrained societal script designed to keep people chasing worth, hustling for validation, and believing that the harder it is, the more it must be worth.

As a Soul Alchemist, you are here to move beyond those distortions. You're here to embody a new paradigm. One where ease, joy, and alignment *are* the path. Where you no longer measure your value by how exhausted you are, how much you've given away, or how long your to-do list is. Struggle is not a badge of honor. Hustle is not a virtue. Burnout is not proof of purpose.

The old system taught us that sacrifice equals significance. That unless you're working ten hours a day, barely resting, constantly proving yourself, you're not doing enough. But that belief is rooted in fear and control. It's based on systems that benefit from your self-abandonment. That profit from your disconnection. That thrive when you forget your true power.

But what if you remembered? What if you remembered that your energy is more powerful than your effort?

Have you ever heard the phrase "work smarter, not harder"? Working smarter doesn't mean manipulating outcomes or cutting corners. It means working in alignment. It means letting your soul lead instead of your schedule. Because when you do what's aligned—what's *meant* for you—it naturally carries more potency, more magnetism, and more impact. One aligned hour in soul resonance will always outperform ten hours of busy work done from pressure and expectation.

So I invite you to consider: What would it feel like to allow ease, joy, and alignment to guide your mission? What would your day look like if, instead of waking up to a long list of things you *should* do, you tuned into your soul and asked, "What am I being called to do today? What feels light, expansive, and alive within me?"

Maybe the guidance that day is to rest. To pause. To meditate. To walk in nature. Or to finish a project you shelved long ago. Or maybe you feel the pull to start something entirely new—a book, a course, an offering you never planned but now feel burning within your chest. Your job isn't to question the guidance. Your job is to *listen*—and trust that what comes through is aligned not just for you, but for those you're meant to serve.

And yes, I know what you might be thinking: "But what about all the things I have to do? I can't just ignore them." But the truth is, yes—you *can*. When the guidance is clear and true, the universe rearranges itself to support you. I've seen it happen again and again.

This book is one of those examples. On June 24th—the day Saturn moved into Aries—I felt this deep, undeniable stirring. Something wanted to come through. I didn't know what at first, but I could feel it building. So I tuned in. I listened. And soon the message came clearly: I was meant to write this book.

The very next day, I started. And as I committed to it, something incredible happened. My normally busy schedule—client calls, agency projects, all of it—suddenly cleared. That week, there were no calls. No urgent requests. It was as if a higher power created space for me to write. So I did. I wrote and wrote. Within a week, I had completed nearly 75% of the book. The following week? Same thing—my calendar remained miraculously open. No emergencies. No interruptions. My clients had nothing pressing. And I was able to finish the book.

That's what soul alignment looks like. When you prioritize what's truly aligned—when you surrender to the expression that wants to move through you—life responds. The field adjusts. Circumstances shift. Time opens. Resources arrive.

This is the magic that happens when you stop hustling and start *listening*. When you stop pushing and start *being*. This is the path of the Soul Alchemist. Not to grind your way to purpose. Not to sacrifice yourself on the altar of impact. But to become the living embodiment of your mission—to let it move through you with grace and coherence.

Because when you act from soul coherence, the field organizes itself around your resonance.

No more struggle. No more proving. No more waiting for permission to rest, to realign, or to choose a different way. You don't need to burn out to be worthy of your soul's work. You already are. And when you let that be enough—when you trust that your presence, your frequency, your light is already doing the work—you create from a place of truth. You become a powerful force not because you're doing more, but because you're doing what *matters most*. That's when your work becomes unstoppable. That's when you *are* your mission.

Creating from Devotion, Not Pressure

When you allow your mission to flow through you rather than trying to force it into form, you begin to experience what I call *soul-led creation*. This is not about executing a plan, hitting milestones, or checking off boxes to prove that you're doing something meaningful.

Soul-led creation is born from presence. It arises not from your mind's timeline, but from your soul's flow. It's intuitive, fluid, and deeply alive.

The energy behind your creations is everything. You can do the same exact thing—launch a program, write a book, share a message—but if one is done from pressure, obligation, or fear of falling behind, and the other is born from devotion, the difference in frequency is undeniable. Devotion carries a vibration of sacredness. It is not rushed. It is not reactive. It comes from a willingness to serve the highest—not just your own ego, but the greater unfolding of consciousness.

When you create from devotion, you're no longer trying to make things happen. You're not chasing timelines or manipulating outcomes. You're responding to the pulse of something greater moving through you. This kind of creation requires trust. It asks you to listen deeply and act only when the energy is ripe—when the nudge is clear, when the moment is alive with possibility. And when you do act, it feels like a blessing. Not a burden. Not a chore. But an offering.

Devotion transforms the entire creative process. Instead of asking, "What should I create to get a result?" you begin to ask, "What is longing to be expressed through me?" And from that question, a sacred dialogue opens between you and your higher self. Sometimes the answer comes as a whisper. Sometimes as an ache. Sometimes it arrives fully formed in a flash of inspiration. But however it comes, you know it by the way it lands in your body. It carries a certain frequency—a resonance that says *this is true*.

And here's the thing: soul-led creation often doesn't make logical sense. It might not be what your audience expects. It might not be what the algorithm rewards. But it's what your soul needs to bring into form. And when you honor that, you're honoring the divine unfolding of your path. You're saying yes to being a vessel. You're saying yes to being used for something greater.

This book, again, is a living example of that. I didn't write it because I thought it would be a strategic move or the right "next step" in my business. I wrote it because I *had* to. It moved through me with a force I couldn't ignore. It didn't come from pressure. It came from purity. From alignment. From devotion to the path I'm here to walk—and the souls I'm here to serve.

So ask yourself: What wants to move through me? What have I been silencing because it doesn't fit the mold? What creations have I delayed because I couldn't justify them logically?

Let those questions linger. Let them stir something deeper. Because when you create from devotion, you stop performing and start transmitting. You stop chasing results and start becoming the frequency of what you're here to embody. That's when your work becomes medicine—not just for others, but for you too.

Your Essence Is the Impact

We all have our own unique energetic signature that carries farther and wider than we can see. As I mentioned earlier, energy precedes matter—and your energetic signature speaks a thousand times louder and clearer than any word you say or any action you take. People can feel your energy. They can feel your authenticity. And they can also feel when there's a disconnect—when something feels off, even if they can't explain why.

This is why alignment is so key. When you are in alignment, you emanate a coherent, clear, and aligned frequency. You become magnetic. But when you're misaligned—when you're not fully in your power or not embodying the truth of who you are—there's friction in your field. A subtle dissonance. An energetic fog that clouds your presence. And the thing is, this dissonance doesn't go unnoticed. Even strangers online—people who come across your content, your words, or your offers—can feel it. They may not know consciously why they feel turned away or confused, but they will sense the lack of resonance.

For the longest time, I wondered why it felt so hard to grow my YouTube channel. I was proud of the videos I created. I knew I was delivering powerful content and speaking from the heart. And yet... the traction wasn't there. The growth felt stalled. And that's because, energetically, I was still holding back. I wasn't fully in my power. I wasn't fully embodying my mission. I was still doubting myself. I felt like an imposter at times. I questioned whether I was really someone who could reach hundreds, let alone thousands. And my energetic signature reflected that. There was friction in my field—and it subtly repelled the very people I was trying to attract.

It wasn't until I owned my path—until I stopped *trying* to be my mission and started *being* it—that things began to shift. The moment I embraced all of who I am and allowed myself to show up fully, unapologetically, and authentically, my energy shifted. My videos began to reach more people. My channel started to grow again. Not because of a new strategy—but because I had become aligned.

Your essence is in direct correlation with the impact you're here to make. The more you embody your authentic self, the more you embody your soul mission. And when you do that, your impact expands—naturally, effortlessly, and often exponentially. You don't have to push. You don't have to chase. You simply have to become more of yourself. That's it.

Let that land for a moment: *Your only job is to become more of who you truly are.*

The more you allow your true self to shine—your energy, your presence, your essence—the more powerful your ripple becomes. And you don't have to do anything grand to make an impact. Every interaction becomes sacred. Every offering becomes a transmission.

Every conversation becomes a portal for transformation—not because you're trying to make it so, but because you *are* the transmission.

There is no need to force. No need to prove. No need to mimic someone else's path. The more you embody your unique energetic blueprint, the more the field around you organizes itself to reflect that coherence. And as I said earlier, energy doesn't lie.

Your essence *is* the message. Your frequency *is* the impact. And your alignment is what activates the world around you.

Divine Timing and the Flow of Your Soul

One of the most powerful shifts you can make on your journey is learning to align with divine timing rather than trying to outrun it. This isn't about sitting back and waiting passively—it's about leaning into trust. It's about attuning to the deeper flow of your soul and following the breadcrumbs it lays out for you one moment at a time.

So often, we've been conditioned to believe that more effort equals more results. That we have to push harder, plan better, hustle more, and stay one step ahead of the curve. But what if that drive to constantly stay ahead is actually pulling you out of alignment? What if it's creating resistance in your field and blocking the very support, flow, and clarity you're calling in?

There is a different way. A way that doesn't ask you to abandon structure or discipline—but invites you to lead with resonance instead of rigidity. It's the way of inspired action. The kind of action that bubbles up from within. That arrives through a whisper, a nudge, a sudden spark that says, *"Do this now."*

Inspired action doesn't come from your mind. It doesn't come from a color-coded content calendar or a perfectly mapped business strategy. It comes from your soul. And when you learn to trust those nudges—to pause, to listen, and then to follow through—that's when the magic begins to unfold.

You've already experienced this. Think back to the times when you followed a feeling rather than a formula—when you acted on intuition rather than obligation. Chances are, things flowed with more ease. The right people showed up. The doors opened. The synchronicities aligned.

That's not a coincidence. That's coherence.

When you act from soul coherence, the field organizes itself around your resonance.

But to access this kind of alignment, you have to slow down. You have to stop grasping. You have to let go of the need to control the timeline and instead surrender into the flow of your becoming. Because divine timing isn't something you can force—it's something you meet with your presence, your trust, and your willingness to let the unfolding happen through you.

And when you do? You begin to feel supported in a way you never have before. You start to notice the subtle alignments, the unexplainable grace, the sense that you're not walking alone. It's as if the entire universe is conspiring to move with you—not because you pushed, but because you aligned.

This is how soul work flows. Not through stress, striving, or force—but through deep inner listening, energetic alignment, and unwavering trust in the unfolding.

You don't have to chase what's already destined. You simply have to become the version of you who is ready to receive it.

Let the Field Rise to Meet You

Soul coherence is the inner alignment that happens when your heart, mind, body, and energy are all moving in the same direction. It's not about perfection or control—it's about harmony. A state where your inner world is no longer fighting against itself, but working as one clear frequency.

This kind of coherence is magnetic. It doesn't just feel good inside—it reshapes how life meets you. When you're in soul coherence, you stop trying to make things happen. You're no longer operating from fear, lack, or misalignment. You're attuned to your higher self. Your energy becomes an organizing principle.

When you act from soul coherence, the field organizes itself around your resonance. That's not just a beautiful phrase. It's how the quantum works. The field doesn't respond to effort or want—it responds to frequency. And when your frequency is clear, aligned, and rooted in truth, everything that matches it begins to find its way to you. You don't have to manipulate timelines. You don't have to exhaust yourself. You don't have to prove anything. Your energy does the heavy lifting.

This is where you stop chasing and start embodying. You stop trying to become and start *being*. The version of you who already lives the reality you desire—who already serves from overflow, who already experiences the impact, the abundance, the ease—is not separate from you. You become her by collapsing the gap and acting from soul coherence now.

And this coherence isn't just for your benefit. It ripples out. It shapes your relationships, your offerings, your presence, your legacy. It's what makes your soul work sustainable. Because you're not creating from depletion or desperation—you're creating from overflow.

You are the vessel, not the source. Your only job is to keep the vessel clear, to stay in integrity with your frequency, and to trust that everything you're meant to impact will feel your signal and find its way to you.

So what if, instead of overworking or over-planning, you simply chose to be the frequency of what you're calling in? What if you let the field rise to meet you, rather than trying to outrun it?

That's the invitation of soul coherence: Let your being lead. Let your frequency speak. Let your aligned energy rearrange reality on your behalf. Because it will.

Closing Incantation - Your Presence Is the Path

Your purpose was never meant to feel like a burden. The soul doesn't demand burnout, sacrifice, or striving to prove its worth. It invites you into deeper alignment, into communion with what already lives within you. You came here not to hustle your way into fulfillment, but to *become* the embodiment of your soul's mission—naturally, powerfully, and without pressure.

When you choose coherence over chaos, devotion over forcing, and embodiment over performance, the path unfolds in ways the mind could never orchestrate. This is not about escaping responsibility—it's about stepping into divine responsibility. The kind that honors your energy, your joy, and your natural rhythm as sacred. You don't have to make things happen when you're in resonance. Your field does the work. Life reorganizes itself around your alignment.

Let this closing incantation bring you back into that knowing. Let it anchor you in the remembrance that your very being is already enough—and from that place, everything flows.

Incantation:

I release the weight of pressure, the illusion of proving.
I no longer hustle for my worth or force my mission into form.
I honor my inner guidance above outside noise.
I trust in divine timing and sacred alignment.
I choose devotion over urgency, coherence over chaos.
I dissolve all distorted patterns of striving and sacrifice
into the nothingness they came from.
I now allow my presence to lead.
I now allow my purpose to unfold through me.
I am the frequency of impact.
I am the living expression of my soul's mission.
So it is.

Chapter 21: Wealth as an Energetic Expression

Receiving, holding, and growing money as a reflection of your frequency

When we talk about wealth, this is often a topic that's frowned upon in many spiritual circles. Wealth is still seen by some as something "not spiritual," something indulgent, ego-driven, or even corrupt. But that narrative is built on centuries of distortion and disempowerment. The truth is—wealth goes far beyond numbers, goals, or external status. Wealth is an energetic expression. It's a reflection of who you are being, what you believe you deserve, and how much radiance your system can hold without collapsing.

You can be wealthy without having millions in the bank. True wealth is not a number, it's an essence you embody. You can feel wealthy right now—exactly as you are—because wealth is a frequency, a state of being, a felt sense of sufficiency and expansion that radiates from the inside out.

The same applies to abundance. So many people chase after abundance, prosperity, and success as if they're distant destinations they have to earn their way toward. But none of these are things you *get* from the outside. They are states you *embody* from within. You become a match for them not through striving, but through energetic alignment.

I want to invite you to pause and really feel into this: What does wealth, abundance, and prosperity mean to you—not on a surface level, but on a soul level?

Go beyond the material things. Not the house, the car, or the money in your account. What do these those things represent? What do they represent? Usually, it's something much deeper—freedom, safety, ease, joy, possibility.

When you say you want more money, it's not really the money you want—it's what the money gives you. More choices. A sense of security. The freedom to do what you want, when you want, without fear or limitation. Money can create space. It can open doors. It can bring a sense of stability and support. But it's not the money itself— it's the *experience* you believe money will create for you.

The same is true in love. Maybe you say you want a partner because you're tired of being alone. But it's not just the person—it's the feeling you long for. To feel supported, seen, loved, and no longer have to do it all alone. To feel joy and connection and belonging. That's the true desire.

And it's the same with success. Maybe you want to be a thriving spiritual entrepreneur, impacting lives around the world. But again, it's not just the success—it's the *feeling* of living in alignment with your purpose. Of being recognized for your gifts. Of feeling deeply fulfilled because what you do matters. And yes, of having the freedom to shape your life and schedule in a way that nourishes your soul. To create abundance on your terms.

In every case—it's never the thing. It's the essence. The feeling. The energy it awakens within you.

So if something outside of you can create a feeling *within* you, then the reverse is also true. When you consciously activate that feeling first—when you become the frequency—you begin to draw that experience into your life. This is the law of reversibility. This is conscious creation in action.

You don't need to wait for a certain income to feel wealthy. You can feel wealthy now. You can practice holding the frequency of sufficiency, of freedom, of ease—whatever it is for you. You decide what wealth means to *you*, and then you embody that essence. That's soul alchemy in motion. You become the radiance you once thought you had to chase.

And when you do that, you shift your magnetism. You're no longer trying to get something to prove your worth. You're simply radiating it. Receiving becomes natural. Holding becomes sustainable. Expansion becomes inevitable.

But to truly step into that space, we must also become aware of the inherited beliefs we're still carrying around money, sacrifice, and proving. These subconscious imprints run deep. We've been conditioned to believe in lack. To believe that wealth must come at a cost. That we must *choose* between this or that instead of *claiming* this and that. We've been taught that we have to sacrifice for success. That we have to earn our way into worthiness.

We've also internalized the idea that wealth must be proven. That we must show the world we're worthy of it by working hard, struggling, or overcoming enough first. These are old imprints, passed down through generations and reinforced by society, culture, and even family systems. But they are not truth. They are distorted filters that color how we receive—or don't receive—abundance.

Maybe you've been told that rich people are greedy. Or that wanting money makes you shallow. Maybe you grew up in a household where money was always tight, where you were taught to be "responsible" and not ask for too much. All of that becomes part of your internal money blueprint. And unless you bring awareness to it, it silently runs the show—keeping you within a certain financial setpoint, never allowing you to expand beyond what feels "safe."

And here's the key: your financial setpoint is not about your job, your business model, or the economy. It's about your *energetic nervous system*. Just like we talked about in earlier chapters—your capacity to hold wealth is deeply tied to your nervous system's ability to feel safe while expanding.

If more money, more opportunities, or greater visibility trigger an unconscious threat response, your system will find ways to sabotage, overspend, undercharge, avoid receiving, or simply block abundance altogether. Not because you're broken—but because your system is trying to keep you safe.

This is why your net worth often mirrors your self-worth. Not because your value is measured in dollars, but because the level of financial abundance you allow in is often directly tied to what you believe you deserve, what feels safe to receive, and what you're energetically willing to hold.

So when money does come in—whether it's a big paycheck, a successful launch, or an unexpected windfall—learn to normalize the experience. Be grateful, yes. Celebrate, yes. But anchor into the knowing that this is your new normal. This is who you are now. Don't make it such a big deal that your nervous system spirals into overwhelm. Because when that happens, the subconscious mind will often find a way to release the "threat" by getting rid of the money—through overspending, unexpected expenses, or energetic collapse.

To expand your wealth, you must expand your radiance. You must expand your ability to receive, to hold, and to sustain higher frequencies of abundance without dimming yourself, shrinking back, or feeling unsafe.

Wealth is not a reward. It is a reflection. It mirrors how fully you've come into your own light. And the more you claim your radiance— the more you allow yourself to become a vessel for your soul's frequency—the more life will meet you with experiences that match that brilliance.

This is the alchemy of wealth. Not chasing it—but becoming it.

The Hidden Ways We Block What We Say We Want

Often, we unconsciously resist or even deflect abundance—not because we don't want it, but because it activates something within us that doesn't feel safe. Abundance, especially when it exceeds what we've been taught is "normal" for us, can trigger the ego's alarm system. It disrupts the energetic setpoint we've grown used to. And when something feels unfamiliar, the body and subconscious often interpret it as unsafe—even when it's something we've deeply desired.

This is why abundance can feel both good and uncomfortable. Yes, it's exciting when things begin to flow—when support shows up, when life surprises us with ease. But beneath the surface, that increase in abundance might also stir feelings of guilt, anxiety, or a need to explain it away. We start to question whether we really deserve it, whether it will last, or what people will think. And that's when the subtle patterns of resistance begin to show. You might say yes on the surface—but your energy says no.

This resistance can show up in the most ordinary moments. Like when someone offers to pay for your dinner—you might accept, but inside you feel unsettled, like you suddenly owe them something. Or you feel the urge to insist, "No, no—I'll get it," not because you truly want to, but because receiving feels vulnerable.

Think about the last time someone gave you a compliment. Did you simply receive it and say thank you? Or did you deflect it by brushing it off or explaining it away with, "Oh, this old thing?" or "Thanks, but I still have a long way to go"? These may seem harmless, but each one is a micro-resistance—a moment where abundance tried to flow in, and you energetically pushed it away.

These patterns are rooted in stories—old beliefs about worthiness, guilt, needing to earn everything, or not wanting to seem too full of yourself. And while those stories may have once served as protection, they now act as filters that block the very things you're calling in. Abundance is not just about money. It's about support, generosity, love, ease, beauty, and flow. And if your nervous system is wired to only allow a limited amount of those things before sounding the alarm, you'll keep bumping up against the same ceiling—no matter how much you desire more.

So what does it actually look like to deepen into the frequency of true receptivity? It means softening your guard and letting go of the need to justify why you're receiving something. It means practicing staying open, even when it feels a little unfamiliar or uncomfortable. True receptivity is an energetic posture. It's not passive—it's open. It's the act of choosing to receive without tension, without guilt, and without the subtle urge to immediately give something back to "balance the scale." It's allowing goodness in and letting it land fully in your body.

This process requires expanding your energetic capacity to hold more. You don't just open to abundance once and then it's done—you live in the energy of receiving. You practice letting compliments land without minimizing them. You let support come through without shrinking. You stop making yourself small so others won't feel uncomfortable. You stop second-guessing whether you've "earned" what's flowing into your life. You learn to say thank you—and actually mean it. You learn to pause and feel what it's like to be supported. You learn to let abundance stay.

And that's what creates more. When you allow the frequency of abundance to move through you without deflecting, justifying, or bracing for it to disappear, you become magnetic. You're no longer just attracting things—you become the space where those things can stay, expand, and multiply. This is soul alchemy in action. It's not just about manifesting desires—it's about becoming the person who can receive them fully, with ease, grace, and zero apology.

You don't need to prove anything. You don't need to earn it harder. You don't have to keep one foot in struggle to feel grounded. You're allowed to thrive. You're allowed to receive more than you need. You're allowed to feel good, even when nothing is going wrong. That's what true receptivity feels like. And the more you practice holding that frequency, the more natural it becomes. Eventually, what once felt like "too much" becomes your new baseline—and from there, you rise again.

Collapsing Timelines Through the Quantum Self

Throughout this book, we've talked about embodiment—the art of becoming the version of yourself who already lives the truth you're here to embody. And as we close in on the final chapters, this embodiment becomes even more important. Because the way you relate to money, wealth, and abundance isn't just a mental or emotional process—it's an energetic one. And that means it also lives in the quantum.

There is already a version of you—right now, in the quantum field—who is wildly wealthy, deeply abundant, radiantly prosperous. That version of you exists in a parallel timeline. And through intention, embodiment, and focused energy, you can connect with that version and begin drawing their frequency into your life *now*.

Let's talk about the quantum field for a moment. The quantum field is the energetic space of infinite possibilities—beyond time, beyond logic, beyond the linear constraints of the 3D world. It holds every version of you that has ever existed, and every version of you that could exist. Think of it as the multiverse: countless realities, all existing simultaneously, each one shaped by a different sequence of choices, beliefs, and energetic frequencies.

In one of those timelines, you're already living the life you dream of. You've already created it. You're living in full alignment, abundance, and joy. You're successful, radiant, fulfilled, and deeply supported. And through a practice called **quantum jumping**, you can energetically step into that timeline—not just to observe it, but to *become* it.

The difference between quantum jumping and simply visualizing your future self is this: when you quantum jump, you're not trying to imagine what your dream life might feel like. You're *experiencing* it. You're stepping into the energetic reality where it already exists, bypassing the doubt, confusion, and limitations of your current identity. And when you connect with that version of you in the quantum field—when you soak in their energy, beliefs, posture, and presence—you collapse the timeline between you and them. You shorten the distance between what you desire and what you experience. That's the power of this work.

Let me walk you through the two practices that will help you connect with your Quantum Self and begin magnetizing wealth, abundance, and all your soul-aligned desires.

Quantum Jumping: Step Into Your Abundant Timeline

Before you begin, get clear on what you want to experience. What timeline are you choosing to step into? Who are you in that reality? Are you an award-winning author? A wealthy healer? A successful entrepreneur? Someone who inherited abundance, or someone who created it from the ground up? Clarity is key—because your intention directs your energy.

Once you're clear, find a comfortable space. Light a candle if you'd like. Play soft, spacious music. Begin with a few deep breaths to drop into your body. Center yourself. Quiet the noise. Drop into your heart and soften your awareness.

When you're ready, set the intention to elevate your consciousness into the quantum field. Feel your awareness rise and expand. Tune in to your body, then your field, then beyond. As you expand, allow yourself to access that infinite, boundless space—the quantum field. It may feel like vast light, spaciousness, or pure presence. There is no beginning, no end. Just infinite potential.

Take a few moments to attune to this space. Then bring your intention back. State it clearly: "I now wish to jump into the timeline where I am… [state your desired identity]." Be open to how this unfolds. You might see a door. A light. A portal. Or you may feel yourself being gently pulled forward. Follow the guidance. Step through.

On the other side, observe. Witness your life in that timeline. See yourself in that version—how you walk, speak, feel, move. What do you believe? How do you carry yourself? What's your energy like? Watch a full day unfold. Soak it in. Be the fly on the wall—but also be present in your body, feeling the energy of that reality move through you.

Feel it. Absorb it. Embody it.

When you feel complete—or when your focus begins to drift—return to the quantum field. Then return to your physical body. But bring that energy *with* you. Anchor it in. Breathe it into your heart, into your cells, into your presence.

The key to this practice isn't just the experience—it's what you *do* with the energy. You must hold that essence. Embody that version.

Begin showing up in your life as the you from that timeline. That's how you collapse time. That's how you mold your current reality to reflect what you've already become.

You can revisit that timeline as often as needed. But don't overdo it—only return when you feel you've dropped out of the essence. If you can hold that frequency for days, weeks, or months, you don't need to jump again. Because you *are* already living it. That's the point: to become your own version of that abundant, radiant self—and let reality adjust around you.

Quantum Field Magnetization: Call It In with Precision and Power

This second practice uses the same entry point as quantum jumping, but instead of stepping into a specific timeline, you work directly with the quantum field to *magnetize* your desires.

Once you're in the field—anchored in the vastness and infinite possibility of that space—bring your focus to your desire. Not the details. Not the how. Focus on the *essence*. Is it freedom? Creative expression? Financial ease? Fulfillment? Let the feeling rise within you.

Now amplify it. Let it grow and expand. Let it fill your body, your field, your awareness. And from that place, draw in the energy of the quantum field to support it. Imagine the desire becoming brighter, bolder, stronger. Let it spread outward, connecting to the field's infinite network of energetic threads.

Feel the quantum field amplifying your desire, infusing it with momentum, and sending it out across all timelines, dimensions, and pathways.

Then speak this intention aloud or silently:

"I now call forth [name your desire] to come to me with ease and grace. I am open. I am receptive. I welcome it now—or something even better."

Release it. Let the desire go. Trust that the field is already working on your behalf.

When you're ready, come back to your body. Breathe deeply. Return to the present moment. And know—you've just set a powerful energetic ripple in motion.

You don't need to repeat this daily. You've already planted the seed. Now your role is to embody the version of you who has already received it. Keep showing up as that version. That's how the field delivers—through resonance, through alignment, through the embodiment of the essence you claimed.

What Are Timelines—and How Do They Collapse?

In the quantum realm, time is not linear. There are infinite timelines all unfolding at once, like threads in a multidimensional web. Each choice you make, each belief you hold, and each energetic shift you embody moves you along a particular timeline. When you align with the energy of your Quantum Self—when you fully become the version of you who already lives what you desire—you collapse the time it would have taken to get there through logic, strategy, or effort alone. You literally jump timelines by aligning with a new energetic frequency.

Instead of moving through the slow, step-by-step progression your mind thinks is necessary, you shortcut the process by shifting who you are being—and reality recalibrates to meet you there. This is quantum manifestation in its truest form. It's not about forcing, chasing, or over-efforting. It's about energetic leadership. It's about becoming so deeply aligned with your future self that the gap between "someday" and *now* dissolves.

You don't hustle your way into abundance—you embody your way there. And the moment you do, everything around you begins to rearrange in response to your new frequency.

The Body as a Vessel for Abundance

Embodiment is the bridge between intention and manifestation. Without embodiment, your desires remain ideas—floating in the field, disconnected from your lived experience. But when you *become* the frequency of what you desire, when your body, energy, and presence align with it—you create a resonance that reality can't help but respond to.

This is especially true when it comes to abundance.

Sustainable abundance isn't created through bursts of action or fleeting manifestations. It's built by becoming someone who can *hold* abundance without collapsing under it, sabotaging it, or shrinking in response to it. And for that, your nervous system is key.

You've already learned that your nervous system has an energetic setpoint—a familiar range of what feels "safe" to receive. That setpoint is shaped by your upbringing, conditioning, trauma, and belief systems. It's the internal thermostat of your life. And unless you expand that range, you'll keep unconsciously regulating your experience back to what feels familiar, even if it's far less than what you desire.

This is why embodiment work matters. It's not just about "thinking wealthy" or "believing in abundance." It's about gradually calibrating your entire being—especially your nervous system—to feel *safe* in expansion. To feel at home in radiance. To feel anchored and grounded while holding more money, more love, more attention, more power, and more visibility.

Because here's the truth: abundance *will* activate you. Visibility *will* trigger you. Success *will* stretch you. Not because you're not ready—but because your body has never experienced those frequencies before. And that's not a failure—it's a doorway.

So the real question becomes: how do you create an internal environment where expansion feels safe enough to stay?

You regulate. You expand. You calibrate. You become.

This is the role of energetic embodiment practices. They're not just rituals—they're rewirings. They help your system reorient itself around a new frequency. They help you stay *with* your body as you grow, rather than leaving it behind.

Breathwork is one of the most accessible tools for this. It helps release trapped energy, regulate the nervous system, and bring you back into your body when expansion feels overwhelming. Just a few minutes of conscious breath can shift you from fight-or-flight into grounded openness—making space for more life to flow through.

Light language activations go even deeper. These energetic transmissions bypass the logical mind and speak directly to your field. They help clear distortions, dissolve resistance, and awaken dormant codes within your system that already *know* how to hold more. You're not learning something new—you're *remembering* what your soul already knows.

Visualization, too, can be powerful—*if* you feel it in your body. This isn't about daydreaming or mentally scripting. It's about sensing. Feeling. Embodying. Seeing yourself in your desired reality and noticing how your body responds. Do you tense up? Do you feel excited? Do you pull back? That feedback is sacred. It shows you where your edges are—so you can breathe through them, soften into them, and expand beyond them.

Embodiment is where the shift becomes sustainable.

You're not trying to "get there" anymore. You're learning to *live there*. You're making the frequency of abundance your baseline, not your breakthrough. You're no longer chasing the next moment of success—you're learning to hold success in your cells. To breathe it. To walk it. To radiate it.

This is the path of the Soul Alchemist—not bypassing the body, but bringing your divinity *into* the body. Not wishing for change, but becoming the space where change happens. Not collapsing under expansion, but learning how to dance with it, hold it, and normalize it until it becomes second nature.

So ask yourself: what am I doing today to help my body feel safe in the life I say I want? What am I doing to normalize abundance, to anchor visibility, to hold wealth not as a fluke—but as a natural reflection of who I am?

You are not just the creator of your life. You are the vessel that holds it. And as your vessel expands, so does everything else.

Money in Motion

Let's talk about something we don't often hear in spiritual conversations about abundance: *spending*. Or more precisely—circulating. Because money is meant to move. To flow. To be received, released, and returned again. But so often, when it's time to spend, invest, or give, what arises is not expansion—but contraction.

You may have felt this before: you're at the store, checking out, and the total is far more than you expected. You have the money, but your chest tightens, your breath catches, and suddenly a subtle panic sets in. Or maybe you see something you really want—something aligned and nourishing—but the thought immediately surfaces: *"I can't afford that. That's too expensive."*

These are very real feelings. And they're deeply tied to a scarcity blueprint many of us were raised with—where money is finite, fragile, and unpredictable. But as a Soul Alchemist, this relationship with money no longer serves you. It's not aligned with your truth.

Scarcity contracts. Soul expands.

A Soul Alchemist doesn't ask, *"Can I afford this?"* She asks, *"Is this aligned?"* And if it is, she trusts that what she needs will arrive, often in ways that the mind couldn't predict. Even if the evidence isn't immediately there, she knows: life supports her. The money flows. The solution exists.

Let me share a personal example. Not long ago, I needed a section of my roof repaired. The quote came back at $3,000—a number that, at the time, felt out of reach. I could have panicked. Spiraled. Wondered how I would make it work. But instead, I paused. I opened up to the possibility of a higher solution and asked if this might qualify as an insurance claim. The roofer agreed to check the rest of the roof—and as it turns out, the damage was far more extensive than I thought. I didn't just need a repair—I needed a full replacement.

Soon after, the insurance adjuster came. They approved the full project, not only covering the roof, but also the damage to my gazebo—something I hadn't even considered. What started as a $3,000 out-of-pocket repair turned into a full $11,000 replacement—completely covered, minus a small deductible.

That's the power of trust. I didn't contract. I didn't scramble. I opened. I aligned. I let a better path reveal itself.

This is what it means to circulate money as a sacred act of alignment. It's not about blind spending. It's about trusting the flow. It's about knowing that you are always supported—and that when something is aligned, the way will be made.

Money is not meant to be clung to or feared. It is meant to move through you, to support your mission, to nourish your body, to uplift others, and to expand your life. When you spend from soul—not from fear—you send a signal to the universe: *I trust life. I trust myself. I know more is coming.*

This is not reckless. This is reverent.

When you invest in something that supports your evolution, your healing, or your joy, you are saying yes to your expansion. When you give from the heart, without fear of depletion, you create a loop of generosity that always finds its way back to you. When you pay bills with gratitude instead of resentment, you shift the frequency of your entire relationship with money.

Money wants to flow. But it cannot flow where there is fear, control, or tightness. Just like breath, just like energy, it needs to circulate freely.

So think of money not as a possession, but as a partner—a co-creative force in your soul's mission. Let it move through your life with reverence. Treat each transaction as an energetic exchange. Each bill as a blessing. Each investment as an activation.

When you embody your Soul Alchemist self, you no longer hoard out of fear—you flow from faith. You release money with the same trust you receive it. You understand that what leaves you returns multiplied, so long as your energy remains clear, open, and aligned.

That is when money becomes a sacred current in your life—not a source of stress, but a mirror of your radiance. Not something to control, but something to dance with. And the more you trust this dance, the more abundance moves through you—not just for you, but for everyone you're here to serve.

Money as a Byproduct of Alignment

Money is the one thing we've been taught to chase from the moment we step into adulthood—sometimes even before. We need it to survive, to eat, to pay bills, to experience joy, to meet our needs. But because it's so tied to our basic survival, money can easily become a looming figure in our lives. It becomes the taskmaster we fear and obey. It's the thing that never seems to stay. We work hard to earn it, and then—just like that—it's gone. Groceries. Rent. Unexpected bills. A few things to treat ourselves. And again, we're back to the grind.

But what if money didn't have to feel so heavy? What if it wasn't the enemy or the boss or the uncatchable prize? What if money could be your friend, your partner, your ally—your supporter?

I want to invite you to examine your current relationship with money. If money were a person, what kind of relationship would you say you have? Is it warm, balanced, and respectful—like a mutual friendship built on trust and reciprocity? Or is it more of a love-hate relationship, where you constantly feel like you need it, but never trust it to stick around? Do you treat it with gratitude and reverence—or with fear, resentment, and anxiety?

Your relationship with money mirrors your relationship with yourself, your worth, and your ability to receive. If you believe that money supports you, that it arrives when you need it, that it loves to flow through you—you will begin to experience exactly that. But if your relationship is rooted in fear, scarcity, and lack, then no matter how much you try to manifest, you will continue to experience money as something unstable, inconsistent, and hard to hold.

This is where we need to shift the paradigm.

What if money wasn't the goal at all—but simply the *byproduct* of your alignment?

When you live in energetic coherence—when your values, your work, your truth, and your actions all point in the same direction—you become magnetic. When you show up in service without agenda, when you create from the joy of your soul's expression, when you live from the frequency of enoughness and purpose, money naturally flows. You're no longer forcing or striving. You're *resonating*.

The clearer your energy, the more receptive your field. And the more deeply you embody your Soul Alchemist self, the more wealth becomes a reflection—not a requirement.

I learned this the hard way.

In the early days of my spiritual business, I did all the things—created offers, posted online, got on calls—all from a place of desperation. I needed clients to survive. I needed money to stay afloat. And that need created friction in my energy that repelled everything I was trying so hard to attract. I wasn't in alignment—I was in panic. And because of that, money felt further and further away.

In 2019, it all collapsed. I got hurt and was barely able to walk for about six months. My business flatlined. I couldn't pay my bills. I had to borrow money from my parents and friends to keep a roof over my son's and my head. It was the lowest point I'd ever experienced. And it was in that darkness that I met the light of surrender.

One day, while outside watering the yard, I realized I had tried everything: job applications, outreach, endless calls, offers, strategy, even calling on my guides for help. Nothing worked. The only thing I hadn't done was fully let go. So I surrendered. I handed it over to something higher. I asked for help. I asked for a way out of the hole I'd dug myself into. And within a few months, I was offered a role as a marketing consultant for a local physical therapy clinic—a contract position that gave me financial stability *and* the freedom to work from home.

That one opportunity led me down a new path—eventually growing into the marketing agency I still run today. It became the stable foundation beneath my spiritual work. And although I resisted that path at first—thinking I had to *choose* between my passion and my practicality—I realized I didn't have to pick one over the other. I get to have both. The marketing work feeds my creativity, my strategy, my love for building things. The spiritual work feeds my soul. Together, they create a beautiful synergy where I'm both grounded and elevated. Rooted and expansive. Logical and intuitive.

And now, money is no longer the driver—it's the reflection. It flows through both sides of my work because I'm in alignment. Because I'm in service. Because I'm *me*.

I want you to know that *you* get to have that too.

You don't have to force money to show up. You don't have to chase it, beg for it, or prove your worth to receive it. You get to live a life that lights you up, that feels like home, that's built from the inside out—and let money flow as a byproduct of your alignment, your embodiment, your radiance.

So don't make money the goal. Make *you* the goal. Make your coherence, your soul alignment, your presence, and your passion the priority. And let money follow the frequency of who you've become.

By now, you know how to embody your future self. You've learned how to become the energetic match for what you desire. If it's wealth you want, then live as the version of you who already has it—not just in thought, but in essence. Show up as her. Think like her. Breathe like her. Choose like her.

Scarcity has no place in your field anymore. You are no longer the one who grasps. You are the one who *receives*. The one who radiates. The one who creates not from need, but from knowing.

And that is the greatest wealth of all.

Becoming the Frequency of Wealth

You've now journeyed deep into the energetic layers of wealth—not as something distant or external, but as a reflection of who you are being. Throughout this chapter, we've explored how your relationship with money mirrors your sense of worth, coherence, and soul alignment. You've seen how scarcity patterns can dissolve when you no longer identify with them, and how abundance flows most naturally when you are rooted in your truth.

Money is not a reward you must earn, nor a test you must pass. It is a frequency that responds to your radiance. When you show up in energetic integrity—honoring your path, serving from a place of devotion, and embodying your highest self—money becomes a natural byproduct of that alignment. There is no longer a need to chase, strive, or prove. Instead, you open, you receive, and you allow wealth to meet you where you are.

The more you live from your essence, the more life rises to support you. You are not here to fear money, fight for it, or shrink in its presence. You are here to partner with it. To circulate it with reverence. To let it flow through you in service to your mission, your joy, and the greater good.

Now, you are ready to stabilize wealth as your new normal—not through force, but through embodiment. Not through control, but through trust. This is the alchemy of abundance. And you hold the codes within you.

Closing Incantation: I Am the Embodiment of Overflow

Wealth isn't something outside of you. It's not a number, a status, or a finish line—it's a frequency you hold. It's the energetic signature of how safe you feel to receive, how deeply you trust yourself, and how fully you allow abundance to move through your life.

This incantation is here to help you stabilize that frequency in your body. To dissolve the patterns of scarcity, self-doubt, and survival that have kept you chasing—and call you back into your power as the source.

Let these words be more than affirmations. Let them be a choice. A decision. A felt shift in your field. Speak them with devotion. Let them land in your cells. Let them rewire your nervous system to expect overflow—not as a fantasy, but as your natural state.

Now, take a breath, soften your body, and claim what is already yours.

Incantation:

I now release all scarcity from my field—
the fear, the grasping, the proving, the lack.
I dissolve every belief that says I am not supported, not safe, not enough.

I choose to remember the truth.
I am abundance. I am radiance. I am the source.

Money flows to me as a reflection of my coherence.
It meets me in my clarity. It expands with my impact.
It multiplies through my joy, my truth, my service.

I no longer chase wealth—I *become* it.
I no longer wait for permission—I *embody* my future self now.

With every breath, I stabilize abundance in my body.
With every choice, I expand what I'm available to receive.
With every act of devotion, I become a magnet for more.

I now circulate money with reverence,
allowing it to flow in, through, and beyond me—
as a sacred partner in my purpose,
as a mirror of my highest alignment,
as a natural extension of who I already am.

I am the frequency of overflow.
And so it is.

Chapter 22: Becoming the Portal for Others

Living as the activation—your legacy is your resonance

Now that we've arrived at the final core chapter of this book, everything begins to come full circle. This is where the shift happens—from doing the work to *being* the work. From seeking transformation to *becoming* the transformation. From learning how to embody the Soul Alchemist path to realizing—you already are it.

At this stage, alignment is no longer something you have to strive for. It's the way you move through life. Your practices are no longer tools you reach for to "get into the right state"—they are simply the way you breathe, live, and express yourself. You're no longer becoming. You have become.

When you reach this level of embodiment, you become the activation. You become the portal through which others remember what's possible. Your energy speaks before you ever say a word. Your presence becomes a transmission. And that, in itself, is the most powerful form of leadership there is.

You don't have to teach, convince, or prove. When you fully embody your truth—when your inner and outer worlds are in alignment—your frequency becomes magnetic. Others may not be able to explain why they're drawn to you. But something about you stirs them, awakens them, shifts something within them. That is the power of radiance. That is the power of coherence. And that is the power of walking in full alignment with your soul.

This kind of leadership isn't about doing more—it's about *being more of who you truly are*. As a Soul Alchemist, a wayshower, a trailblazer, you lead not by fixing others or carrying them forward, but by holding a higher frequency that others naturally calibrate to. You model what's possible, and by doing so, you invite others into their own remembering.

You are no longer responsible for pulling people along. That was the old paradigm. In this new way, you lead through embodiment. You serve as the lighthouse—anchored, radiant, unwavering—so others can find their own way home.

You guide not through handholding, but through holding presence. You mentor not through control, but through resonance. You activate not through teaching alone, but by standing fully in your truth, allowing your energy to speak louder than your words ever could.

This is the essence of energetic leadership. Your frequency becomes your service. Your coherence becomes your legacy.

And when you show up in that state of deep authenticity, life responds. People, opportunities, abundance, and joy begin to flow toward you—not because you chase them, but because your resonance calls them in. This is the magnetism that emerges when you are unapologetically aligned with your soul's truth.

Becoming a Soul Alchemist is not a final destination. It is a lifelong journey of refinement, of deepening, of returning home to yourself again and again. But from this point forward, it's no longer just about what you're transforming within—it's about what you're radiating out.

You are meant to be the light for others. Not the rescuer, not the savior—but the mirror and the map. You are the portal. Your life becomes the invitation. Your presence becomes the space through which others remember who they are.

This book was a portal you were led to because your soul knew you were ready. Now, it becomes a guide you carry with you—not to repeat step by step, but to *live* as a transmission. Soul alchemy is no longer something you do. It is something you *are*. Something you emanate. Something you offer the world simply by being fully, unapologetically you.

Legacy Through Resonance

As one continues walking the path of soul alchemy, the question of legacy inevitably begins to arise. But legacy, in this awakened space, is no longer about what one accomplishes in the traditional sense. It's not about how much one does, achieves, or builds—it's about the resonance left behind. It's about the imprint that one's essence leaves on others, often in ways that defy logic or explanation.

Every time your presence impacts another soul—whether through a word, a gaze, a transmission, or simply through your beingness— that moment becomes a seed planted. It may seem small, perhaps even unnoticed, but the energetic ripple carries far beyond what the mind can grasp. And that ripple is legacy. That frequency—your frequency—is what lingers, what echoes, what continues to activate long after you've moved on.

The deepest form of impact is not something you can measure or quantify. It lives in the invisible, in the energetic. You can touch someone's life in a way they may not even be able to explain—but they'll remember it. They'll feel it. They'll carry it forward. And in that carrying, your essence lives on.

Even when you create something in the physical—a book, a course, a piece of art, a body of work—what leaves the mark is not the format or the structure. It's the energy you infused into the creation. When something is birthed through soul, when it's saturated with truth, frequency, and alignment, it becomes more than a product. It becomes a portal. A transmission. An activation in its own right.

This book is that for me. It didn't come from my mind—it came from something deeper. There was a calling within me that grew so strong it could no longer be ignored. My soul needed to bring this work into the world. And I didn't just write words—I poured my essence into every chapter, every page. My stories, my voice, my energy, my truth—it's all here, woven into every line. And my hope is that you didn't just *read* these words—but that you *felt* them. That something stirred within you. That this book didn't speak to your mind alone—but to your soul.

That is what legacy feels like. Not a monument or a milestone, but an *awakening* that continues beyond you.

You, too, are here to leave a legacy. And that legacy is not something you have to build through effort. It's something you *become* through alignment. Through coherence. Through presence. You leave a mark on the world not just through what you do—but through who you *are being* in every moment. The more embodied you are, the more potent your presence becomes. Your energy starts to speak louder than your actions, louder than your words, louder than your name.

Every soul who chooses the path of awakening leaves a mark—not because of how visible they are, or how many people know their name—but because their frequency shifted the collective field. Because their energy helped lift the veil for someone else. Because their presence made it safer for others to come home to themselves.

This is what it means to lead through resonance. This is how your soul's frequency lives on.

You are The Map and the Mirror

To live as both the map and the mirror means embodying your future self so fully that your entire presence becomes a guidepost for others. You no longer need to explain how you got there—your energy shows the way. Your life becomes the proof. Your alignment becomes the compass.

When someone truly lives from their embodied future timeline— when they become the essence of the reality they once desired—they naturally lead by example. That embodiment becomes the map. Others can observe the way they walk, speak, choose, and create. They feel the coherence. They see the embodiment. And even if they can't explain it, they begin to understand what it means to live in conscious alignment.

The map is not about giving directions. It's about *being* the direction.

But in the same breath, you also become the mirror. Not only do others see what's possible through your embodiment—they also see themselves reflected back. Sometimes that reflection is expansive and inspiring. They see their own potential through you. They remember what they're capable of.

Other times, your embodiment will stir up everything they've been avoiding. Your light may reflect their shadows. Your confidence may bring up their self-doubt. Your visibility may trigger their fear of being seen. Your abundance may surface their lack. This is not because you are doing anything wrong—it's because your frequency is *revealing* something. And that, too, is part of the work.

You don't reflect their limitation—you reflect their disconnection from what's possible. And that reflection becomes the spark that initiates their next evolution.

This is the power of vibrational leadership.

When someone embodies their future self—when they claim their highest timeline and align with it energetically—their entire frequency rises. They begin to radiate a specific vibrational signature, one that holds the codes of coherence, self-trust, abundance, and alignment. And when they maintain that frequency—especially in the presence of others—they create a field that is both stabilizing and activating.

Vibrational leadership doesn't require titles or platforms. It requires presence. When someone holds the frequency of their future self without collapsing, wavering, or diluting to make others comfortable, they become a living invitation. They don't pull others up—they inspire others to rise. Their field creates an unconscious calibration point for everyone they encounter. Simply being in their energy makes others *remember* what's possible.

That is the quiet power of coherence. It speaks louder than strategy. It reaches deeper than words. It creates a ripple through the energetic field that touches people in ways they may never be able to articulate—but they'll feel it. They'll be changed by it.

And the more consistently someone holds that frequency—the more they stabilize in their embodied timeline—the more powerful their field becomes. They become the anchor, the mirror, the map, and the portal. They become the transmission.

This is what it means to walk as a Soul Alchemist—not just transforming yourself, but radiating a frequency that initiates transformation in others. Not through effort, but through being. Not through teaching, but through resonance. Not through control, but through unwavering embodiment.

Coherence as Transmission

When someone fully embodies alignment, it creates a sense of core stability that cannot be shaken by external noise. There's a groundedness that comes—not from rigid control, but from deep integration. And that coherence becomes palpable. It's not loud. It doesn't announce itself. But it's felt.

The more someone lives in alignment with their soul, the more stable their inner frequency becomes. That stability radiates outward and creates a field of safety, clarity, and expansion that others immediately pick up on, even if they can't name it. People feel calmer in your presence. They feel safe, held, and seen. They feel like they can exhale. And that's not because you said anything—it's because your field said, *"You're okay here. You're home."*

This coherence creates a resonance that gently awakens others. It makes space for them to find their own clarity. To feel their own truth. To remember what alignment feels like within *them*. You're not pulling them. You're not rescuing them. But your very presence becomes an anchor—steady, calm, and rooted—and that allows them to expand. It's not a lifeline. It's not dependence. It's energetic stability. You become the mirror of what's possible, and in that reflection, others remember their own potential.

That's why it's so important to walk this path fully. Because when you commit to your own embodiment—when you integrate your own truth and become the living transmission of what you teach—you don't just transform your own life. You become the catalyst for others. You become the energetic portal that calls them forward, not through force or persuasion, but through radiance.

And this is not something that can be captured in a title.

You are not just a coach, a healer, or a guide. None of those labels can contain the magnitude of what you're here to do—or more importantly, who you're here to *be*. Your essence is the activation.

Your frequency is the medicine. And your embodiment is the message.

There was a time in my own journey when I struggled to define what I did. I had certifications. I had skills. I had tools. But no title ever felt like it fit. I tried on many—transformational coach, Akashic Record guide, intuitive healer, light language channel, divine messenger. But each one felt like it put me in a box too small to hold what I truly offered. It wasn't until my guides gave me the title *Soul Alchemist* that everything clicked. Because I don't just coach. I don't just deliver messages. I don't just channel. I *alchemize*. I *activate*. I *transmit*. I *embody*. And more than anything—I become the frequency I came here to carry.

If you've ever felt confined by titles, by roles, or by expectations of what you "should" be—this is your invitation to let all of that go. You are not here to fit into a mold. You are here to *radiate your truth*. And your truth cannot be labeled. It can only be felt.

This is soul alchemy embodied.

Your presence is the gift. Your coherence is the legacy. And your way of being is what opens the path for others to come home to themselves. The more stable and integrated your own energy becomes, the more others will find stability in your field. Not because they lean on you—but because your frequency reminds them how to root into their own. That is coherence as transmission. That is vibrational leadership. And that is the quiet, sacred power of being fully, unapologetically you.

The Power of Quiet Presence

There's a common belief in the world—especially in spiritual and personal development spaces—that leadership must be loud, visible, and performative in order to be meaningful. That in order to make an impact, you have to speak on stages, post regularly online, guide large communities, or be constantly seen. But the truth is, some of the most profound activations don't come from visibility at all. They come from presence—quiet, anchored, unwavering presence.

You don't need to be loud to lead. You don't need a title or platform to create transformation. You don't even need to be outwardly doing anything. The simple act of being—of showing up in your authenticity, in your frequency, and in your coherence—has the power to ripple through lives in ways that are felt far more deeply than anything that can be said or explained.

When someone is deeply anchored in their own frequency, when they walk with integrity, clarity, and steadiness, they naturally become a stabilizing force for those around them. Others feel more grounded, more open, more at peace—not because anything was taught or explained, but because something in the field shifted. The coherence of a single person can become a lighthouse for many. This isn't about control or leadership in the traditional sense. It's about presence that speaks without sound, energy that awakens without force, and alignment that radiates without seeking attention.

Many souls are not here to lead in the way the world traditionally defines leadership. They are not meant to be out in front, on a stage, or in the public eye. They are here to hold frequency—to anchor light. That alone is sacred service. By stabilizing their own field, they make it safer for others to expand. Their frequency supports those who are called to step into more visible roles, not by directing or teaching them, but by being the silent anchor that allows those missions to unfold.

Some of you reading this may feel the call to be more public, to speak, to teach, or to guide. Others may feel called to remain inward, rooted in stillness, without needing to be seen. Both paths are equally important. Both are necessary. Because no matter how visible or behind-the-scenes your role may be, you are here to be the stabilizer, the ignition point, the field through which others remember who they are.

Stillness, when it arises from embodied alignment, becomes its own transmission. Integrity, when lived without needing recognition, becomes a stabilizing code in the collective field. And quiet presence, when it holds the vibration of truth, often creates more lasting impact than the most forceful words or elaborate teachings ever could.

Impact is not measured by reach. It's measured by resonance. And resonance cannot be faked. It comes from truth. It comes from presence. It comes from the lived embodiment of who you really are. You don't need to call yourself a leader to lead. You don't need a platform to activate. And you don't need a following to make a difference.

Your beingness is your offering. Your coherence is your medicine. And your presence—exactly as it is—is more than enough.

Walking as the Portal

When you open yourself fully—when you become more intentional, more anchored in your soul—you stop simply doing the work and instead *become* the work. You walk as the portal itself, the threshold where old patterns dissolve and new potentials begin. That is the true alchemy. That is the power of soul embodiment.

Just imagine how many people you will impact simply by continuing to walk this path, by being the living embodiment of your soul. When you hold your head high—not in arrogance, but in quiet devotion— you begin modeling a new way of being. You become the presence that says, *life doesn't have to be this hard.* You show, through your energy and way of being, that there is a more vibrant, heart-centered, easeful way to live—a way that is rich in magic, beauty, and truth.

By now, you've walked through your own inner shadows, released the patterns that once held you back, and integrated higher timelines into your being. You've become the embodiment of your future self—not as an idea, but as a lived experience. And in doing so, you've become a portal for others. You carry a frequency that serves as an invitation. Not everyone will walk through it. Some may sense the doorway and hesitate. Some will look away entirely, because they are not yet ready to awaken. But for those who are ready—those whose souls have been quietly calling for a new way—you will become the threshold that beckons them forward.

And that's the beauty of walking as a portal. It's never about pushing others to change or trying to convince them to grow. Everyone awakens in their own time. Some souls have chosen longer journeys filled with dense experiences before their human self becomes ready to step into the light. And no matter how much you want to help them, it is not your role to save anyone. It's not your job to fix them—because no one is broken. Just as you were never broken, they are simply navigating the human experience through the lens of old programming and survival-based patterns.

You don't need to do anything but *be*. Your presence, your essence, your embodiment is enough. That's how you lead. That's how you guide—not by handholding, but by holding open the space. You become the lighthouse. The ones who are ready will see you, feel your frequency, and be drawn to cross the threshold on their own.

This is something I had to learn the hard way. In the earlier stages of my business, I worked with many clients one-on-one, and although I did help them shift and grow, it felt exhausting. I realized I was trying to *help* them, trying to lead them step-by-step, trying to hold their hand through every moment—and it drained me. That wasn't my role. My soul wasn't here to walk for them. I was meant to activate, not fix. To ignite, not carry.

Once I made peace with that, everything changed. I began calling in clients who were ready—truly ready—to take ownership of their evolution. Clients who didn't want a guide to fix them, but a space where they could be activated and uplifted. That's when I truly stepped into my power as a Soul Alchemist. That's when my work began to feel joyful, expansive, and aligned.

And that is what this book is. It's not just a collection of teachings or personal stories—it's a portal. A living activation encoded with frequency, written for the part of you that is ready to awaken and rise. The question is: are you ready to step through?

There is no rush. If now is not the time, that is perfectly okay. The path will call again when your soul is ready. But know this: the portal will remain open. I will continue holding this space for you—whether consciously or from afar—and whenever your soul whispers "yes," I'll be here, resonating, waiting, walking beside you in frequency. You've already felt it. You've already started. The next step is yours to choose.

Your Energetic Legacy

You may never fully know the impact your essence has on the world around you. You may never see all the lives that shift simply because you chose to live in alignment with your truth. And yet—your legacy is being written in every moment you choose embodiment over performance, presence over proving, and truth over fear.

This book was never about teaching you how to do more or be more. It was always about remembering. Returning. Reclaiming what has always lived within you.

You are not here to perform your purpose, to earn your place, or to prove your worth. You are here to be the living transmission of your soul. Your frequency *is* your message. Your coherence *is* your gift. Your embodiment *is* your legacy.

No one can take that from you. And no one else can offer the exact frequency you hold.

Every moment you choose presence, you become a stabilizer in this world. Every moment you choose integrity, you become a beacon. Every moment you honor your soul's rhythm, you create ripples that stretch far beyond what the mind can grasp. That is how timelines shift. That is how the world changes. That is how a new paradigm is birthed—one embodied being at a time.

You are here to be a portal.

Not a destination, not a guide with a map, but a walking transmission of what's possible. A threshold through which others remember their own light, their own truth, their own power. You don't need to force that. You don't need to try. You simply need to be.

And this is where the path of the Soul Alchemist brings you—not to a finish line, but to a beginning.

The journey doesn't end here. It expands. It deepens. It becomes more real. More lived. More radiant. This book was only ever a reflection of *you*. It was your soul that brought you here. Your frequency that responded. Your inner truth that recognized itself in these words.

You are the alchemist. You are the embodiment. You are the portal.

Now… walk as one.

Closing Incantation: I Am the Portal

There is no turning back from the truth you've reclaimed.

The path of the Soul Alchemist is not a role you take on or a label you carry—it is a state of being. A frequency. A resonance that now lives in your cells, your choices, your breath, your presence. And it cannot be undone.

You have walked through the layers. You've seen what was hidden, faced what was uncomfortable, and reclaimed what was never truly lost. You've moved from doing the work to becoming the work. You are no longer striving for the future self—you are living it now. You are no longer searching for the activation—you are the activation. And those who are meant to find you will.

This chapter was never meant to teach—it was meant to remember. To stir what you already know. You came here for more than survival. More than healing. You came here to hold the codes for a new way of being. And as you continue living from this frequency, your very presence becomes a silent invitation for others to rise.

Let these final words not be an ending, but a threshold. A threshold into deeper embodiment, into unwavering coherence, into living as the transmission your soul came here to offer.

You are not here to wait for permission. You are here to walk as the portal.

Now, speak these words as a declaration of who you are and who you choose to remain.

Incantation: I Am the Portal

I no longer seek the path—I *am* the path.
I no longer wait for the activation—I *am* the activation.
I no longer perform my truth—I *embody* it.
I walk as the portal through which old patterns end and new worlds begin.

I stand as the threshold where others awaken—not by force, but by frequency.

I am the resonance that realigns, the light that reveals, the mirror that reflects possibility.

I hold nothing back. I dim nothing down. I dilute nothing to make others comfortable.

I am rooted, open, aligned, and unshakable.

This is my legacy—not what I do, but who I am.

I now choose to walk as the living embodiment of my soul's truth.

And so it is.

Chapter 23: Co-Creating with the Quantum Field

Mastering reality creation through frequency, embodiment, and energetic alignment

---

There comes a point on the soul alchemist's path where creation no longer happens through effort, but through frequency—where desires are not chased, but called, not forced, but received. This is the space where you shift from hoping life will meet you to knowing you are already aligned with all that you seek.

You are no longer here to passively wait for miracles—you are here to become the field in which they arise.

This final chapter is not a conclusion but an invitation. An invitation to consciously partner with the quantum field, to shape reality not through willpower but through embodiment. This is where energy becomes form, and form becomes fluid again. Where you learn not only to desire, but to hold, receive, and live as the version of yourself who already lives what you once longed for.

Let's begin by grounding into what the quantum field really is—and how it responds to your identity.

What Is the Quantum Field—and How Does It Respond to Identity?

The quantum field is not a place, but a field of infinite potential. It is the energetic matrix from which all realities emerge—the formless intelligence that responds not to what you say you want, but to who you are being.

Every thought, emotion, belief, and embodiment pattern you carry emits a frequency. That frequency becomes your request to the quantum field. And the field, being neutral and responsive, reflects back a reality that aligns with that frequency—no exceptions, no judgment, no delays. Not what you affirm, but what you expect. Not what you envision once, but what you embody consistently.

This is why identity is the cornerstone of co-creation. You are not manifesting from your conscious desires alone; you are manifesting from your dominant identity—your self-concept, the internal story you carry about who you are and what is possible for you. You don't manifest what you want. You manifest what you are. And who you consistently are determines which version of reality you are tuned into.

If you continue to identify as someone who is healing, striving, trying, or waiting, the field will mirror those states back to you. But the moment you shift into being someone who already holds, already receives, already lives the outcome—that's when timelines collapse. That's when the field reorganizes to match your coherence.

This chapter will walk you through practices that shift you into that frequency. But remember, techniques alone are not enough. They work when the energy behind them is clear, congruent, and anchored in identity. That is the foundation of quantum creation—not just visualizing a new life, but becoming the version of you who lives it now.

The Role of Observation, Emotion, and Frequency in Creating Reality

At the quantum level, everything exists as probability until it is observed. This means that every potential version of your life already exists—every timeline, every possibility, every outcome. The moment you place your attention on one of those possibilities, you begin drawing it into form. Observation collapses the wave into matter. But it's not just any kind of observation—it's the quality of your focus, your emotion, and your frequency that determines what takes shape.

This is why passive wanting doesn't create change. It's not enough to wish for something while simultaneously holding fear, doubt, or separation. The quantum field responds to your energetic state, not your conscious preference. Your emotional frequency is the fuel. Your focus is the steering wheel. Your embodiment is the anchor.

When you observe a reality with conviction—when you feel it as real and align your frequency to match—it becomes magnetic. That emotion infuses your field with power. That clarity imprints the blueprint. And that consistency keeps you tuned into the signal of what you desire long enough for it to materialize.

The more coherent your frequency—meaning the more unified your thoughts, feelings, and embodiment—the faster the quantum field reflects it back. Coherence is the signal that reality listens to. And when that signal is strong, unwavering, and embodied, timelines collapse into now.

Quantum Jumping, the Law of Assumption, and Timeline Work

At the heart of reality creation lies a radical truth: you do not become your future self by chasing it—you merge with it now.

Quantum jumping is the practice of shifting into a parallel version of yourself that already lives the life you desire. In the quantum field, every version of you already exists. There's a version who is already wealthy, healthy, deeply fulfilled, living in love, radiating purpose. That version is not separate from you—it's simply vibrating at a different frequency. When you tune your thoughts, emotions, and embodiment to that version, you collapse time and step into alignment with that reality.

The **Law of Assumption**, made popular by Neville Goddard, teaches that what you assume to be true becomes your lived experience. It bypasses wishful thinking and instead asks: what if you *knew* it was already done? What if you fully assumed the identity of the one who already has the thing you desire? From that assumption, everything else begins to rearrange itself.

Timeline work invites you to consciously choose which version of reality you want to align with. Rather than waiting for proof or evidence, you become the anchor of the frequency you want to live. Each choice, each thought, each emotional response becomes a vote for a specific timeline. This is energetic leadership—choosing the timeline of expansion, of radiance, of your highest soul expression—and refusing to collapse back into the timeline of fear, lack, or waiting.

When you commit to living as the embodied self who already has what you desire, you stop oscillating between timelines. You stabilize. You solidify the signal. You become magnetic to the version of life that already belongs to you.

Living from the End (Neville Goddard)

To live from the end means to assume the state of the wish fulfilled. Rather than focusing on what's missing, or trying to figure out how your desires will manifest, you anchor into the feeling that it is already done. You become the version of you who has it—and you live as them now.

Neville Goddard taught that imagination is the creative force of the universe, and that what you feel to be true within yourself will eventually externalize in your world. But it's not just about imagining once and then waiting. It's about consistently occupying the state of the fulfilled version of you. You speak, act, think, and feel from the outcome—not toward it.

This is not delusion. It's quantum alignment.

You aren't pretending or faking it—you're embodying the truth that your desired reality already exists. You are simply catching up to it by aligning your frequency and identity with it now. When you live from the end, you stop needing proof. Your certainty becomes the activator. Your beingness becomes the bridge.

The mind may resist this at first, demanding evidence, doubting your certainty, or pulling you back into old versions of yourself. But when you persist in the feeling of the wish fulfilled, even before anything in your external world confirms it, you bend reality. You collapse time. You step fully into the timeline of your chosen future.

Quantum Scripting

Quantum scripting is the practice of writing from the perspective of your desired reality as if it has already manifested. Unlike journaling your current thoughts or feelings, scripting is about stepping into the identity of your future self and letting them speak. You're not writing about your dreams—you're writing as the version of you who is already living them.

This isn't just a mindset tool; it's a quantum frequency transmission. As you script, you generate the emotions, thoughts, and energetic signals of the life you're calling in. You're activating neural pathways and aligning your field with your desired timeline. The more vividly and emotionally you script, the stronger the signal you emit into the quantum field.

For example, rather than writing "I want to feel more confident," you write, "I am so deeply grounded in my inner knowing. Every room I walk into, I feel magnetic and certain." This subtle shift rewires your inner narrative and reconditions your energy. Over time, your external reality begins to reflect what you've already claimed on paper.

Scripting can be used daily, as part of a larger manifestation ritual, or simply when you feel disconnected from your vision. You can script your day ahead, your dream life, or the energy you want to walk in that week. What matters most is how it feels as you write. The goal is not to get it perfect, but to embody the state you wish to inhabit.

Your words become spells. Your pen becomes a wand. Through intentional language and presence, you literally write yourself into a new reality.

State Akin to Sleep (SATS)

The State Akin to Sleep, or SATS, is a powerful manifesting technique taught by Neville Goddard that allows you to impress your desired reality onto the subconscious mind. It's based on the principle that the subconscious accepts as true whatever is felt vividly and emotionally—especially in the relaxed state between wakefulness and sleep.

In SATS, you enter a deeply relaxed state—just as your body begins to fall asleep, but your awareness remains intact. This liminal space is where your conscious mind softens, and your subconscious becomes more receptive. From this state, you visualize a specific scene that would be true if your desire were already fulfilled. Not a vague wish or hope—but a clear, vivid moment that implies completion. A moment after the manifestation.

You might imagine yourself hugging a friend and celebrating your new home. Or seeing your name on a published book. Or receiving a loving message from a soulmate. The key is to feel it as real—not as if it will happen, but as if it already has. What would you hear? What would you see? How would it feel in your body?

The more you repeat this scene in the drowsy state, the more it imprints onto your subconscious. And because your subconscious shapes your perception, behaviors, and attraction point, your outer world naturally begins to conform.

SATS is not just a visualization technique. It's a way of planting new seeds in the soil of your being. It's an act of creation through felt experience.

Use it nightly. Use it intentionally. Let the final thoughts before you drift into sleep be of your future lived now.

Energetic Rehearsing

Energetic rehearsing is the art of pre-experiencing your desired reality—not through thought alone, but through full-body, full-soul embodiment. It goes beyond visualization and taps into frequency alignment. You are not just imagining the life you want; you are rehearsing what it feels like to live it now.

This is how you become familiar with the unfamiliar future.

Think of it like preparing for a performance—not just memorizing the lines, but stepping into the character. Feeling their presence, emotions, and posture. When you energetically rehearse your future self, you begin to carry their certainty, confidence, and clarity into your now. This doesn't mean pretending—it means practicing alignment until it becomes embodied truth.

You can do this through movement, voice, ritual, or meditation. Walk through your house as the version of you who already lives in overflow. Speak aloud your affirmations as if you're already living that timeline. Feel how it shifts your posture, your tone, your energy.

This is more than play—it is calibration. You're training your body, your nervous system, and your energy field to recognize success, love, freedom, and abundance as your new normal. You are signaling to the quantum field: "This is who I am. This is what I'm available for."

Energetic rehearsing dissolves resistance. It closes the gap between now and next. And it places your focus not on what's missing, but on what's already vibrating within you—ready to unfold in form.

Becoming the Embodied Attractor Field

You are always attracting—not from what you want, but from who you are. Desire alone doesn't magnetize reality into form; embodiment does. The quantum field responds to the frequency you carry, the identity you inhabit, and the coherence between your thoughts, emotions, and energy.

To become an attractor field means to live as the version of you who already has what you desire. Not someday. Not when things fall into place. But now.

This is the energetic posture of "I already am."

When you become the embodiment of love, abundance, creativity, or purpose, those realities cannot help but respond. You collapse the timeline between longing and living because your frequency no longer signals separation—it radiates fulfillment.

This isn't about perfection or performing spiritual identity. It's about coherence. Wholeness. Integrity. Alignment. You become magnetic to all that matches your essence because your field is clear, resonant, and rooted.

You're no longer chasing. You're emanating.

Every thought, every breath, every step becomes an invitation to reality to reorganize around your being. You're not waiting for proof—you're becoming the proof. You walk into rooms and shift the frequency. You speak and something stirs in others. You create, and your essence lingers in the space long after your words are gone.

This is the path of the Soul Alchemist. Not to attract by effort—but to allow through embodiment.

Quantum Jumping to Magnetize Your Desires

Quantum jumping is a powerful way to align with the version of you who already lives the life you desire. It's not about escaping your current reality—it's about collapsing timelines by stepping into resonance with what's already available to you in the quantum field. Every version of you already exists. Your role is to consciously *choose* the one you are ready to embody.

Before you begin, take a moment to get clear. What reality are you jumping into? Who are you in that timeline? Are you thriving in your soul mission? Are you financially free, deeply in love, fully expressed? Clarity anchors your intention. The clearer you are, the more direct your quantum leap will be.

To begin the jump, create a calm and open space. Dim the lights, light a candle if you like, or play soft music—whatever helps you drop into presence. Take a few deep breaths to center yourself. Let your mind quiet and your awareness shift from thinking to feeling. Drop into your heart. Set the intention to expand your consciousness into the quantum field.

As your awareness expands, imagine yourself lifting, rising, stretching beyond your current physical body into a space that feels infinite and alive. The quantum field may feel like vast light, spaciousness, or a subtle energetic hum. It is timeless, boundless, and filled with possibility. Simply allow yourself to *be* in that space. Feel it. Attune to it.

Then, with a clear heart and focused mind, speak your intention: "I now choose to jump into the timeline where I am..." and complete the sentence with the reality you desire. You might see a light appear before you, a door, or you may simply feel your body being pulled forward. Follow the experience. Walk into the light. Open the door. Step through.

On the other side, you'll enter the timeline you've chosen. Observe everything. See yourself already living that life—what are you doing, how are you moving, what do you believe, how do you speak, what do you feel? Be the fly on the wall and let your senses absorb the experience fully. The goal isn't just to watch—it's to *feel* what it's like to be that version of you. Let the energy of that life imprint into your being.

When the experience begins to fade, or when you feel complete, return to the vastness of the quantum field. From there, return to your body, bringing with you the essence, frequency, and felt experience of that timeline. Breathe it in. Let it settle into your cells, your field, your consciousness.

The key is to *hold* the frequency. That essence you just embodied— who you became in that other timeline—must now live within you here. Embody it. Think like them. Move like them. Speak like them. Let your current life adjust itself to reflect who you have chosen to become.

You can repeat this practice anytime you feel disconnected from the essence or need a refresher. But if you're able to maintain the resonance for days, weeks, or even longer, you'll find yourself naturally making different choices, showing up in new ways, and magnetizing opportunities that align with your new vibration.

This is conscious creation through quantum embodiment.

You don't attract by reaching—you attract by *being*.

Quantum Field Magnetization

While quantum jumping allows you to experience a version of yourself already living your desired reality, magnetizing through the quantum field is about activating your energetic signal in the here and now to attract those realities into form. Instead of stepping into another version of you, this practice calls your desires *toward you*—by becoming a vibrational match for their fulfillment.

Begin as you would with the quantum jump: prepare a calm, grounded space. Breathe deeply, center your awareness, and set the intention to enter the quantum field. As your consciousness expands, allow yourself to sense the vastness of this field—an infinite web of possibility that stretches across all timelines, realities, and dimensions.

Now, rather than seeking a specific version of yourself, connect with the **essence** of what you desire. Let go of the details—the how, the when, the through-whom—and instead anchor into the *feeling state* your desire would evoke. Is it joy, safety, expansion, freedom, radiance, love? Whatever it is, summon that emotion. Let it rise in you. Let it swell. Let it take up space.

Once the essence is alive within you, draw upon the energy of the quantum field to amplify it. Imagine this desire growing in strength, vibrating throughout your body, radiating outward into the quantum field. Let it ripple beyond you, spreading wide like waves through water, carried by the field to every energetic intersection it needs to reach.

Speak into the field with presence and authority: **"I now call forth [state your desire] to come to me with ease and grace. I am open. I am receptive. I welcome this into my life in this or an even better way."**

Feel the resonance of those words. Then let go. Release the desire into the field. Trust that it's been received and is already in motion.

This practice doesn't require daily repetition. The call has been made. The desire has been sent. Your role now is to become the *embodiment* of its fulfillment—living, acting, and showing up as the version of you who already has it.

When you live as her, when you walk with that frequency, the quantum field responds accordingly. It bends time. It accelerates convergence. It collapses the perceived distance between you and what you desire.

That's the beauty of timeline work. Time, in the quantum realm, isn't linear. Every outcome already exists in a parallel stream of possibility. The "you" who has everything you desire is not far away in the future—it is a frequency match away. When you embody that energy, you shift timelines. You jump tracks. You no longer wait—you *align*.

This is how the quantum field supports manifestation—not through force, but through frequency. Not through waiting, but through *being*. And when your being aligns with your vision, life begins to mirror that essence back to you in ways that feel miraculous, yet completely natural.

Bringing It All Together

As you've now seen, manifestation is not about pushing, striving, or convincing the Universe to give you what you want. It's about alignment. It's about energetic integrity. It's about becoming the version of you who already lives the life you're calling in—and letting that version lead the way.

The quantum field doesn't respond to what you *say* you want. It responds to who you are being. To what you embody. To the emotional and energetic signature you carry each day.

Whether you choose to quantum jump, script your future into form, visualize from the end, or simply sit in the frequency of what you desire, the core principle remains the same: you are the creator. You are the portal. Your life is a mirror of the frequency you hold.

This final chapter was never meant to give you a rigid formula or a new set of rules. It was meant to give you tools—pathways back to your own creative power. Techniques to help you deepen into the truth that's been with you all along:

You don't manifest what you chase. You magnetize what you are. And now, you have everything you need to begin.

This Is Just the Beginning

You made it. You walked with me through the deepest layers of your becoming, through the thresholds of release, remembrance, embodiment, and radiance. And yet... this is not the end. This is the beginning of everything.

You didn't just read a book. You activated something within yourself. Something ancient. Something alive. Something that was always meant to awaken through this journey.

My intention with every word was never to teach you something new, but to help you remember what's always been inside you. Your truth. Your essence. Your soul's frequency. That spark that kept whispering that there's more. That you were made for something deeper. Brighter. Realer. And now... you know.

This is the moment you begin to walk differently in the world. Not because you've become someone else, but because you've finally allowed yourself to be all of who you already are. The path ahead will still stretch you. It will still invite you to shed, to rise, to remember again and again. But now you know the way. You are the way. You carry the codes of your own transformation. You are the alchemist. The portal. The transmission.

Thank you for saying yes to this journey. Thank you for being willing to face what was hidden. To reclaim what was lost. To embody what was always meant to shine through you.

I wrote this book not just to be read—but to be felt. To be lived. And to walk beside you on the journey home to yourself.

And even though these are the final pages, my presence, my essence, my frequency walks with you still. In the moments when you feel like slipping back into the old. In the thresholds when you are asked to rise again. In the sacred ordinary of your becoming.

You are not alone. You were never alone. So take a breath. Feel into your being. And remember…

This is just the beginning.

✧ The Alchemist Commitment ✧

A sacred devotion to living your truth, transmuting your limitations, and embodying the fullness of who you are.

The path of the Soul Alchemist is not about striving to become someone new. It is a journey of remembrance — a sacred return to the truth of who you already are beneath the layers of fear, conditioning, and fragmentation. Rather than reaching outward for something more, this path invites you inward, calling you to reclaim what was once forgotten or pushed aside in the name of survival, acceptance, or belonging.

To walk this path is to enter into a conscious relationship with transformation. It means no longer turning away from discomfort or bypassing your pain with false light. Instead, you meet your shadows with grace. You sit with what's real. You transmute the heaviness of the past into the gold of your becoming. This is the alchemy — not something you study from afar, but something you live, breathe, and embody from the inside out.

Being a Soul Alchemist is not a passive title or an abstract identity. It is a living, breathing devotion — a daily commitment to walk in alignment with your truth, to live with intention, and to embody your highest frequency even when it would be easier to shrink back into the familiar. It asks you to show up fully for yourself and for the world, not just in moments of clarity or inspiration, but in the quiet, uncomfortable spaces where real transformation is forged.

If you feel called to this work, then let it become your vow. Speak the words aloud. Let them root into your body and ripple through your field. This is your energetic signature — your declaration to walk the path not just in theory, but in practice. Let it seal something sacred within you.

My Commitment as a Soul Alchemist

I choose to walk the path of remembrance.
To shed the layers I've outgrown.
To release the masks, the lies, the shoulds, and the survival patterns.
To reclaim every piece of myself I abandoned to feel safe or accepted.

I choose to meet my shadows with compassion.
To feel what I used to numb.
To see what I used to avoid.
To bring light to what once lived in the dark.

I choose aligned action.
To follow the wisdom of my soul over the noise of the world.
To move not from fear or force, but from resonance and truth.
To speak, create, and show up in full energetic congruence.

I choose to live in devotion to my highest frequency.
To let joy be sacred.
To let rest be powerful.
To let my life become the alchemy.

I choose to lead from within.
To become the embodiment of what I once sought outside myself.
To radiate what I came here to activate.
To be the mirror that awakens others to their own light.

I choose the path of the Soul Alchemist.
And I walk it with reverence, with courage, and with an open heart.

Continue Your Soul Alchemy Journey

If this book stirred something within you, if you felt the resonance and remembered something long-forgotten, then your journey is just beginning.

Transcendence is where that journey continues.

This is my sacred membership space for soul-aligned expansion, multidimensional healing, and quantum embodiment. It's where we go beyond information and into transformation—together. If you're ready to deepen your inner alchemy, raise your frequency, and live from your divine truth in every area of your life, Transcendence is here to hold you.

Inside, you'll receive:

- A **12-week Soul Alchemy Journey** to activate your next level of becoming

- **Weekly live sessions** that alternate between powerful Energy Calibration Sessions—designed to activate and recalibrate you at the deepest energetic level through Light Language transmissions—and Integration Sessions that support you in anchoring those shifts, embodying the activation, and experiencing real transformation in your everyday life.

- Access to a **growing library of energetic activations**, healing tools, and deep-dive workshops

- A vibrant, soul-aligned **community** of conscious beings on the path

- Bonus courses, summit replays, and practices to help you embody your light and live your purpose

This is not just a membership—it's an energetic space for remembrance, resonance, and radiant becoming.

If your soul is nudging you forward…

If you feel ready to step more fully into the alchemist you came here to be…

Then I invite you to explore what's waiting for you inside.

Join us here: **www.kaysanders.com/transcendence**

You are no longer walking alone. This is your path of power. And we're walking it with you.

With love and gratitude,

Kay Sanders

About the Author

Kay Sanders is a Soul Alchemist, Light Language Channel, and spiritual guide devoted to activating awakening souls into the truth of who they are. Her work isn't traditional coaching or healing—it's an energetic transmission. Through channeled light codes, deep soul remembrance, and powerful frequency work, Kay helps others awaken their inner alchemist and embody the radiance of their soul.

She is the founder of Transcendence, a sacred membership space for soul-aligned expansion, where energy mastery, embodiment, and quantum creation converge. Kay's presence alone serves as a catalyst—activating those who are ready to rise, reclaim their light, and lead with truth.

To explore Kay's offerings and stay connected, visit:

Website: www.kaysanders.com
YouTube: Kay Sanders – Soul Alchemist
Membership: www.kaysanders.com/transcendence